Politics As You Like It

Commentary From The Internet
An Example of Writing from the World Wide Web

Politics As You Like It

Commentary From The Internet
An Example of Writing from the World Wide Web

By

Bernard Paul

ISBN: 1-58820-603-3

This book is printed on acid free paper.

This book may also be ordered directly from the author by writing to
P.O. Box 20511 Port Richmond Station
Staten Island, New York, 10302

Please when ordering include an additional five dollars to cover the cost
of shipping and handling.

1stBooks – rev. 7/06/01

Bernard Paul

Introduction of Book
For Publication

"Politics As You Like It"; "Commentary From The Internet"; is a collection of commentaries this author wrote on his website at The World Wide Web during the years 1997, 1998 and 1999. The subject matter covers a variety of topics from political commentary, and biographies of some public figures to sports.

The initial concept was to put up a weekly commentary where the topic would be chosen by the visitors to the website. Over the three year period I was writing these commentaries the original intention could not be realized for not too many visitors to "Politics As You Like It" made suggestions for commentaries they would have like to have seen written. So, by necessity, the topics for the most part were chosen by the webmaster for the page.

The first commentary written about Noam Chomsky, went up in late July of 1997. When I started the concept of an Internet Zine; (which "Politics As You Like It' essentially was) was very new. The amount of people on the World Wide Web since I began writing on the Web has almost doubled to over fifty million people here in The Untied States currently. The website received almost ten thousand visitors and averaged about one-hundred visitors a week. Commentaries were written weekly for the first year and then bi-weekly after that.

This book is an example of what a novice could do in terms of presenting his or her work on The Internet and thus as Andy Warhol said, (paraphrased) "have his or her ten minutes of fame".

These days, professional Internet Zine's like Michael Kingsley's; "Slate" and hosts of other successful Zines infuse the Internet with a spirit of life of it's own.

Some of my commentaries may offend, others may enlighten the reader. For example, a commentary on the execution of convicted Texas murderer, Karla Faye Tucker, broght a strong reader reaction to both the pro and the cons of the death penalty. Another commentary on the tragic Columbine shootings brought some crazies in the pro-gun movement who could not respect my anti-gun stance taken in the commentary written shortly after the Columbine incident. A commentary that I wrote on FEMA, (The Federal Emergency Management Agency) shocked many people and was published in 1999 in "American Dissident" Magazine based in Concord, New Hampshire.

For the most part, I enjoyed putting some of my ideas up on The Internet for mass consumption and would hope others would try to do the same. For too long, the average, Joe and Jane out there, have not had the means, connections or will to have their ideas listened to due to the mainstream media dominating the stage and the means to distribute news and ideas. The Internet has changed all that and has become a formidable tool for the dissemination of ideas from those who in the past were unable to do so. In that spirit I have put what I have written on The World Wide Web into the conventional publishing format, (Hardcover, Softcover and Electronic Publishing) to sound the alarm to my potential reader or this wonderful technological revolution available to all of us. "Politics As You Like It" was a labor of love that I think you will enjoy reading. Have Fun!

Author
Bernard Paul
New York, New York
October 2000

Politics As You Like It:
Commentary From The Internet
An Example of Writing from the World Wide Web

Bernard Paul

Table of Contents

Bernard Paul

Bernard Paul

Politics As You Like It:
Commentary From The Internet
An Example of Writing from the World Wide Web

Bernard Paul

Introduction To Book

In early February of 1997, having never even remotely thought of the value of owning a computer, I went out and bought what I guess was the next best thing, a Web TV Terminal and Keyboard manufactured by Phillips-Magnavox. I really could not afford at that time a desktop computer so I settled for what is almost a computer. The prime limitation of Web TV was it's inability to download, a feature that many who are computer savy value.

A few months later in early April of 1997, I was up late one night trying to come up with an idea that not only would empower me but the general public at large. I like many had grown tired of being force fed news stories and having a political angle attached to a lot of news coverage I was being exposed to. Since the conventional media was going the way of "Tabloid" news the quality of news coverage had diminished to the point where the profession of broadcast and print journalism had a black eye that would not heal. I was going to try to change all that by writing commentaries on the Internet which not only presented the issues on both sides of the story, but would encourage visitors to my webiste, "Politics As You Like It" to sign in with their comments in a guestbook on the website.

What happened over the next 29 months was sheer magic and far surpassed any expectations I had for my website when I first went online on July 27th 1997. Hundreds of people from all over the world were sending me comments on what I was writing and with some I took the debate further, e-mailing further comments of my own, based on their initial entries to my websites guestbook. Portions of that guestbook are included in this book. In all I produced fifty commentaries in a little under two and one half years. The subject matter in this book does not confine itself to one area but rather is a mix of topics. Research time for each commentary written online was at least 10 hours per week. For the first year I published weekly and after that bi-weekly.

Two of my readers, Jeff Gersten from Monticello, New York, and Linda Peruki from Novell, Michigan, at my invitation also wrote guest commentaries. Politics As You Like It was an adventure in freedom of the press, without, the influence that advertisers can and do exert over a publication or broadcast news entity, or the private political agendas that many news directors and editors have put on them by the owners of the concerns they work for. Our news is always colored by wealthy powerful men who want to shape the publics mind the way they want it to be and for the most part the general public, thinks as they are told to think, with a lot of mis-information in the conventional news business being thrown their way. This book is a wake-up call to our conventional media to clean up it's act. While what I have done in empowering myself with this wonderful new technology is good, this book falls short of a full blown indictment of conventional news media because I realize there are many dedicated professional journalists who are just being told what to do and write by their editors and news directors. People have to eat right?

I encourage the readers of this book to empower themselves as I have by joining the World Wide Web technological revolution and with that power take back control of many parts of your life, which have been in the hands of institutions which have very little accountability or loyalty to their viewers or readers. Instead the prime loyalty many news organizations continue to have

I

is to the corporate bottom line, profits and that bottom line ultimately, does not allow for responsible reporting of the news in many, many, cases. There are exceptions to my premise, but you would have to look very hard and close to find those exceptions in the world of journalism today.

This book is really not about the subject matter, but it's theme is what you can do with The Internet to get some ideas out to the public at large. In the past doing what took huge sums of money and connections in a field which is for the most part closed to the majority of the public. Do they really care what we have to say or think or do the conventional media mavens care about only the bottom line, profits at all costs? I'll let you the reader answer that question.

Finally, this book is the product of three and one half years work and thousand of hours of research. I sincerely hope that you the reader enjoy reading some of these commentaries as much as I enjoyed writing them.

Bernard Wax
March 2001
New York, New York

Bernard Paul

Commentaries

Politics As You Like It:
Commentary From The Internet
An Example of Writing from the World Wide Web

Bernard Paul

DEDICATION

This Book is dedicated to Eric & Denise Andresen The Webmasters of Internet Website
Web Tv Sig
Published on The Internet from their home in Davenport, Iowa In The United States of America.

Politics As You Like It:
Commentary From The Internet
An Example of Writing from the World Wide Web

Bernard Paul

VOLUME 1 NO. 1
POLITICS AS YOU LIKE IT
"CHOMSKY"

After careful thought for many weeks, on a topic to open this my first column with, I came up with a virtually ignored political genius, and thought he would be an excellent way to start things here. So, a spotlight and hats off to Noam Chomsky, Insiitute Professor of Linguistics at The Massachusetts Insitute of Technology. He is truly a political commentator of vast demensions, who for the most part the mainstream and conventional media refuse to recognize or cover.

The author of many, many books, on domestic and international governmental policy, Chomsky, like many free thinkers who combine, logic, and a keen analysis, along with common sense, is seen as an abberation, most on the right would prefer not to deal with. On the left he is also seen as much too controversial to pay any attention to. So one must be politically aware to know of him. The humor to this treatment of Chomsky, is and most would agree, logic and common sense are the last thing most mainstream politicians would care to think about, since it conflicts, perhaps, with their own dollars and cents survival, and the effectiveness they must have to the special interest groups, they give most of their attention to.

In Chomsky's book "Keeping The Rabble In Line" his genius as always shines. When asked to comment on race, class and gender bias he replies: (parapharsed) "objective power is concentrated". Objective power lies in various places: in patriarchy, in race. Crucially, it lies in ownership. In terms of opression, this form is worth overcoming. When we talk about what is at the core of the system of oppression and what is not, the degree of suffering is where the distinction lies. If you think about the way society works in general, it pretty much works the way our founding fathers said it should. Society should be governed by those who own it" So as much as we may think that American society has changed, (for the better or worse) the same forces of domination that were in effect in this country in the 1820's continue to run the show in 1997. This cannot and does not by any strecth of the imagination constitute government by the people or for the people, but rather government by the few for the few.

By the few for the few, means, the few with the money to buy and control our political process, and manipulate American society to their specific interests, which oft times do not coincide with the interests of the majority of the rest of American society. If we are to be a truly free and democratic nation, this distortion of freedom cannot continue. To do such can have dire consequences and will erode The United States position as the leader of the free world and most important degrade further the negative opinion that many Americans have of their country at this time.

How politicains came to be intensely disliked here in The United States, (when we are supposed to look up to our politicians as leaders and men and women of virtue) is a whole different story, in of itself. Self-interest can be downplayed for the good of our country. Not to do so, may leave us without any country at all!

VOL. 1 NO. 2

POLITICS AS YOU LIKE IT
"DOMESTIC TERRORISM AND ACTS OF WAR"

This week, here in my hometown, New York City, something out of a "James Bond" thriller came to pass. More so, of surreal proportions!. It seems, simply put, that there were a bunch of guys, holed up in some apartment in Brooklyn, that were making bombs and had decided to bomb one of the busiest subway stations here in New York City, at the height of the morning rush hour, last Friday morning.

One of this group of characters, called The FBI and that is how this plot in the name of freedom for Palestinians in The Mid-East was learned of and prevented. Tributes for quick and decisive action in this matter should go out with the heartfelt gratitude of all American people, (and those who suffer terrorist acts overseas) to agents of The FBI and The FBI and New York City Police Departments Joint Terrorist Task Force headquarted here in New York City. Their heroic actions prevented the major loss of lives and many hundreds more being wounded, were the terrorists plans brought to fruition.

Would the planned actions of these alledged terrorists, here in New York City, serve their interests in the Mid-East? The answer to that is, an unequivocal, yes, at least as far as the alledged terrorists are concerned. The United States as a result of its association with Israel, is responible! However, most rational people understand that The United States has for a long time worked with Israel, to reslove The Palestinian probelm and has strongly promoted efforts to achieve peace between Israel and The PLO.

So, some innocent subway rider, on their way to work in the morning, should have to lose his or her, life, so the Palestinian problem in The Mid-East can be resloved in a more expeditious fashion? Really! Oh yeh? What remains to be resloved here, is how The United States Immigration and Naturalization Service, (heretoafter referrred to as The INS) could have allowed these suspected terrorists or for that matter over two-hundred suspected terrorists who were kicked out of their countries, into this country.

When an accusation of suspected terrorism is made by a foriegn country, whether proven or not, this designation, should send a red flag to every other country in the world that wishes to combat and eradicate terrorism. Apparently The U.S. INS, did not see the designation, (or refused to recognize it) of some two-hundred possible terrorists, as worthy of it's close examination and thus, preventive action, by the INS. What more would The INS require to take preventive action? Certainly, there has been over the past twenty-five years more than enough incidents of domestic terrorism, (The World Trade Center bombing, here in New York City in 1993, is one example of many) and international terrorism, to warrent tighter restrictions on individuals who are suspected of such horrible acts, or could be seen as having the potential to committ such acts.

The question remains at this time is why the remaining individuals who are now in this country, with prior designations as suspected terrorists, are still here, or for that matter, why they are not being monitored by The FBI. Certainly, the reason exists to do so. I don't think anyone, Americans included should not have to wake up with the thought, that somewhere, near where they live, are a bunch of people, mixing chemicals in the middle of the night, that will blow us all to kingdom, come, especially, when we have the information and intelligence to prevent this.

Finally, this commentators tribute to an extraordinary public servant James Kallstrom, Assistant Director of The FBI here in New York City. The agents and officers who caught the people who were going to commit this act of terrorism, came within a hairs breath away, of being, blown up themselves, when they came upon these terrorists. Both alledged terrorists tried to activate the bombs when the New York City Police and FBI agents came upon them. Only quick thinking, by the police and agents present, stopped from occuring.

We in this country have the wherewithall to prevent these things from happening. Lets begin to use them for the safety of all. The United States should be the last country in the world where someone or some group of people should feel safe to plan and commit terrorist acts and this is the clear message to all who would think that they could do so, that The United States must send to these barbarians. See Ya All Next Time. Your comments are welcome in the guestbook for this page.

Bernard Paul

VOL. 1 NO. 3

POLITICS AS YOU LIKE IT
"THE UNITED PARCEL SERVICE STRIKE (UPS)"
THE ISSUES: FROM BOTH SIDES: MANAGEMENT AND LABOR

This weeks topic for my column comes by request of Steven E. Vogel from Denver, Colorado.

Last week, one-hundred and eighty five thousand workers with The United Parcel Service, (heretoafter referred to as UPS) were ordered out on strike by the union that represents them, The International Brotherhood of Teamsters. UPS, handles eighty percent of all package deliveries in The United States. In 1996, UPS earned over one billion dollars in profit.

At the heart of the strike is the use of part-time workers by UPS. At the time of the walkout sixty-two percent of all UPS workers were part-timers. Many in the labor movement feel that the practice of using part-timers represents a hidden form of downsizing. UPS mangement contends that the part-time workers do quite well, earning, for part-time work, with benifits, seventeen dollars an hour. UPS offers to settle the current strike, by creating another one-thousand full-time positions. The Teamsters Union representing UPS workers wants ten thousand new full-time jobs created. Additionally, UPS management wants control of the billion dollar UPS worker pension fund, which is currently under the control of The Teamsters Union.

Negotiations to settle the strike have broken down and according to Federal Mediator John Calhoun Wells, "President Clinton would like both sides to negotiate a settlement as soon as possible" The President has declined to order the workers to resume work, in the early stages of this strike, instead adopting a wait and see attitude. President Clinton has at his disposal the use of The Taft-Hartly Act, which would force UPS workers to go back to work, while both sides would continue to negotiate toward a settlement.

UPS management is threatning to cut fifteen thousand jobs, whenever the strike ends to offset some of the huge losses they are incurring as a result of the strike. Wages for part-time workers at UPS have been frozen for the past fifteen years. (since 1982)

5

As this cat and mouse game continues, between both sides in this dispute, the potential damage to our nations economy is being downplayed. After all we do have a roboust and surging economy at this time, right? Fine, if that premise is acceptable, then the question to UPS management is, if your not going to create more full-time jobs, then what is the problem with doing such, in an economy that is seen by many, as the best in the past thirty years?

In the meantime, several major corporations, including Wal-Mart have written a collective letter to President Clinton, asking him to intervene in the strike. UPS is reporting losses of fifty million dollars a day as the strike continues. For those on strike, benifits of fifty-five dollars a week are to begin this week. Many companies have lost thousands of dollars worth of business, because they were unable to guarantee twenty-four hour delivery to their customers. UPS, with the exception of The U..S. Postal Service is the only concern that guarantees twenty-four hour delivery of packages.

What is the purpose of refusing to reclassify part-timers when UPS, could well afford to do so at this time? Behind most corporate downsizing in the past five years, were fears of a weakened economy and thus to maintain profit margins, many corporations choose the downsizing road. Workers are supposed to grow with their company. It seems that UPS management has run the compnay in the past two years as though we were in a recession. So the paramount issue of this strike, would then seem to be a valid argument on behalf of those who are out on strike.

In a booming economy, where Wall Street has hit historic heights, and UPS is highly profitable, there is no reason why part-timers should not be reclassified and offered full-time positions. Many observers of the labor movement feel this will be a long strike. With unions, having lost over fifty percent of their membership over the past twenty years and thus, a lot of the power that they used to yield, the current strike becomes more than just a UPS-Worker, dispute.

Some would believe that the outcome of this strike in the favor of the workers is essential to the survival of the labor movement in The United States, which has suffered heavy damage in the recent past. Certainly, considering the positive economic indicators at this time, if a powerful union like The Teamsters could not prevail in this current strike, labors position in

The United States would be further, significantly undermined, perhaps irreparably so.

The President of The International Brotherhood of Teamsters, Ron Carey, has had vast experience with The United Parcel Service company. He was President of Teamsters Local # 804 in Long Island City, New York, for over twenty years, before becoming the first elected International Teamsters Union President in 1993. Mr. Carey's New York City local, represented UPS workers, in The New York Metropolitan area. When he ran for the International Teamsters presidency, Mr. Carey ran on a platform of reforming The Teamsters Union and ridding the union of organized crime elements and their influenece over union affairs.

Mr, Carey in the past three and one half years has personally, dismissed officials of Teamster Union locals that had ties to organized crime. He is seen by many in the labor union movement and by the members of his union, (the most powerful union in The United States and Canada with twelve million dues paying members) as one of the most honest and fair union leaders in the history of The Teamsters Union.

Finally, many UPS part-time workers feel they have earned the right to a full-time job, by working as part-timers for many, many years. While many UPS part-time workers appreciate the benifits package they receive which puts their hourly compensation at seventeen dollars an hour, many cannot continue to support their families, on the eight dollars an hour they receive before taxes as part-timers, and thus desparately need the reclassification to full-time worker and the increased pay that would come with that reclassification, to surrvive.

Considering all factors present in this walkout by UPS, mangements position seems to be inconsistent with the facts and fairness to the workers position in this strike. In the meantime, we the average consumer, when this strike is settled, will as always wind up paying out of our pocketbooks, (in the form of higher prices in the marketpalce) for the inflexibility of both sides in this strike. Not a pretty picture, indeed! See ya all next time. Your comments are welcome in the guestbook for this page.

VOL. 1 NO. 4

POLITICS AS YOU LIKE IT

TED KOPELL AND "CHEAP TECHNOLOGY" THE JOURNALISTS OF TOMORROW

Several weeks ago, some interesting comments were made at The Metropolitan Club in New York City, at a fourm on the news media, sponsored by Quinnipac College. The comments were made by ABC News, "Nightline" anchor, Ted Kopell, to an audience of fellow ABC News anchorpersons and a group of ABC News executives of news programs which included, the former President of ABC News, Roone Arledge.Sam Donaldson, Barbara Walters and Peter Jennings.

Mr. Kopell's comments were broadacst by C-Span, a cable channel which sees itself as a station of poltical record. C-Span presents daily live coverage of The United States Senate and The United States Congress from Washington D.C.

I could not help but smile a bit after listening to Mr. Kopell's comments to the gathering assembled. For after all what I do here is a form of journalism, using a most restrained definition of such.

Essentailly, the esteemed anchor of "Nightline" for the past eighteen years, seemed to feel that. the mainstream media, (the networks, ABC, NBC and CBS) had lost a lot of credibility, with the viewing public, in recent years, due to the increased competition, by cable news stations, (such as CNN, Bloomberg News, ect. ect.) and the poliferation of "cheap technology" on The Internet.

Mr. Kopell went on to say, (parapharsed) that the public did not know who to believe anymore! Furthermore, he felt, due to "this cheap technology" available to millions on The Internet, that everyone soon, would be a journalist.

In defense of The Internet, and the many great idaes and homepages that are there, this commentator must note, that if the mainstream media in the past and present had really listened to their audiences, ideas and concerns, and had given ample opportunity for presentation of those ideas and concerns, instead of advancing their political agendas and caving into pressure from their advertisers and other special interests, many people like myself, who write about various topics, on The Internet, would probably not do so.

I find it distressing to hear Mr. Kopell, basically say, that it was his message we should pay attention to and that any message produced with this "cheap technology" should be suspect.

However, as long as the mainstream news media continues to try its maintainence of a monopoly on the coverage and presentation of the news, the way they see it, thousands of people like myself will attempt to find a vehicle for their ideas about the news. These ideas, presented by so-called novices, (this so-called novice commentator holds a Bachelors Degree in Media Studies with a Broadacst and Print Journalism Emphasis from Fordham University) should not receive short-shrift, because they are not coming from the major networks.

In closing here, if the process of mass communications were an open one to begin with, my comments here would not be neccessary. To own a televison or radio station costs millions. To obtain a job in the news business for the mainstream media is like searching for water in the desert.

If your lucky enough to land a job covering the news for presentation to the public, your final product, is severely compromised by editors, and higher ups and business considerations of the entity you are working for.

You would'nt even recognize your own news story after editors get through with it. So presentation of ideas through this "cheap technology" should be welcome by journalists like Ted Kopell, whose support of The First Amendment for everyone is essential by virtue of the positions held by top anchor newspersons.

Instead, what, I'm hearing, is that unless you listen to my message, (the networks and conventional mainstream media) then don't listen, because my message should be the only message that can be trusted.

While ABC News is excellent at getting to the truth in a story, (journalism at its heart, is the finding and quest for the truth) ABC News and Ted Kopell do not have a lock on being able to determine what the truth is in a story at any given moment.

There are some who have never worked for a formal news organization who are also very good at finding the truth. Thanks Mr.Kopell thats just the problem, too many Americans have experienced.

They have listened to one mesage for too long and that message has been clouded and distorted by politics, money and special-interests.

This is why people are looking elsewhere for their ideas and news. Tunnel vision does not represent a free press. Mr. Kopell should be saying, that the networks welcome all competition and the audiences will gravitate toward those with the most interesting, unbiased and objective reports.

I don't see why my ideas or reports as an Internet commentator and journalist should be deminished, because, the venue I have chosen to present my ideas is, classified, by the mainstream media, as being "cheap technology".

Cheap Technology my foot! This "cheap technology" (The Internet) is currently being used by fifty million people, here in The United States. The Internet is a force to be reckoned with and where tomorrows Ted Kopells will come from.

Sorry, to respectfully inform Mr. Kopell of ABC News, that some people may listen to what I have to say also. If that means that your ratings will lose, one-tenth of one-percent of a point, then try changing your message a little. See Ya All Next Time. Your comments are welcome in the guestbook for this page.

Bernard Paul

VOL. 1 NO. 5

POLITICS AS YOU LIKE IT

P.T. BARNUM REVISITED:WELFARE REFORM:ONE YEAR LATER:AN EXPERIMENT PROGRAMMED TO RUN AMOK

Another brainstorm just waiting to blossom, is welfare reform. Last year in the middle of a Presidential campaign, President Clinton fullfilled a campaign promise he had made when running for election the first time. "We're going to end welfare as we know it" proclaimed candidate Clinton.

So, with Republican Presidential candidate Bob Dole breathing down his neck, President Clinton signed The Welfare Reform Act of 1996.

Now, there are few people who would'nt agree that this nations welfare system needed an overhaul. Generations of dependency had been fostered by this system which became a revolving door to remain in poverty. for those recipients in the welfare system.

So the effort at reforming welfare systems around The United States could only be seen as a noble and ideal effort on the part of those who would attempt to do so, right? Well not exactly! For this like many issues are not just black and white, or right and wrong, many gray areas exist, which also must be examined to obtain the whole picture here. To do this, we must first ackowledge some givens, that have occurred during the past five years.

One, thousands of experienced workers have lost their jobs, in massive downsizing at many different companies in our country.

Two, many of these displaced workers have not been able to find another job or comparable work to their previous employment in the past five years.

Three, thousand of college graduates from the years 1992, 1993,1994 and 1995, have been unable to find jobs comensurate to their level of education, because of the downsizing and backup of people who lost their jobs during the downsizing of America. The current resurgence in The American economy, is due to a glut of low paying service sector jobs, with which one can hardly support oneself on, let alone a family.

Where does this leave the millions of welfare recipients, currently nationwide, who have been converted by their various states and municipalities, to workfare? Well, to begin with, even while performing work for their benifits, most welfare recipients are being told, that they may collect benifits for only two to five years.

Note that the majority of these current welfare recipients, lack the skills, education, experience or interpersonal skills, to satsify the requirments of almost all entry-level jobs in todays corporate world. Perhaps my point is beginnng to dawn here a bit.

Several weeks ago, President Clinton, at a conference in Detroit, asked once again, that major corporations hire welfare recipients to help end the cycle of dependency.

Question 1-How can a company even consider hiring someone with no education, marketable skills, or experience in the workplace?

Question 2-What about the thousands of people who had jobs who are skilled with good educations, and are now victims of downsizing, and looking to re-enter the job market?

Question 3-How about the thousands of people who have lost jobs that have gone to Mexico, Europe and Canada, due to NAFTA,(North American Free Trade Agreement instituted during The Clinton Administration) and other legislation that make it easy for an American corporation to leave The United States to obtain cheap labor elsewhere?

Theres really no point in continuing to present my argument here when some simple mathematics will give us the outcome of welfare reform.

How is someone whose welfare benifits expire going to find a job of any kind, that they can support themselves with, considering that the aforementioned groups of people cannot find anything decent?

After the limits to receive welfare benifits run out, thousands of human beings and their children will be out in the street. The money that was saved by using their labor at reduced costs in workfare programs, will be far eclipsed by huge expenditures to pay for the social consequences of thousands of people more without means of support.

My final question is this: Did not our politicians realize this when they agreed to this suicidal piece of legislation last year?

If we agree they did, then is the real agenda, to move people from the welfare rolls to the work rolls, as productive tax-paying citizens, or move them from workfare, (a system being classified a salvery of sorts by many today) to a prison cell, where their labor would then be absolutely without cost to the state.

What is the real aim of welfare reform, retribution or rehabilitation of a public ward.

In, New York City, thirty-eight thousand people are currently in the workfare program. Less than ten have found jobs of any kind. Welfare recipients who are lucky enough to be attending community college at the same time, are being told by The City of New York, that they must quit college, to fullfill their workfare assignments if the two conflict.

Not one workfare participant is beimg told that they will even have an outside shot at a job with New York City, once their welfare benifits expire.

To sum up, did you the public think that workfare was a noble idea whose time had come? How about the triple taxes you will have to pay when the social consequnces of all this come to light, almost certainly down the road?

During the next three to five years, the mainstream media will partcipate in this experiment doomed to fail, by continuing to demonize the poor and the homeless and for the most part those who are without power to fight back.

This mis-infornation will erode any public support for these so-called marginal groups in our society.

I use, the term so-called, becuase more than sixty million people in The United States today live below the poverty line. At the same time, government funding to organizations that assist the poor are being drastically cut. Talk about being up the river without a paddle.

So, what we have is the criminalization of poverty. There are solutions to the cycle of welfare dependency and I will address those solutions in a future column.

Without any fear whatsoever of being criticized for my views here, note, that as far as I'm concerned welfare reform as it stands, is, immoral, unetchical, possibly unconstitutional and irresponible on the part of those who have instituted it, full well knowing it cannot succeed and will lead ultimately to the destruction of thousands of innocent peoples lives.

Oh yes, in case any of you have forgotton, our lawmakers write laws to help our lives become better.

Government is supposed to help, not hurt its own people, right? Welfare reform! Legislation designed to run amok. Wonderful, just wonderful.

If I was a lawmaker and asked to write a bill that would get rid of the poor, The Welfare Reform Act of 1996, would be perfect for achieving just that. What a compassionate country we live in these days, that this could be done to our own people.

In future commentaries I will also address the complete sell-out in the past five years of the middle-class American worker, white collar and blue collar, the new poor in America and the import to our country of products produced by slave labor in China which of course has more American workers without jobs. See Ya All Next Time. Your comments are welcome in the guestbook for this page.

VOL. 1 NO.6

POLITICS AS YOU LIKE IT
PERHAPS FORGOTTON GRACES
IN A TIME OF RUDENESS

Many would feel that all human beings have universal needs. Some of those needs would include, love, respect, dignity and the need to be productive and make a contribution to ones society, so it would be a better place for everyone to live in.

After all on an emotional level, we are human beings. The difference we are told between animals and human beings is that human beings have the ability to think and reason, and therefore, human beings should above all species, act in the best interests of one another.

We would always expect such of those in authority and to those to whom we give a public trust. Unfortunately, as one goes down the road of life, it can become apparent that things are not as simple as we thought them to be. A variety of, cultural, sociological, demographic, class, gender, age, and racial factors, tend to work against my theme here. Perhaps, the points I try to make, are givens in America, today, however judging by peoples actions, the basic skills needed in interpersonal relationships (to avoid serious problems and conflict) seem to be lost in too many people today.

Animals react, with no thought involved in the process and human beings reason, with acquired intellect, which allows one to think before acting against ones self-interest.

However, what if we have an education system in The United States, (considered to be the best in the world) that for the most part, only teaches us to obey, follow directions and does not encorage the learned behavior of thinking. Has thinking become a lost art?

In recent weeks, several police officers in the place where I live, New York City have been accused of vile, horrendous acts of brutality against one man.

These alledged acts have sparked protests and once again those who represent authority look like predatory animals, rather than role models, that the public they are supposed to protect, should look up to and take pride in.

Does aggressive law enforcement include police brutality? If one is poor, or from a different culture or race, should that be a signal, that they are ripe for abuse from any authoritarian entity? I would hope not!

Summing up here, the respect you give to others is the respect you will receive. This is a lesson that some of my readers would tell me is better reserved for children. However, lately in our country and the world, perhaps the lesson should be renewed for those who are supposed to know better, adults.

Law enforcement is an important part of any community. They are there to protect us from those who would harm us. Nobody should fear the police unless they are involved in criminal activity.

Forgotton graces, such as, the words please, excuse me, thank you, appreciate, good morning, how are you seem to be missing or lost in action, in day to day life.

What are we, as human beings, in a perpetual state of war with one another declared or undeclared? The power of an apology, where one has wronged another, seem to have been lost also, especially in the law enforcement community. I've seen too many situations, where, police, prosecutors, judges and other law enforcement personnel, have been dead wrong about a case, where an innocent person had been falsely accused.

The current case of Richard Jewell, who was falsely accused of The Olympic Park bombing, at last years Olympics, in Atlanta, Georgia, by The FBi, is one example.

What is the problem with The FBI and The United States Department of Justice, issuing, a clear public apology to Mr. Jewell? His life was disrupted beyond belief. Mr. Jewell, a year after this happened is unable to find employment anywhere.

Is a half-hearted apology from The Attorney General of The United States, Janet Reno, sufficient?

Does respect for law enforcement become undermined, when these apologies are not forthcoming? I would think so! It is usually the criminal that is without remorse or sociopathic. Is unremorsefullness the charcteristic of

most criminals when they do wrong? Yes it is! Therefore, that characteristic, should not be one displaying itself in an institution representing virtue

Law enforcement is not above the law.

Finally, and most important, it is not neccesary to break the law, in order to enforce the law. Law is written to be enforced as is, not to be reinvented or ad libbed by the cop on the beat

Must one be a criminal to catch a criminal? That thought is revolting. Lets all go back to some basics in life, and maybe instead of pointing fingers, we can all try to respect one another. Human beings have that capability and we owe each other these basics as we go along in life. A return to civility, would certainly not be against anyones interest. See Ya All Next Time. Your comments are welcome in the guestbook for this page.

VOL. 1 NO. 7

POLITICS AS YOU LIKE IT

PRINCESS DIANA:QUEEN OF HEARTS:"A CANDLE IN THE WIND":1961-1997-MOTHER THERESA-"THE SAINT OF THE GUTTERS":1910-1997

In a week that can be seen as nothing less than extraordinary, our world has lost two kind, gentle and compassionate souls. At the conclusion of last weeks column, I wrote of more, "civility" between people. I usually write this column on Sunday afternoons, and last week, while writing my column, had not yet learned of Princess Diana's death, which appears to have occured under very uncivil circumstances.

A week ago, Sunday, Princess Diana, The Princess of Wales, 36, died in an early morning car crash in Paris, France. At the time of her death, her car was being chased by numerous paparazzi, (photographers) on motorcycles,who earn a living, with the pictures they take of famous people.

Also killed with Princess Diana, was her boyfriend, Dodi Al-Fayed, 41, the son Mohammed Al-Fayed, the billionaire owner of Harods Department Store, in Great Britain. Princess Diana's driver was also killed in the crash and her bodyguard, who survived the accident, remains in critical condition in a Paris hospital.

The conditions under which this incident happened are still under investigation as is, whom and what were directly responible for this tragedy. Mixed reports from the world-wide media covering this story, have the speedometer of the dark blue Mercedes-Benz automobile, involved in the crash, as being frozen at 121 miles an hour, at the time of the crash and some have reported that the speedometer was at zero, when the car crashed.

There are further reports, that the driver of the car, had a blood-acohol level, that exceeded by six times the normal blood-alcohol level.

In otherwords, the driver of the car is alledged to have been, dead drunk. What many of us who mourn Princess Diana do know, is that a light in the world has been extinquished.

With more than ease, Princess Diana, could have lived her life on a mountain of wealth and power, accumulated through her family and her 1981 marriage to Prince Charles, of The British Monarchy, and son of Queen Elizabeth.

She, however, and to her credit, choose not to. Instaed, she campaigned and used her station in life, to advocate, relentlessly, a variety of causes, which included, the disease Aids, and the removal of land mines, which were in abundance in war-torn countries such as Bosnia, and still killing many people, years after the conflicts had ceased.

Princess Diana, traveled the world, and everywhere she went, she left those with whom she came in contact with, feeling better.

We must all remember that Princess Diana was only human and subject to all of the imperfections that go with that designation. Should it be determined down the road, that aggressive paparazzi were responible for this tragedy, then certainly,the way the photo press, with impunity, invades the lives of people of reknown, will have to be evalauted and possibly, laws written, to protect the privacy and well being of public figures.

The fact that one may be a public figure, which the world would wish to see photos of, dose not justify the animalistic invasions of privacy that produce many of these photos. This does not come with the territory and famous people have the right to live their lives in peace and privacy also.

That an incident, such as this which occured to Princess Diana, would be neccesary, to highlight this point and have something done about it, is very sad indeed.

Nevertheless, something will have to be done, even if ultimately, after all the facts come out, the paparazzi are found not to be responible for this incident. Millions of people, including, this commentator have sent their condolences to the families and friends of Princess Diana.

In these less compassionate times, we have truly lost a woman who was a shining light to all who had the pleasure of seeing her and a person, who beleived in, faith, hope, charity and love. What is it, that we elevate our heros to unprecedented heights, where we worship and adore them, only to tear them down, in displays which are disgraceful?

Princess Diana, leaves behind two young sons, (heirs to the British throne) who one day might be Kings of England.

Yesterdays funeral was watched by billions of people all over the world and the procession in England was attended by millions. If the world learns anything by Princess Diana's passing, perhaps it will be, to try to be more civil, a little nicer to other human beings. Rest in Peace, Princess Diana, for your light will continue to shine for a long, long, time.

Additionally, another of our worlds gems, passed away this week, Mother Theresa at the age of 87.

Mother Theresa, called, "the saint of the gutters" helped and comforted the poorest of the worlds poor.

A 1979 Nobel Peace Prize winner, Mother Theresa when she accepted the award, did so in behalf of "the unwanted, unloved and uncared for" in the world. A Catholic Nun, whose missions went from the streets of Calcutta, India, to the mean streets of the South, Bronx in New York City. she and her order The Missionaries of Charity, tended and gave love, to lepers, starving people in Ethiopia, Aids victims, and earthquake victims in Armenia.

Mother Theresa also established a world-wide network of homes for the homeless and though she was only five feet tall, her works of mercy over many years made her one of the most admired women in the world.

Pope John Paul said a mass for Mother Theresa outside his summer home in Rome, last Friday.

President Clinton, commented, that "the world has lost one of the giants of our time". I guess to live ones life, unloved, or not to have loved, is not good.

To many of the worlds poor and unloved, Mother Theresa was the one light that gave purpose and meaning to their lives. She was an Angel To The Poor

Surely, Mother Theresa will be elevated to Sainthood, once that process begins.

Finally, surely, we can all understand how short life can be. Once, many accumalate, what life has to offer, and have taken care of the needs of our

families and friends, then to be truly fulfilled as human beings, one must turn to trying to make someone elses life a little better.

Neither of these two extraordinary and gifted women, Princess Diana and Mother Theresa, were, deaf, dumb or blind. Both had twenty-twenty vision, heard very clearly, and were full of humanity. Both choose to make a difference in thousands of peoples lives and the world is a much better place to live as a result of their having been here.

Everyone who has watched what has occured this past week remains in a state of shock. Rest in Peace Mother Theresa.

This week the entire world mourns two, gems and angels. See You All Next Time. Your comments are welcome in the guestbook for this page.

VOL. 1 NO. 8

POLITICS AS YOU LIKE IT

HAPPY BIRTHDAY: WEB TV NETWORKS INC: A YEAR OLD AND GOING STRONG

My column this week will be brief, in order to allow you my readers to have center stage. Web Tv is coming up on its first birthday as a product which revolutionized access to The Internet, E-Mail and many other wonderful features which were made available to many who, otherwise would have never had the opportunity to have this incredible world open to them.

I ask and encourage my readers this week to sign my guestbook with their thoughts and comments on how Web Tv has improved, and or changed their lives, and what they like the most about Web Tv. Lets all celebrate this aniversary together.

HAPPY BIRTHDAY WEB TV NETWORKS INC.-ONE YEAR OLD AND GOING STRONG

Bernard Paul

VOL. 1 NO. 9

POLITICS AS YOU LIKE IT

PUBLIC EDUCATION:EDUCATION OR DE-EDUCATION:JUST WHERE ARE WE GOING?

This weeks topic for my column comes by request of Jeffery Gersten from Monticello, New York. Mr. Gersten has been a member of his local school board for a little over one year.

There has been a crisis in public education for some time. Some of the barriers to genuine progress have included, overcrowded classrooms, schools with not enough room for students, who should maintain control, (Federal, State or Local entities) the level of educational standards that should be maintained, and raising those standards to meet current and future technological needs of an increasingly demanding society and workplace.

While this writer is not a parent with children in school, he can certainly understand the importance of a quality public school education, so the youth of today can compete and be of value to society in the future and thus be able to make a significant contribution to society.

I have felt for a long time, that entrenched bureaucracies which were directly responible for administration of various school systems, were primarily at fault, for the lack of progress in public education. There also has, in recent years, been a mass exodus of experienced teachers at all levels of public education, that has compounded the problems in public education. There are serious questions that must be addressed here.

I will use as an example The New York City School system, for since I reside in New York City, I am more familiar with that situation. In, the New York City public school system, (the largest in the nation) over a million students attend class every day.

Currently, there are no classroom seats for eighty-eight thousand of those students. New York City public school teachers earn an average yearly salary of forty-eight thousand dollars, (the second highest salary in The United States of all geographic areas) but cannot produce an acceptable reading level of over fifty percent in the students they teach. Now this just does not make sense! If New York City, and other areas that suffer from the same problems, are paying top dollar for teachers, then why should it not be possible to obtain, top results? Many would think that a top salary paid to a teacher would bring good if not excellent results in students.

However, the lower reading scores in many schools are occuring even with a lower standard of education in place. Control, (who makes the day to day decisions about the operations of schools) is an important issue also. In New York City, a central Board of Education, with thousands of entrenched bureaucrats, has been charged with this responibility for quite a long time. Local school boards have some power, in New York City, but not much. I feel that local school boards should have the majority of power in running their individual schools and also should have to the power to draw up the budgets required to run their schools.

Central control of school systems has proven itself to be self-defeating in the purpose of putting the childrens education, first and bureaucratic interests, second.

With local school board control. interests of students and the immeadiate community, in which many of the students live, will be addressed with more intensity.

A local school board, is not a faceless, emotionless bureaucracy, run by a multitude of political appointees and therefore would, just by its makeup and nature, be nore effective in achieving results. What I'm writing of, more simply put, is that if politics is removed from public education on a marcro level and shifted to a micro level, that the levels of accountability to the students should rise and therefore the levels and standards of education would rise also.

Then one, must also look for with caution. that in micro-managing a school, through total school board control, that the same bureaucratic pathology does not appear on a smaller level. However, I doubt that micro-management would produce the same problems we have had, with mangement from a huge central bureaucracy, even though, that would be possible, if local school boards were not watched closely. Micro management has long been the hallmark of the counterpart of public education, private education which is seen as very successful in comparison to public education.

There is a light at the end of the tunnel here. Recent proposals, by The New York State Department of Education would raise the requirments needed to graduate with a Regents diploma in all public schools in New York State. These raised standards for a Regents diploma could also have the effect of increasing the dropout rate for those who cannot meet the higher standard planned to graduate.

Support and funding is in place, to give every student in public education a computer at his or her desk by the year 2000. This is very important.

Computer literacy will be one of the many new requirments in most all wrokplaces in the 21st century. Finally, there is also a drive on, in the education field, to have teachers, take and pass re-certification exams, in their particular subject areas, that they teach, every five years. This is an excellent idea and would prevent teacher complacency, once they had obtained tenure or become vested in their jobs.

This writer is far from an expert in the field of public education and I have just written of some of the probelms apparent in public education today.

However, I do feel strongly about huge bureaucracies being a bar to progress in public education.

Our children do deserve the best we can give them and therefore this topic does demand close attention, further examination, and most of all, positive results. If this column and commentary, has helped to achieve those ends in any way at all, then I feel good about that, for a journalists job, is to shine light, sometimes where there is no light.

We may not like what we see, when the light allows us to look, however at that point, at least we have a choice, as to whether or not we wish to do what is proper, to makes things a little better, for others. See Ya All Next Time. Your Comments Are Welcome In The Guestbook For This Page.

VOL. 1 NO. 10

POLITICS AS YOU LIKE IT

THE WILDEST:WILD CARD IN BASEBALL:THE NEW YORK YANKEES:WORLD CHAMPIONS OF BASEBALL:1996 AND MAYBE 1997?: A LONGSHOT TO GO ALL THE WAY?:WELL, NOT REALLY!

I know! Your all saying, what is he doing this week writing about, sports. What does that have to do with politics? Well my readers, politics is an aspect of the sports world, like elsewhere and a reader has requested this weeks topic. So normally, I would'nt be writing about sports,however my readers receive priority on any topics they wish to see written about and this weekly column is really for the topics my readers wish to see written about. Only in weeks where no topic has been suggested by a reader, do I choose the topic for coverage.

This weeks topic for my column comes by request of Charlie Cancellieri from, Queens, New York. In a week where sportscaster Marv Albert had had the spotlight Mr. Cancellieri, stressed in his topic request, (parapharsed) "please, no Marv Albert". Perhaps the Marv Albert story has received too much coverage in the past two weeks. So the spotlight, here, goes to one of the greatest sports franchises in history,

The New York Yankees, or as their fans affectionately have called them for years, "The Bronx Bombers". For those readers not from New York City, The Bronx is one of five sections in New York City and where The Yankees play their home games. Aside from the usual politics going on in the Yankee front office, between hands-on owner George Stienbrenner, his General Manager, Bob Watson, and field manager Joe Torre, on this last day of the 1997, baseball season, The Yankees are in good shape and much more than their "wild card" status might indicate. On the other hand when attempting to focus on whats going on with The Yankees at any given moment, we should rememebr, that this is "The Bronx Zoo"; a term coined by former Yankee relief pitcher extraordinaire, Sparkey Lyle, who authored a book of the same name.

In otherwords, with The Yankees, one really never knows which way the wind is blowing. However, I do know this much. The Yankesss were 1996 World Champions of baseball. Tradition and history indicate that this ballclub is one tough customer when the chips are down, in a playoff or World Series. So, while most baseball fans marvel at The Baltimore Orioles, (with the best won-lost percentage in major leauge baseball this year) or The Atlanta Braves, (last years National Leauge Champions, and division leader this year) the real sleeper of the 1997 baseball season are The Yankees. They should not be counted out of going all the way to their second consecutive world championship, in as many years. Why? Well for one, this wild card entry into The American Leauge playoffs, toady, the last day of the baseball season, has the third best record in major leauge baeball, having won 96 games and lost 66 for a .593 percenatge

. There are six divisions in major leauge baseball, and The Yankees finished this season in second place, in The American Leauge Eastern Division, with a better record than first place finishers in four of six of those divisions. Only Atlanta and Baltimore have better records. The Yankees record of games won and lost this season would usuallly have a team finishing the season in first place, and having everyone who folows baseball, calling the team excellent.

Another factor to consider in the overall outcome of this situation is that The Yankees have the second highest team batting average in The American Leauge, .286. Thats better than twelve other teams in The American Leauge, including The Baltimore Orioles. and are tied with the National Leauges Colorado Rockies for the second highest team batting average out of twenty-eight teams in major leauge baseball. Further, The Yankees have the lowest earned run average in the fourteen team American Leauge and rank fifth in all of major leauge baseball, in team, pitching, earned run average, 3.87. One more very important statistic to take note of is that The Yankees, out of twenty-eight teams in major leauge baseball, are ranked third in team, runs batted in, (RBI'S) with 833 runs batted in. With men on base, The Yankess score runs and runs win baseball games, lots of them!

These are not the statistics of wild card teams. Rather, these statistics would represent by most standards a bona fide strong contender for The World Championship of baseball. This coming Tuesday evening here in New York City, The Yankees open the first round of The American League playoffs against The Cleveland Indians.The Indians have been to The World Series only twice in the past 43 yaers. 1954 and 1995.They have very little experience in post-season play, though they have become a power to be dealt with in the American Leauge for the past five years.

At the top of The Central Division of The American Leauge East, Cleveland has won ten less games, this season than The Yankees. With ace pitcher David Cone and fastballer Andy Pettitte set to pitch the first two games of this series for the Yankees, I doubt that The Yankees will have any problems disptaching The Indians into oblvion. Both Cone and Pettite are seasoned post-game pitchers. The 1997 Yankees are just as talented, if not more talented than The World Champion 1996 Yankess. The 1997 Yankees have had pitching problems and even with these problems, finish the season with an excellent record.

They have won 13 out of the last 16 games for a .812 won-lost percenatge, going into Tuesday's playoff series. Ultimately, The Yankees will have to get by Baltimore, to once again earn the right to play for The World Championship in The World Series. In an eight game, home and home series with Baltimore earlier this month, The Yankees played .500 ball, losing three out of four in New York, and winning three out of four in Baltimore. With a little extra push The Yankees can beat Baltimore in a playoff series also. Then serious attention must be paid to The Seattle Mariners as a possible playoff opponent of The Yankees and their talented leader Ken Griffey Jr. who has hit 55 home runs this season. The Yankees have their work cut out for them. So the diminished respect a wild card team would normally receive in baseball, cannot in all fairness be attributed to The Yankees, this year.

They must and should be taken very seriously, as post-season play begins. I pick The Yankess to be in The World Series for the second year in a row and then its anybodys guess, what happens next. While the owner of The Yankees flirts with New York City officials about moving the team out of New York, (perhaps to New Jersey) or to the West Side of Manhattan, (the section of Manhattan is considered in New York City to be the crown jewel of five sections of New York City) The Yankees are truly where they belong, in The Bronx, doing what they have done better than any other baseball team in the history of baseball, winning championships.

History and tradition bear out that The Yankees, when the moneys down on the table, do not choke. So, they are this years wild card, a designation not taken too seriously by most baseball fans, but watch them, they are very likely

Bernard Paul

to repeat as World Champions in 1997. See Ya All Next time. Your Comments Are Welcome In The Guestbook For This Page.

VOL. 1 NO. 11

POLITICS AS YOU LIKE IT

THE UNITED STATES SENATE TAKES ON THE IRS:FOR A CHANGE:THE INTERNAL REVENUE SERVICE GETS TAKEN TO THE CLEANERS:TAXMAN MIGHT BITE THE DUST

The suggestion for this weeks topic comes by request of *Edward Simmons from Downey, California.* What strikes most Americans taxpayers with fear? Just mention The IRS, (Internal Revenue Service) and people begin to tremble. As bureaucratic terrorists, The IRS, remains second to none in most peoples minds. Now don't get me wrong, here. I like many Americans feel that The IRS serves a vital function in collecting the $1.5 trillion dollars in taxes it takes in every year. These monies are required to run our country.

What many question, is some of the methods The IRS uses to collect the taxes. In, 1819, United States Supreme Court Justice John Marshall wrote, "the power to tax involves the power to destroy". Our nations first income tax came into being in 1862 and was instituted to pay for the expenses of The Civil War. The Civil War tax expired ten years later and was not re-instituted until 1894, but that income tax was ruled unconstitutional by The United States Supreme Court. For the next seventeen years, there was no income tax. Don't ask me how during this period the country managed to run itself, for quite honestly, I don't know!

In 1913, with ratification of The 16th Amendment to The United States Consitution, the income tax was here to stay. Back in 1913, a tax form for paying taxes was only two pages long and the Tax Code, which regulated the paying of taxes was fifteen pages long. Today the tax code is over eighty thousand pages long. An entire office of accountants and lawyers would have difficulty understanding the current tax code. Now, many people have been calling for tax reform for quite some time.

I can remember a few years back, when Jerry Brown of California was running for President of The United States, throwing the entire tax code into a garbage can and screaming for tax reform, at one of his campaign stops.

Along with reform of the tax code, what is also needed is reform of the abusive way in general taxpayers have been treated by The IRS. At long last, this dream, which many have talked about, and done very little, looks like it may become reality in the near future. During the past three weeks in Washington, The Senate Finance Committee,of The United States Senate has been holding hearings and conducting an investigation into the way The IRS treats taxpapyers. Some very interesting revelations have come out in these hearings! For one, it was established by testimony at the hearing, that the all feared audit, (thats where The IRS calls you in and looks at you with a microscope and asks that you justify every nickel and deduction on your tax return) is primarily practiced against poor people. The IRS's justification for this practice, was that poor people could not fight back, and lacked the resources to mount any substantial opposition, to any IRS action taken against them.

Perhaps. sound reasoning from a business standpoint, because the IRS would not have to spend it's money to recover any monies owed it from this group of people. However, enforcement of the law in this way is highly illegal and a clear violation of Section 1986 of The Civil Rights Act, that prohibits the enforcement of the law, against only one particular group, and not another group as well.

So here we go again, a Federal bureaucarcy, breaking the law to enforce the law. Great example put forth by those with whom we entrust to collect our taxes. Apparently, this problem of Federal agencies running afoul of the law is not an isolated incident. The problem is serious enough that The House Judiciary Committee along with Rep. George Gekas (R-Pa) and Rep. Barney Frank (D-Mass) and twelve other members of The House of Represenatives are sponsoring a bill called "the Federal Agency Compliance Act" which if passed by The Congress and The Senate and signed by President Clinton, would <u>further mandate,</u> that Federal agencies follow established law and precedent, in their day to day operations.

The fact that this bill which would create a new law, is even necessary, is a shame. As far as governmental entities are concerned a lot of people would expect on the Federal level, a better delivery of services and most certainly a strict adherence to the law and regulations that would govern the running of that agency. The fact that "The Federal Agency Compliance Act" is even being proposed means that its just not The IRS violating the laws, rules and regulations.

If we can't trust Uncle Sam to follow the law, just where are we going as a country? Further incidents of abuse of taxpapyers came out in stunning comments by cuurent IRS agent, Jennifer Long, who works with the Houston, Texas office of The IRS. Speaking on The CBS News program, "Face The Nation" last Sunday as to how bad IRS wrongdoing is, Agent Long, said, "I feel like its pretty widespread. I have had so many people tell me about suicides.......(of taxpayers)I really think somebody should look into how many people have committed suicide because of the IRS's actions. I think the statistics might be quite shocking." Agent Long went on to say that she knew of at least five suicides of taxpayers, though she was not the agent involved with those cases.

Newsweek magazine reported last week, that several IRS District office managers had been suspended in Arkansas and Oklahoma for allegedly breaking the law, by evaluating agents in their offices on the basis of how many levis and seizures were made of taxpapyers money and property. In otherwords, an illegal quota system was in place. United States Senator Daniel Patrick Moynihan (D-NY) offered an insightful and interesting comment last week. Senator Moynihan felt, (parapharsed) that because The IRS is both a collection agency and law enforcement agency that this was a bad combination and could not work. I agree one-hundred percent with that conclusion. Further abuses bt The IRS in dealing with taxpayers, have included in many cases the strange suspension of due process. Strange, because, most all decisions sent to a citizen by any Federal, State or Local, agency are subject to an appeal of that determination if the citizen decides to exercise that right guaranteed him or her under the 14th Amendment of The UNited States Consitution.

It seems IRS has chosen in many, many cases to ignore the right of appeal by taxpapers in a variety of decisions The IRS has issued in the past. I don't think for a second any American taxpayer has a problem with paying his or her fair share of taxes to help run our government, however all this aforementioned stuff is not part of the program and uncalled for. <u>Administrators of the law must follow the law, for people to have any respect for the law.</u> Anarchy, in the way Federal agencies manage their affaris is just unacceptable and should cease if we are to have a govenment worthy of anyones respect.

And the band plays on or when it rains it pours. The IRS currently operates with over one-hundred and thirty thousand employess, far more than they really need to conduct business. An over-staffed, overfunded, den of lawlessness run amok. Many, in Washington feel The IRS could do its job just as well with just thirty thousand employees. They will chase taxpayers who cannot defend themselves for a nickel, however consider these additional facts. Last year The IRS spent over four billion dollars of taxpayers money on a computer that would improve the implementation of the current tax code. Ready for this folks? You guessed it! The computer lost and the taxpayers got nothing for the four billion dollars of their money spent on trying to develop a computer to collect taxes more efficiently. The computer could not figure out the tax code or keep up with it. Four Billion dollars probably would represent several thousand IRS employees, annual salaries. Why not get rid of several thousand IRS employees to cover the four billion lost here?

No, folks, they remain on the job. If I owed the IRS four billion dollars they would chase me around the world, look under manhole covers for me, and hound me into my grave, or until they knew I was in my grave. <u>Excuse, me,</u> I'm of the opinion that they would hound me in the aforementioned manner for a few hundred dollars if I owed that to them. So four billion dollars is spent by The IRS on a failed project and nothing is done about that. Where is the accountability, responibility?

Summing up here, Acting IRS Commissioner Michael Dolan, started the reform process, by making a public apology to the many people who had been mistreated by The IRS, and said, "Clearly there are problems"

Now I have no problem with Acting Commissioner Dolans public apology. What I question, was the need for United States Senate public hearings, to have something done about these,"problems". Just who are these people who work for the IRS? Does an out-of-control bureaucracy have a conscience in dealing with its fellow American citizens? The answer to that question, in my opinion is no and in this case, no, until the light of a Senate investigation forces them to be human.

Acting IRS Commissioner Dolan has now promised to end the quota system used to collect money and which acted as an incentive for IRS agents to gouge taxpayers. In a further promise, Acting IRS Commissioner Dolan has also promised unprecedented direct access to thirty-three district managers of

IRS offices around the country, to taxpayers in those regions, who could present their complaints, one day a month, directly to those district managers. These district managers have real authority to reslove any complaints that would be brought directly to them.

This is a start, but without a significant overall change in the atitude towards taxpayers that a lot of the employees of The IRS have, no marked change can occur. The kind of tax we all pay is being reviewed on Capitol Hill also, income tax, flat tax, or consumer tax, however, I'll have to save that for another column. President Clinton recently signed "The Taxpayer Relief Act of 1997"

I will reserve comment on that until I call a friend that is a specialist in deciphering Egyptian hyrogliphics. See Ya All Next Time. Your Comments Are Welcome In The Guestbook For This Page.

Bernard Paul

VOL. 1 NO. 12

POLITICS AS YOU LIKE IT

THE DEATH PENALTY IN NEW YORK STATE:POLITICS ON THE BACK BURNER PLEASE

Law which is of value to a society, that is not enforced, becomes an insult to those who draft it and to the society the law is meant to protect. New York States Death Penalty law, seems to qualify to be defined as to the aformentioned.

In 1995, after many years of a Governor who refused to support a death penalty law, on moral and religious grounds, (Former New York State Governor Mario Cuomo) New York State got its first death penalty law on the books in a long time. A little known former prosecutor from Dutchess County, New York, and a virtual unknown in New York State politics at that time, George Pataki, had made the enactment of the death penalty, the central theme of his campaign for Governor, in 1994.

Now, I for one have not been a strong supporter of the death penalty. However, I do believe, that in certain circumstances, the death penalty should be sought and carried out. My rationale behind this feeling, is that there are just some crimes committed, that are so reprehensible, that not to seek the death penalty in such cases, represents an affront to the people,(society and the public) in any jurisdiction.

An example of the way I feel about the imposition of the death penalty, was the horrendous crime committed by Colin Fergerson on The Long Island Railroad, a few Christmas's back, where he boarded an evening rush hour train going out to Long Island from New York City and then just stood up and started firing a gun indiscriminately at passengers on the train. Several innocent people were killed and many more injured. At the time this happened, New York State had no daeth penalty law. In subsequent Court proceedings, held in Nassau County, New York, Mr. Fergerson, claimed, representing himself pro se, "that they had the wrong man". He was found gulity after a trial and sentenced to several consecutive life terms in prison.

Now the taxpayers must pay millions of dollars to house and feed, this animal for the rest of his life. For those readers who have a problem with the use of the term, "animal" here, what else can you call a guy who opens fire with a handgun, indicrimnately, on a railroad and kills and hurts innocent people, a human being? During this case in Nassau County, New York, an official, (Nassau County Executive Thomas Gulotta) had called Colin Fergerson, an animal and then was forced to retract his statement, due to a public outcry from groups that called, the Nassau County officials designation of the killer, as being racist.

Skin color has nothing to do with the circumstances in this case, period! Why should mercy be shown towards such an individual. An individual who did'nt express the slightest degree of remorse for the horrible crime he committed.

I, further believe, that in the pre-meditated murder of a police officer, the death penalty should be imposed. This is where New York States, current Republican Governor George Pataki, has shown himself to be, one-hundred percent politician. He ran and was elected for the office of Governor in New York State promising the reimposition of the death penalty, should he be elected. On the strength of that promise he was overwhelmely elected.

In his first year New Yorkers got the death penalty law, Governor Pataki, had promised. From that point on it was all downhill. In a case last year, in The Bronx, where a police officer was killed, The Bronx District Attorney, (the man responible for prosecuting crimes in that area of New York City) Robert Johnson, refused to seek the death penalty, citing philosphical and moral grounds. Governor Pataki maintained that D.A. Johnson's personal feelings about imposing the death penalty, should have been kept out of his decision and in not doing so, D.A. Johnson was not following the law. Robert Johnson is the first balck, District Attorney in The Bronx. His race became a possible issue when contrasted with how Governor Pataki, reacted to two similiar situations. An outraged Governor Pataki, demanded that D.A. Johnson seek the death penalty, or he would have him removed from the case and appoint a special prosecutor that would seek the death penalty. D.A. Johnson held steadfast to his position and Governor Pataki, had him removed from the case, and a special prosecutor was appointed to pursue the case, on behalf of The People of The State of New York.

It should be noted that Governor Pataki's decision to remove D.A. Johnson from the case, so the death penalty could be sought, is currently under appeal, by D.A. Johnson.

In the contrasting case, where a highly decorated veteran police officer was murdered, Governor Pataki, did a flip-flop. This time the District Attorney involved was the esteemed District Attorney of New York County, (Manhttan) Robert Morghenthau, who also opposes the imposition of the death penalty on philisophical and moral grounds. The case involved a man who had worked for his fathers clothing business, years ago, and had been caught stealing and fired from his job by his father. Earlier, this year, the son, returned to his fathers house on the West Side of Manhattan with the intention of robbing him again. The police were called and P.O. Anthony Sanchez, in confronting the son on the stairs of the building was shot and killed, exchanging gunfire with the suspect. A pretty clear case of pre-meditated murder, if I ever saw one.

Last week, D.A. Morghenthau, announced, _he would not see the death penalty in the murder of P.O. Sanchez._ In making his annouement, D.A. Morghenthau, gave no reason for his decision not to seek the death penalty. Governor Pataki, in this situation, agreed with D.A. Morghenthau, and called the fallen police oficers family to say, that life in prison was the proper penalty, to be sought in the case. Now, if you were the average cop on the beat, every day, trying to make your area safe and livable for the people on your beat, how would you feel about your job after learning of Governor Pataki's decision.

The message sent, in not seeking the death penaly for the pre-meditated murder of a police officer, is that you can get away with the murder of a police officer.

Behind the scenes of this case, are the commentators who have speculated, that Governor Patki caved into politics with this case in agreeing with D.A. Morghenthau, because he was scared of just how powerful Morghenthau is! So an alleged cop killer, does not get the penalty that is appropriate, becuae a District Attorney is more powerful than a sitting Governor of New York State.

As far as I'm concerned, (and I'm sure a lot of people would agree with me) that is a clear cut perversion of the law as it was intended to be imposed, and _very absurd._ What good is a death penalty law, if we cannot even have it vigorously, sought in the murder of a police officer? Then New York States, death penalty law, becomes a joke, and can be defined as what our current Governor in New York State, used to get himself elected, despite his outrage and actions in The Bronx case, involving D.A, Johnson. There is no justice in the position Governor Pataki has taken in the recent case. Politics be dammed, especially, where the clear cut pre-meditated murder of a police officer is concerned. Our police should be backed up, one-hundred percent. Instead they report to work, having to think about politically motivated decisions, made by politicians, which in the long run, compromises their effectiveness as police officers along with diminishing their morale.

In these situations, politics should be placed on the "back burner" out of respect to those who try their best to protect us every day, our police officers. If Governor Pataki had chosen to take the same position he took in The Bronx matter, when dealing with the Manhattan matter, at least we could feel he was being consistant and a lot of people offended by his recent decision, would feel a lot safer and better. The death penalty law in New York State was not meant to be a paper tiger. That certainly was not the legislative intent of those who wrote the law and voted for it's enactment in The New York State Legislature.

Essentially, that is what New York States Death Penalty Law, has become, two and one half years after its enactment. This must change if we are truly interested in lowering crime on a permanent basis. See Ya All Next Time. Your Comments Are Welcome In The Guestbook For this Page.

VOL. 1 NO. 13

POLITICS AS YOU LIKE IT

THE WIZARD OF OZ: OUR AMERICAN ECONOMY: FANTASY OR REALITY

This past week, Federal Reserve Chairman Alan Greenspan, said; (parapharsed) That he felt, "the ongoing unprecedented surge in the stock market, could not go on forever". The primary function of The Federal Reserve Bank is to set interest rates, which then dictate the amount major banks must charge their customers to borrow money. The Federal Reserve Bank is also concerned with our nations money supply. Too little money in circulation causes problems, as too much money in circulation, also can cause problems for our economy.

I tend to disagree with Chairman Greenspan's assessment of how long the stock market can continue to be bullish. It is my feeeling, that the curent stock market boom can continue, getting better, indefinitely. This stock market, further in my opinion, is not being fueled by a booming American economy, taking place here in our country. It is being fueled by numerous overseas markets for a variety of products. that are no longer being manufactured here in The United States. Yes, John Q. Public, you can have a booming stock market, along with double-digit unemployment. In the Sunday edition of The New York Daily News, nationally syndicated columnist, Jim Dwyer, writes; "In fact unemployment in the city, (New York City) is way above the national rates." Dwyer goes on to write, "work is easy to find, if you have an advanced degree in computer science, or can get by on six dollars an hour from a chain store."

Now for the readers of this commentary who are not or have never lived in my home town, currently, New York City, let me shine a further light on Mr. Dwyer's statement in his Sunday column. To begin with, six dollars an hour for the normal forty hour week, comes out to two-hundred and forty dollars a week before taxes or twelve-thousand four-hundred and eighty dollars a year

Secondly, how many people have advanced degrees in computer science?

Now remains the question, of how an individual let alone a small family is expected to live on $240.00 a week in a city where the average rent for a small apartment is well above $700.00 a month. Well you say, theres plenty of six dollar an hour jobs to go around, so let the guy work two jobs, for six an hour and his wife, work one job for six an hour, and the problems taken care of, now as a family, they earn before taxes thirty-six thousand dollars a year and change. Sounds good, right!

However, New York City at this time in the middle of a race for Mayor has an unemployment rate of eleven percent, the highest of any other city in The United States. At the same time we here in New York City are being told that our cities economy is booming, in most part, due to the tremendous Wall Street, stock market. With the nations highest municipal unemployment rate, no candidate for Mayor, (including the incumbent Mayor, Rudolph Giuliani) have said one word about unemployment in New York City, or how if re-elected or elected to be Mayor, they would help create new jobs, or help bring back, the four-hundred thousand jobs, that have left New York City, since the year 1980.

New York Daily News columnist, Jim Dwyer, also writes in his Sunday column, "so much of the economy is a mirage." I could'nt agree more! For those readers who at this point of my column, who would say, "well, New York's problems are not mine"; you would be sadly mistaken, for New York City and how well it is doing, pretty much sets the tone for how the entire nation will do in the future.

Now I'm not an economist or an expert in the way the economy functions. I'm just an average guy, offering his commentary and or opinion, on a variety of topics, every week in this commentary.

In doing such, I try very hard, every week, to let common sense and logic dictate what I write about. Being human, sometimes I am dead wrong in my opinion, and sometimes, I'm right on target. My commentaries are not written to satisfy the consensus or justify the status quo at any given moment, but are guided, by experience in life and keen observation of what is going on around me. I've taken the time to stop, look, listen and evalaute. The process is called, "thinking"; something not taught in the good majority of schools in our country anymore.

In, the legendary movie, "The Wizard of Oz", the principal character, Dorothy, (played so wonderfully, by actress, Judy Garland) comes upon, what she thought to be an omnipresent, all powerful Wizard, only to find, that the Wizard was far less than she had thought him to be. Our current American economy is the same thing Dorothy came to see, when she completed her journey, down the yellow brick road, *one huge mirage.* Yes, our economy is booming, however, most people who live in our country are not the benificiaries of this booming economy and here's why they are not.

Two and two, will add up to four here. First of all, since 1987, hundreds of thousands of Americans have lost good paying jobs, in the most massive layoffs, (called downsizing by American corporations) to have ever occured in the history of our nation, including The Great Depression of 1929. Very few of these people have been able to return to the level of earnings they enjoyed, before they were downsized. Many, today, if they were lucky enough to find another job, are working for less than half of what they had earned before they had lost their jobs.

Second, fueled by bi-partisan support in Washington, laws were passed that made it easy for American corporations to set up shop, in Mexico, Canada and a variety of European countries, where labor costs are very low, in comparison, to what they were for American corporations here in the United States. In the name of profits, at levels hundreds of times higher than they were making here in The United States, multi-national corporations, basically, declared, The American Worker, "expendable" and headed for greener pastures.

In terms of profits, (the bottom line in all business ventures) this makes sense. However, in terms of the loyalty, most would expect from an American corporation, doing business, here in The United States, it's absurd! Not only has The American worker been *totally "sold out" and left up the stream without a paddle,* the potential of The American market for the sale of goods manufactured overseas by American corporations has also been forsaken. Case in point!

If I own a company, that manufactures color television sets here in The United States and it costs me with all my overhaed, (expenses to manufacture the product) $200.00 a television set, why not go to Mexico, whwre I can manufacture the same set for $30.00. The difference goes into my pocket. I can then lower the price on my television set, and still maintain a profit margin, much higher than I had achieved in The United States and The

American market be dammed too, I'll market my product overseas, in Europe or Asia. This all started with *The North American Free Trade Agreement, (NAFTA)* and has'nt shown any signs of subsiding.

This is how and why Wall Street booms and will continue to boom, indefintely in my opinion. Now what happens to all The American people who have lost jobs and cannot find jobs of any substance as a result of the aforementioned? Ask the companies who have set up shop in Mexico how they feel about that, while you flip hamburgers for McDonalds with your college degree, for six dollars an hour, or with the skills you tried to learn so you would not fall victim to this *sellout, extraordinaire,*

In closing, yes Wall Street is going very well, but that success will not help create jobs that are sorely needed at this time. The good portion of Wall Streets money is also overseas. Wall Street today, is essentially, an island by itself. They say, "no man is an island", however Wall Street, feels being an island is no problem. I wish the solution I could offer, would be to advise everyone who wanted a good job here in The United States to just go back to school and learn computer science.

I don't know if its that simple! In the newspaper today, I also saw a photograph of a 51 year old woman, who sweeps the parks here in New York City to earn her welfare check. She is part of New York Cities answer to Welfare Reform, workfare, The Work Experience Program or WEP. She's paid $15.12 a day, earning her welfare check. The postscript here, is that this woman, went to school and earned a two year degree in computer science from, SUNY, The State University of New York. After graduation, she could not find a job! Lets all stop fooling ourselves. Thers something profoundly wrong with our economy and I for one, can't be told anything by my political leaders and just accept it or beleive it. Our American Corprations have an obligation to The American worker and the same laws that allowed them to go, can force them to come back' if just re-written! See Ya All Next Time.

Bernard Paul

VOL. 1 NO. 14

POLITICS AS YOU LIKE IT
HUMAN RIGHTS?

This week I extend a special invitation to all of my readers for a little help.

The help I require, (on the eve of a an important meeting between, President Clinton and The President of China) is an explanation of why the leader of the free world is sitting down, (or bending over) to talk with a leader from a country that currently has seven million people, (human beings) working in slave camps?

Furthermore why are the fruits of these modern day slaves being allowed to flood our American market? I like most average American people thought for a long, long time that the idea of salvery, was not only outlawed, but a replusive one. Indeed, perhaps I was wrong in thinking so! The fact that Amnesty International has been investigating various human rights violations, for many years in our country, puts a little more salt in the wound. I'll get into that, in a future column and mention that only to highlight that The United States is also alledged to be a violater of human rights, but certainly not to the extent that China has been proven to be.

This situation in China looks like a race between, human rights and capitalism, with human rights finishing a distant second. It seems that The United States will try to maintain good relations at all costs with China, which also includes the killing of many students, a few years back, when the students demonstrated in Tianiman Square, in China, for some of the freedoms we are blessed with here in The United States

While China is a major power and player on the world scene, they cannot be permitted to get away with flagrant human rights violations and in doing this use the American market, to sell the goods produced by slaves. I for one, when discovering that a product I'm about to buy, is made in China, get a funny feeling in my stomach, and put the product back and refuse to buy it. It is my hope that this week as President Clinton talks with China's leaders that he will ask that this situation be addressed, not because it looks bad, but rather, because, China's slave policy is an insult to what modern day America stands for. All human beings deserve to be treated with respect and have a right to dignity. China's slave policy brings us all down one notch in life. To know of this policy and not vigorously condemm it is to remain silent in the face of a practice that has long been met with contempt in most of the world we all live in.

The principles that make The United States, the greatest country on earth, cannot be compromised for the sake of the dollar bill. If so, we are made to look like a bunch of clowns whose words, ideas and principles are not to be taken seriously, by the rest of the world, and most important by our own people here in this country.

It is possible to conduct business and foriegn trade with China, and have a conscience at the same time. China continues to enjoy as a trade partner of The United States. a privileged and most favored nation status with our country and unlimited access to the huge market here in The United States. Aside from the aforementioned, China enjoys this status, even while it continues to sell missles to Iran, an enemy of The United States and nuclear technology to Pakistan.

China's recent arrest of a Catholic bishop, along with it's intense persecution of Christians in China, add to a long list of human rights violations.

Finally, China, maintains a policy of steep tarrifs and taxes on U.S. products we wish to market in China. President Clinton earlier this year finally, addressed a simliar uneven trade situation with Japan, which for years was restricting the marketing of American trade products in Japan.

Imagine, all of the products that The United States has allowed Japan to market here in America, and then when we want to market our products in Japan, thats no good. What kind of a trade policy was that? It seemed to benefit only, Japan.

The United States is not a doormat or a vechile for world wide domination of the market, by Japan, China, Hong Kong, Maylaysia and Pakistan. The word "trade" conotates, *a two way* street. Japans current trade surplus with The United States is close to sixty-billion dollars a year. What is our trade surplus with Japan? We currently have no trade surplus with Japan, only a huge trade deficit.

Bernard Paul

As these countries continue to spit in America's eye, Prseident Clinton pretends not to notice. Well it's high time he took notice, so our economic security here in The United States, does not permanently fall into the hands of external forces. We saw an example of this last week, when the Hong Kong stock market, triggered a three-hundred point drop in The Dow-Jones Industrial average here in The United States. So, President Cilnton, has a pretty big agenda with China, this week and I sincerely, hope he comes away from this historic meeting, with some meaningful progess and reform.

Our current trade situation with China, is just unacceptable, and not in the best interests, either short-term or long-term of our country. Good Luck, this week, President Clinton. See Ya All Next Time.

VOL. 1 NO. 15

POLITICS AS YOU LIKE IT

THE UNITED STATES OF MICROSOFT

This weeks material and topic come courtesy of Efrem Violin who lives in Culver City, California. Mr. Violin is active in assisting the musical arts in his home town.

I found it amusing and laughable when a few weeks back Attorney General of The United States Janet Reno threatened Microsoft Chairman Bill Gates and his company, Microsoft Inc. with fines of one million dollars a day, for giving away his browser, Internet Explorer, (Internet Explorer is Microsoft developed software and is used to search the Internet for a variety of subject areas) free of charge.

This giveaway ordered by Chairman Gates was to stimulate Microsoft's business, against Netscape, their number one competitor. Attorney General Reno was saying, that essentially, Microsoft was gaining an unfair market advanatge and attempting to create a monopoly, in violation of anti-trust laws, by not charging for his browser. Now everyone knows that Bill Gates is not trying to create a monopoly but only *trying to take over the entire planet earth, and then some, thats all!*

In honor of Bill Gates, (probably the greatest genius to come along in a very long time) I reprint below, an article forwarded to me last week by Mr. Violin. In doing so, I hope to provide my readers with a little laugh this week.The day of Attorney General Reno's announcement the price of Micrsofts stock went up four points. Apparently, the threat of a possible one million dollar a day fine, did not damage Microsofts stock market position, one bit. Below a little more admirable fun poked at a guy you can't help but like, Bill Gates and his company Microsoft who also, by the way own Web Tv Networks Inc.; the venue this column appears through. Just kidding Mr. Gates, okay? Love Ya, Bill Gates!

REDMOND, Wash. Oct 21, 1997-

In direct response to accusations, made by the Department of Justice, the Microsoft Corp. announced today, that it will be acquirring the federal government of the United States of America for an undisclosed sum.

Bernard Paul

"It's actually a logical extension of our planned growth", said Microsoft chairman Bill Gates. "It really is going to be a positive arrangement for everyone". Microsoft representatives held a briefing in the oval office of the White House, with U.S. President Bill Clinton, and assured members of the press that changes will be "minimal". The United States will be managed as a wholly owned division of Microsoft

. An initial public offering is planned for July of next year and the federal government is expected to be profitable by "Q4 1999 at latest"; according to Microsoft president, Steve Ballman. In a related announcement, Bill Clinton stated that he had " willenly and enthusiastically accepted a position as a vice-president with Microsoft, and will continue to manage the United States government, reporting directly to Bill Gates.

When asked how it felt to give up the mantle of authority to Gates, Clinton smiled and referred to it as "a relief" He went on to say, that Gates has "a proven track record" and that U.S. citizens should offer Gates their; "full support and confidence."

Clinton will reportedly be earning several the times $200,000 anually he has earned as U.S. president, in his new role at Microsoft.

Gates dismissed a suggestion that the U.S. Capitol be moved to Redmond, as "silly"; though did say that he would make executive decisions for the U.S. government from his exisiting office at Microsoft headquarters. <u>Gates went on to say that the House and Senate would "of course" be abolished!</u> "Microsoft isn't a democarcy" he observed; " and look at how well we're doing." When asked if the rumored acquistion of Canada, was proceeding, Gates, said, "We don't deny that discussions are taking palce."

Microsoft represenatives closed the conference by stating, that United States citizens will be able to expect lower taxes; increases in government services and discounts on all Microsoft products. <u>About Microsoft</u> Founded in 1975, Microsoft (NASDAQ "MSFT") is the world-wide leader in software for personal computers, and democratic government.

The company offers a wide range of products and services for public, business and personal use, each designed with the mission, of making it easier and more enjoyable for people to take advantage of the full power of personal computing and free society every day. <u>About The United States</u>

Founded in 1789, the United States of America, is the most successful nation in the history of the world, and has been a beacon of democracy and opportunity for over 200 years. Headquarted in Washington D.C.; the United States is <u>a wholly owned subsidiary of Microsoft Corporation.</u>

Well there you have it folks! In case you did'nt know it already, Bill Gates and his Microsoft Corporation are not only running The United States Government, <u>they own it too!</u> Hail Gates! See Ya All Next Time and Don't

Forget to __VOTE__ in your elections this coming Tuesday. It does make a difference

Bernard Paul

VOL. 1. NO. 16

POLITICS AS YOU LIKE IT

"FAST TRACK" LEGISLATION IN WASHINGTON:NAFTA REVISITED:FAST TRACK TO THE BREAD LINE IN OUR SO-CALLED BOOMING ECONOMY

This past weekend, Congress was in a rare special session to decide the fate of President Clinton's "fast track" legislation. Essentially, "fast track" if approved by Congress, (there are enough votes to approve the bill in The Senate) would give President Clinton the authority to submit his version of trade deals, which then Congress would accept as submitted by President Clinton, or vote down.

No changes in the trade deals submitted would be permitted by Congress. This almost amounts to trade deals with foriegn countries, like Mexico, Canada, China, Maylaysia and Japan by executive presidential fiat.

If Congress did not like what The President was submitting to them, the option to turn it down, if exercised would slow down progress in any trade deals sought by The President.

A few days ago, President Clinton said, (parapharsed) "that if "fast track" failed to pass, it would be an immense setback for The United State's position in international trade.

The fast track bill is being opposed by organized labor, for the same reasons the 1993 NAFTA, *(The North American Free Trade Agreement)* was. *Jobs* with a capital J. This commentator as the average joe who cares about his country also opposes "fast track" for the following reasons.

Currently enough jobs have left our country. While everyone in Washington, since the passage of the 1993 NAFTA bill, has been saying that NAFTA would not cost Americans any jobs, it has. Several weeks ago The U.S. Department of Labor finally admitted the truth. It has been conceded that since NAFTA passed in 1993, that 124,000 American jobs have left the country for Mexico.

On the day Congress passed NAFTA in 1993, 550,000 Mexicans worked across the American border in low wage factories owned mostly by American companies. The Mexican workers average pay in 1993 was $6.00 a day. Just four years after NAFTA was enacted, there are currently over 940,000 workers just across the border working for less, because of the devaluation of the Mexican peso.

The same methods that helped send all these jobs to Mexico with NAFTA in 1993 would be employed to do the same thing, with "fast track" if it passes. This is just unacceptable.

Have'nt we lost enough jobs to foriegn competition in the past ten years? This "fast track" legislation must be killed to insure whatever morale the American worker has left and to endorse his and her survival. President Clinton is just going in the wrong direction with this corporate pork, "fast track" bill. Instead, President Clinton should be sending Congress and The Senate bills which would impose severe monetary penalties, on any American company that would leave The United States to do business elsewhere. The monies collected by this *"corporate exit tax"* would then go into a fund, that would help create more jobs here in The United States, not to retrain workers, who won't be able to find jobs with their new skills.

Fine, you want to sell out the American worker and our country, pay for it, and pay for it dearly. A flat-tax could be imposed on the average profits of any company that choose to leave The United States, on the preceding five years of gross profit which would be paid into The United States Treasury when a company would choose to leave The United States.

Employers here in The United Staes have threatened to close plants where workers have wanted to join unions, and set up shop in Mexico. How anxious would these employers be to leave if they were required to pay a hefty, *"exit tax"*?

Finally, "fast tarck" would not impose any penalty whatsoever for the use of slave labor. Rob your investors, and rip off your labor! Is this the corporate credo that we go into the 21st century with? One hell of an example to the next generation! When Vice-President Al Gore debated, Texas businessman and Vice-Presidential candidate Ross Perot, over NAFTA, many years ago, Perot, correctly commented with great foresight, that,(parapharsed) "NAFTA would create a great sucking sound of jobs lost to Mexico". No one cared to listen to Perot, calling him some kind of a nut

Many, Many, Americans have seen their friends or relatives, lose good paying jobs in the past five years only to be re-employed in low wage or part-time jobs, with no benefits, that pay less than half of what they had previously earned. Imagine, having a good paying job of $35,000 a year and after downsizing and laws like NAFTA. now having to work for $16,000 a year, so companies instead of making a 600 percent profit, leave the country to make a 1600 percent profit.

In this commentators opinion, "fast track" will speed up only one thing, the trip to the unemployment office to file for benefits. Of course Wall Street will love "fast track". Last week after it was announced that unemployment here in the United States is at a 24 year low, The Dow-Jones Industrial average fell over one-hundred points. One final note! Last weeks unemployment figures do not take into account the millions of Americans who have given up looking for work. So we are told we have a 4.2 percent unemployment rate. To use an old expression, _BALDERDASH!_

Fast Track must be defeated and I urge my readers to call or E-Mail, their Congressperson, and express their disatisfaction with this attempted further rape of the American worker. See Ya All Next Time!

VOL. 1 NO. 17

POLITICS AS YOU LIKE IT

1984:BIG BROTHER IS HERE

Civil liberterians, this week in New York City, are having fits, and choking on their pastrami sandwichs. New York City, which has led the nation in producing dramatic decreases in crime, is considering, "big brother" tactics, in high crime areas and in the most prominent park in New York City, Central Park.

Not many today would argue strongly, that giving up some constitutional rights, to achieve a safer society is something they could live with. This past week here in the New York City, the newly re-elected Republican Mayor of New York City, Rudolph Gulliani, announced that it would be a good idea to put cameras in high crime areas of the city, and Central Park.

Mayor Gulliani did not include in his announcement, the placing of cameras in every police station in New York City, where police abuses of the public in 1996 have cost the City of New York over thirty million dollars, in lawsuit settlements. I strongly disagree with idea of placing cameras in high-crime areas and Central Park. Futhermore, I find the idea of doing such, repulsive. Mayor Gulliani, said last week, in making his announcement, "that no one could have an expectation of privacy while in public". I like most people support effcetive, just and swift, law enforcement. I am even willing to give up some constitutional rights to become a benificiary of a safer place to live in.

However, I also feel that Mayor Gulliani's idea to put cameras in public araes is just a pretext to take away other freedoms that are enjoyed in the future. No one has anything to fear, if they are not doing anything wrong, I'm told. The issue here is much larger than that. A paranoid govenment that does'nt trust its own people, will ultimately produce a paranoid populace. Government for the people Mayor Gulliani, not Government against the people, under the pretext of being for the people.

While New York Cities Mayor should be commended for the results he has obtained in reducing crime in his first term as mayor, this camera stuff is overkill. It is my fear that cameras in high crime areas of New York City, will force the criminals to go to low crime areas to commit their crimes, thus of course making it necessary to put more cameras there.

Significant reductions in crime have already been achieved in high crime areas, without cameras. Why can't the methods used to obtain those reductions just be increased?

Finally, I'm not comfortable with the idea that the cameras would be placed in only poor neighborhoods where supposedly the majority of crime is being committed and also where a good many people of color live in New York City. Why not put cameras in low crime middle-class areas of the city, where crime is also committed, but not at the levels of high crime areas? If the basic agenda is zero tolerance for crime, the cameras could be justified in low crime white middle class areas also, no?

Sorry, Charlie, I'm not going for this camera stuff. Too many times, I've seen idaes and programs, that were meant to benefit do the exact oppositie. My column last week, about NAFTA, (The North American Free Trade Agreement) and the proposed, "Fast Track" legislation in Washington, gave a prime example of that.

Norman Siegel, Executive Director of The New York City Civil Liberties Union said the placing of cameras in public araes, "raises the Orwellian specter of Big Brother spying on citizens". In George Orwells classic novel, entitled, "1984", Orwell describes a futuristic society, which includes an all seeing, all knowing government which spys on every action and movement of its population. Is this what we really all want? Think about where it will lead. See Ya All Next Time

VOL. 1 NO. 19

POLITICS AS YOU LIKE IT

CAN I GET SOME DISCIPLINE FOR A THIRTY-TWO MILLION DOLLAR CONTRACT?: THE NATIONAL BASKETBALL ASSOCIATION AND GOLDEN STATE WARRIORS GUARD LATRELL SPREWELL

This column is written under the "I thought I saw everything department". Perhaps the principals last name in this recent debacle had dictated his destiny._Sprewell_ He was it seems, if we take several puns and definitions of his last name, to have a _"spree"_ done _well"_; at one time in his life.

Well, last Monday, the professional basketball world was made victim to a spree of sorts by one of its star players. With twenty witnesses to this sad event, Golden State Warrior guard, Latrell Sprewell, assaulted his coach, last Monady during a team practice. The form of the assault, was an attempt to choke Golden State Warriors head coach, P.J. Carlesimo, by puting his hands around the coaches neck. After the incident, Sprewell also reportedly threatned to kill, the former Fordham University head basketball coach.

Coach Carlesimo. In defense of his actions, Sprewell was quoted as saying, "I could'nt take the verbal abuse that he's, (Coach Carlesimo) given the guys the past month or so". Up to this point, Sprewell has not said he was sorry for what he did.No public apology has been forthcoming, only a private apology to his freinds and family. Certainly, Coach Carlesimo is due a sincere public apology from Sprewell. No circumstances I know of can justify Sprewells actions.

Latrell Sprewell is paid 7.7 million dollars a year to play basketball. The Golden State Warriors basketball team, who employ Sprewell currently have the third worst won-lost record in the twenty-nine team,National Basketball Association. In the nine team Pacific division, Golden State is in last palce having won one game and losing fourteen games.

In this unprecented action by a player against his coach, The NBA has suspended Sprewell for one year and the team he plays for has terminated his contract. Even if another team would want Sprewell to play for them, he cannot, under the terms of the suspension, play in the NBA until December of next year. David Stern, the Commissiner of The National Basketball

Association and the leauge should be commended for taking this disciplinary action against Sprewell. A clear message must be sent throughout the sports world, (not only basketball) that this type of behavior as demonstrated by Sprewell's assault of his coach,will not be tolerated and that severe penalities will be suffered by anyone who would act in the aforementioned manner. The penalties and sanctions given to Latrell Sprewell in this matter are very appropriate and not at all harsh. In professional sports there is no room for unprofessional conduct of any kind.

This commentator along with many others who have written about this incident, feels that Sprewell crossed a line, which should not be crossed, by doing what he did.

Moreso, and very important are the youngsters who support and watch professonal sports, who must not be left with the idea that what Sprewell did was okay! God knows, we have more than enough mindless violence here in The United States already.

Finally, and briefly, Major Leauge Baseball should take a cue from the disciplinary action in this matter by The National Basketball Association. The Roberto Alomar incident, several years ago, comes to mind. Alomar had spit in an umpires face during a game, and received a nominal slap on the wrist from Major Leauge Baseball for doing that. Many, including, this writer felt Alomar, should have received a harsher penalty for what he did. There must be consistancey in the way these type of incidents are dealt with, so the message sent out in professional sports is a consistant one also. Furthermore, the message sent, is one that is not confined to professional sports, but to living ones life, in general, across the board, in all walks of life, that this type of behavior is *totally unacceptable.* The response, when these types of incidents occur, no matter where they happen, should be a uniform one.No amount of spin contorl can mitigate this type of outrageous behavior.

In closing, if I were paid 7.7 millon dollars a year on a thirty-two million dollar multi-year contract, I certainly would have sufficient discipline to take whatever my coach had to say to me, even if it was abusive. You keep your mouth shut and do your job! In todays era of prima-donna sports stars ,who for the most part are very spoiled, I guess thats too much to expect. It is my opinion that when someone pays you 7.7 million dollars a year, (or even a lot less than that) you listen and produce and are very apprecative for the

opportunity to do so. No one likes verbal abuse. Sometimes it comes with the territory. Good riddens to Latrell Sprewell, who can't keep his hands off his coach, for a thirty-two million dollar, 7.7 million dollar a yaer contract in professional basketball. I'm supposed to feel sorry for this guy? See ya All Next Time!

Bernard Paul

VOL.1 NO. 20

POLITICS AS YOU LIKE IT

HYPHENATED AMERICANS AND MULTICULTURAL EDUCATION: A HIDDEN AGENDA ON ALL SIDES

During the past two months, on several occasions, readers have asked me to do a column on hyphenated-Americans. In declining to do so, I cited my lack of knowldge regarding the subject matter. After a bit of research on the topic, which included questions of people who knew of the current hyphenated-American debate, I felt that at this time a commentary could be written about this new area of thought. Credit for suggesting this topic goes to Mr. Efrem Violin of Culver City, California and Mr. Jeffy Gersten of Monticello, New York.

Both Mr. Violin and Mr. Gersten are politically active in their respective communities. Mr. Violin, (a musician for thirty years) lobbies The Culver City Arts Committee and The City Council of Culver City, California, for fair and just appropiations for the musical arts. Mr. Gersten, is a member of his local school board and attends many conferences and meetings that relate to his school board membership.

At the heart of this issue is the desire to have people, call themselves just plain Americans and not identify their origin by ethnicity first and being American second. For example, according to this conservative proposal, people would no longer call themselves, Afro-American, Hispanic-American, Polish-American, Irish-American, Italian-American Jewish-American, Russian-American ect. ect. ect.; but just American.

The idea here, in proposing this way of identifying one's heritage, is that in taking out the ethnic portion of one's identification, our country would be more unified and become stronger as a nation. It is my opinion after examining this proposal, that it sounds like a potential type of <u>McCarthyism,</u> if put into practice.

To begin with, I see no problem or reason with Americans exercising their right to identify with their ethnic origins first and their geographical station, second. Most people are proud of where they came from, or where members of the family they belong to originated. History has demonstrated that countries that have rallied around a nationalism of sorts, have run into serious problems. Then I fear, that some conservatives, (who are seen as extreme, by many people in the political world, which is the basis for my premise here) would call Americans, who refused to go along with this line of thinking, as somehow disloyal to America, and therefore doing a dis-service to their country.

This country does not become weaker by the wonderful and tremendous diversity of people that live and work here. To the contrary, that diversity, is one of the reasons The United States is one of the greatest places on the face of the earth. Americans should be allowed to express their pride in the ethnic origins they have, without reservation, and in doing so, should not be subject to any attempt to stimatize such identification. Many people derive a great deal of self-esteem from identifying with their ethnic origins as I'm sure they also feel proud to be Americans.

Regarding this issue, I strongly support the status-quo and feel that those who wish people to identify themselves as only American are out of step with the reality of our times. We have had enough of institutional prejudice in America. There is more than enough enlightenment in America to allow for the individuality of people who live and work here. Any attempt to take that away, in my opinion, is an attempt to futher erode the freedoms we are fortunate enough to have in America.

Those who identify themselves using a hyphenated-American defintion of themselves are cool with me.

Secondly, I attempt to address the state of multi-cultural education in schools. I can understand the need for multi-cultural education. However, from what I've read and seen, the intent and purpose of multi-cultural education is not being carried out by educators or the school systems they work with here in America. When multi-cultural education becomes a vechile to bash our country, I cannot support it. Too often, multi-cultural education has repleced American history, or whatever American history being taught along side multi-cultural history, is for the most part a negative account of the history of America.

Now, I'm not saying that negative portions of American history should not be taught to students. What, I am saying is that multi-cultural education should not be the only history taught, and that the good and bad of American history should be taught, also. Many people would concede that history is usually a reflection of those who write that history, and not necessarily, accurate. The purpose of allowing multi-cultural education into our schools was not to replace American history and then bash America when teaching multi-cultural subjects.

This way of teaching history is divisive, and a distortion of facts. What is multi-cultural educations agenda, to produce citizens, that hate America? The teaching of multi-cultural subjects should be consistant with one of the purposes of education to begin with, and that is, producing good citizens, who will particpate and have productive lives here in America. How will a youngster come away with the self-esteem she or he needs to compete for a good job, if they are being taught to dislike the country they live in.

It looks to me like multi-cultural education and the way it is being implemented currently, will produce a lot of anti-social kids which would produce more problems for society.

Finally, multi-cultural education, can be important to the education process, if taught in a manner which is not self-defeating to the general purpose of education to begin with. See Ya All Next Time

VOL. 1 NO. 21

POLITICS AS YOU LIKE IT

THE JOKER IS WILD:AND NOW WE HAVE PRINCE HASEEM HAMED:FEATHERWEIGHT BOXING CHAMPION OF THE WORLD AND HBO (HOME BOX OFFICE)

Seth Abraham, the head of sports promotions for the cable network, HBO, really outdid himself this time.

In a contract that will run for six televised fights, Abraham, has continued to perpetuate the slease factor in professional boxing by signing Prince Haseem Hamed. Hamed, a virtual unknown in the fight world, will certainly get his five mnutes of fame now, especially. after last Friday evenings excuse for a fight promotion.

The class act of the night, was the appearence of current heavyweight champion Evander Holyfield, who accepted an award from Madison Square Garden President Dave Checketts, commemorating Holyfield's first professional fight, which had taken palce at Madision Square Garden, a long time ago.

With 11,954 paying customers attending the fight, Prince Haseem, (he likes to be called Has by his friends) knocked out New York City native Kevin Kelly at two minutes and twenty-seven seconds of the fourth round. There were six knockdowns during the four rounds. Madison Square Garden, in this heavily promoted and publicized boxing match, had 7,550 empty seats for the contest.

Professional boxing in this writers opinion, has become an absolute joke! I would have to agree with the late and great boxing analyst and commentator, Howard Cosell, in calling for the sport to be banned. I spend, (like most people) my week dealing with a host of difficulties that one must face in life. Come Friday or Saturday evening, I would like to sit down and relax, perhaps enjoying a good program. Since cable has a better line-up of programs at most times, I check my cable listing to see that a boxing match is on at 9 P.M. Eastern Standard Time. Now, I like a good boxing match like any other guy out there. So I raid my fridge, for a cold one, turn on the televsion and this is what I get.

Bernard Paul

"Prince Naseem Hamed stood behind a curtain leading to a runway where he would enter the Madison Square Garden ring for his United States debut. All the fans could see was the Prince's silhouetted figure behind the curtain. As some rap music balred, the Prince danced for over twelve minutes keeping the challenger, Kevin Kelly waiting in the ring. As the crowd screamed, "Naseem, Naseem", Kevin Kelly and his trainer hopped up on the ring ropes gesturing for Haseem to enter the ring. Finally, the Prince did, Down the ramp he came, with some more dancing, (which looked like a hedonistic tribute to himself) to the ring apron, where the Prince finally entered the ring, with a double-somersault from the outside of the ring. Then the Prince danced around inside the ring for another five minutes, before ring announcer Michael Buffer, (the second quality act of the night behind Evander Holyfield) began the intoductions of the principles."(parapharsed excerpt from The New York Daily News-Saturday-December 20th 1997)

Prince Naseem is a boxing champion of the world or maybe, I am the chump of the universe for allowing this spectacle into my living room. If I had'nt looked at the T.V. Guide, I would have thought I had tuned into Ringling Brothers, Barnum and Bailey Circus. If what I saw was a sports contest then my name is Bill Clinton. (another entity that represents slease also, by the way)

Seth Abraham at HBO Sports, who will ask me to watch the Prince five more times. Can I get something for my money? Well I guess this is the holiday season, and many people have fun and party during the holidays. So, maybe HBO wanted to give me a party, disguised as a boxing match. If so, please accept my sincere apology, HBO Sports, because it was a great party but not a boxing contest.

In the laugh department on a scale of 100 with 100 being the highest rating I rate the boxing match a zero and the sidebar antics a 100. I know, I did'nt have to watch. However, I thought there was some degree of professionalism left in boxing and then there is always, another clown to watch, 48 year old, HBO boxing analyst George Foreman, who is an act by himself. So, all in all, I got a few good laughs, but where was the beef.

At the end of the fight, after exhausting 3 brews, I threw an empty beer can at my televsion set. My televsion set responded by running into some

temporary technical difficulties. Life in America has become so complex, has'nt it? Happy Holidays everyone. See Ya All Next Time

VOL. 1 NO. 22

POLITICS AS YOU LIKE IT

"PAROLEWATCH"
A DIAMOND IN THE ROUGH
AN IDEA WHOSE TIME HAS COME AND LONG OVERDUE:CITIZENS
FIGHT BACK AGAINST CRIME

It oft times seems for some reason that good ideas don't come from where they should, our elected officials and the leaders who work with them. From almost totally outside this realm comes a gentleman who has come up with an idea which is long overdue, and he has taken the idea and brought it to fruition.

Joe Diamond who hails from Brooklyn, New York, has started an Internet website, entitled "Parolewatch" "Parolewatch" is a spin-off organization from another organization Mr. Diamond started in 1994, called "Take Back New York". In co-operation with The New York State Department of Correctional Sevices, (which administers New York States prison system) "Parolewatch" allows anyone with access to The Internet, to view a database which contains release dates of convicted violent felons, who have been convicted of violent crimes, in nine different catagories. In assisting Mr. Diamond, The New York State Department Correctional Services provided "Parolewatch" with a 37,000 inmate database of convicted violent felons.

In the current database at "Parolewatch" convicted violent felons who are to appear before The New York State Parole Board in April of 1998, for release consideration, are listed according to the crime they have committed and were convicted of. Additional information provided on each inmate is, their name, the current prison they are serving their sentence in, the crime they were convicted of, the area of New York State in which they committed their crime and were convicted, and their sentence.Though based in New York City, "Parolewatch" provides information from all 51 counties located within New York State.

What "Parolewatch" will do is allow the general public, imput, into just whom is released back into their respective communities. With the knowledge "Parolewatch" provides, letters against an inmates release could be written to The Parole Board, letters or phone calls to District Attorneys, offices, objecting to an inmates release could be made and letters indicating whether or not parole should be granted could also be written to the sentencing judges in the particular jurisdictions involved.

"Parolewatch", currently is in its formative stages in New York State, however its potential as a tool for public safety is tremendous. Mr. Diamond, who himself was a victim of a violent crime in 1992, (armed robbery) is a 1989 graduate of Brooklyn College where he majored in political science. During, 1989, he worked for six months as an aide, on the current Mayor of New York Cities, mayoral campaign. Mr. Diamond,came away from his experience working on that campaign, impressed with Rudolph Gulliani's committment to lowering crime in New York City. New York City, currently leads the nation in the reduction of crime for the past five years in all catagories of violent crime.

The basis for Mr. Diamonds first organization, "Take Back New York" which evolved into "Parolewatch" was the advocation for victims at various stages of the criminal justice process and the training of grassroot advocates to regularly monitor court proceedings and parole hearings. The major inspiration for the foundng of "Parolewatch" was a similiar database in New Jersey, (which has been on-line a little under one year) entitled, "New Jersey Parole Eligiblity Website". Visitors to Mr. Diamonds website can also, at this time access, four dfferent links to related websites, which include victims advocacy groups, state corrections agencies, state parole boards and law enforcement sites. The links include several other states, and what they are doing in the area that Mr. Diamond is involved in.

Further information that can be accessed on "Parolewatch" include a biography on each member of The New York State Parole Board, and a letter in support of "Parolewatch" by Marc Klass, the father of Polly Klass, who was brutally murdered by a California convicted violent felon who had been released on parole.

Finally, Mr. Diamond through his website, "Parolewatch" is attempting to obtain a million signatures, opposing the parole of convicted child murderer Joel Stienberg, convicetd in 1987 of the brutal murder of his adopted daughter Lisa, which took place in New York City. Stienberg is to appear for release consideration before The New York State Parole Board during the second week of January 1998. Stienberg is serving a sentence of eight and a third years to twenty-five years and has been denied parole once before by The Parole Board. A disbarred attorney, Stienberg sued The New York State Parole Board in early 1996 for refusing to release him and lost. He will have served ten and one-third years of his twenty-five year sentence, when he appears for release consideration, next month.

Certainly, the wrong message is sent when people like Stienberg are granted parole, without serving a good majority of their sentences. In Stienbergs case, New York State would be forced to release him, under law, after completion of two-thirds of his sentence, or sixteen years and eight months. I would feel that appropriate considering the gravity and nature of Joel Steinberg's crime.

In my opinion, the legislative intent behind the parole laws in New York State, were not meant, to have an early release granted to a guy who was convicetd of beating his adopted daughter to death while high on cocanie. All in all, "Parolewatch" is a great idea whose time has come. Should you wish to contact, Mr. Diamond for further information, his E-Mail Address is:

Wave3@parolewatch.org

and his organization can be reached by telephone at

1-212-340-1192

The "Parolewatch" website can be reached at URL

http:www.parolewatch.org

Take my word for it, its certainly worth a few minutes of your time to see what Mr. Diamond has done here. If it has not been done where you live, it might be a good idea to contact your legislators to lobby for such a website. Hats off to Joe Diamond, a guy who cared and did something about it. We need a lot more people like him. Thank you Joe. This citizen appreciates what you have done and recognizes the importance of what you will be able to accomplish with "Parolewatch".

Joe Diamonds website is a "diamond in the rough" which will shine very brightly in the future. See Ya All Next Time and A Very Happy and Healthy New Year To You, Friends and Family. May 1998 Be A Good Year For You.

VOL. 1 NO. 23

POLITICS AS YOU LIKE IT

ROCK AND ROLL IS HERE TO STAY AND I THINK FOLK MUSIC TOO: BOB DYLAN: AN AMERICAN LEGEND IN HIS OWN TIME

Generational politics is something I've never been very good at. Coming from the baby-boomer Vietnam-Era generation, the generation gap between, my parents, (I call them The World War II crowd) and my generation was always very real and intense.

However, like any generation of youngsters, we had all the answers, and we were going to change the world. The problem with this, as far as my generation was concerned, was that we were dead serious at obtaining results for our idealism and actually wound up changing the world a little bit.

Surrounding all this, as a motivation and catalyst was my generations music, which was held in contempt and disdain by the older generation at that time. Rock and Roll was the work of the devil many from the World War II crowd preached. It was too loud and it was vulgar to boot. Frank Sinatra, Benny Goodman, Artie Shaw, Louie Armstrong, Pearl Bailey, Judy Garland, Glenn Miller, Guy Lombardo, Josephine Baker, Billie Holiday, Paul Whiteman, Xavier Cugat, Dean Martin, well they were okay. Elvis Presley, Little Richard, Chuck Berry, Fats Domino,and Bo Diddley and then The Rolling Stones and The Beatles with Chubby Checker and Fabian, and Bobby Darin, in-between, *no good, said Mom and Pop of the 1950's*

There has been a puritanical repression of expression in The United States going back to The Mayflower, that perhaps explains many peoples reluctance to accept new forms of ideas and music.We remain a very repressed country on all fronts, due to this puritanism, which does not encourage progress. It also frowns on people having a good time and enjoying themseveles.

Then came the 1960's, an unbelievable time in our countries history. Suddenly a lot of people turned against their government and flaunted convention to the upteenth degree. A huge counter-culture arose to challenge the establishment. I must admit while all this was going on, I sort of missed the boat. After a stint in the military, I came home looked around and thought my country had turned into an insane asylum. Even today, there are many things that occured in the 1960's that I do not understand. So I write this column as one who was totally outside the counterculture.

However, that does not mean I fully agreed with the establishment, at that time either. On the other hand, I never have believed that overt displays of disatisfaction was the way to obtain change. A lot of people in my generation felt differently.

Bob Dylan, was sort of adopted by the counter-culture of the 1960's and never really felt himself to be a spokeman of the left in the 1960's. The warnings that indeed "The Times Were a Changing" came in a strange form. Rather, a small, fragile looking guy from Minnesota, with a very nasel voice, backing himself up with a guitar and harmonica and some incredible lyrics and music, was to be one of the pied pipers of an entire generation.

Bob Dylan, was his name, (his real name was Bob Zimmerman) Usually, in wars involving the people against their own government, and the generation in power, there are a lot of victims among the upstarts. However, thirty-two years after all this happened, Bob Dylan, remains a true survivor, of the turmoil during the 1960's and is just as, if not more popular today, than he was then.

At the age of 56, Dylan has returned to the top of the music charts with a brand new album, containing all new material. Last May, during one of the one-hundred tour concert dates he does every year, Dylan was hospitalized with a viral infection, around the sac in his heart and almost died. Several tour dates had to be cancelled and his record company, Columbia Records, received over five-hundred calls inquiring about his condition. He made a recovery (though not a complete one) in two months and was back on tour. What is very impressive is the level of interest in this mans music and life. It is nothing short of phenomenal.

In September of last year at the request of *Pope John Paul* at a eucharistic conference in Bologna, Italy, Dylan, performed "Knocking' On Heavans Door", "A Hard Rain's A-Gonna Fall" and "Forever Young". The Pope, listened with eyes closed loving every minute of Dylan's private performance for him.

Three weeks ago in Washington, with President Clinton in attendance, Dylan, received a Kennedy Center Honors award, given to those who have more than distinguished themselves in the arts, here in The United States. In 1992, at The 30th Aniversary Tribute To Bob Dyaln Concert,(sold-out concert) at Madison Square Garden, in New York City, a virtual who's who, of the rock world paid their homage to Dylan. Included in the incredible array of talent present, were, George Harrison of "The Beatles", Stevie Wonder, Tom Petty of the group, "Tom Petty and The Heartbreakers", Tracy Chapman, The O'Jays, John Cougar Mellencamp, Eric Clapton, Neil Young, Mary Chapin Carpenter, Chrissie Hynde, of the group, "The Pretenders", Willie Nelson, Kris Kristofferson and lengendary studio musician, G.E. Smith, who is an act all by himself.

They all got together and sang some of Dyaln's classics. For those of my readers who are not familiar with G.E. Smith, he was the musical director and lead guitarist for the popular weekly television program, "Saturday Night Live" for fourteen years.

Dylan who had left the music scene for ten years began rebuilding his career in 1988, with an album which was not received well entitled, "Down In The Groove". In that same year he got together with the late music legend, Roy Orbison, George Harrison and Tom Petty for the very successful, "Traveling Wilburys" album. In an appeerence at "Woodstock '94, Dylan, held his own against such modern rock groups, like, Metallica and Nine Inch Nails.

His son, Jakob, member of the group "The Wallflowers" is a huge star in his own right and has sold a lot of albums too. However, father Bob, keeps his distance from his son, Jakob Dylan, in the creative department. Re-inventing one's self and maintaining a popularity base across generations is never an easy thing to accomplish. An artist must make many concessions in his work and final product to achieve this. Not only has Bob Dylan, done this very well, but I would specualte at this time, that perhaps a hundred years from now, his words and music will be standards, akin to the staying power that many classical composers, like Mozart, Bach, ect. act. have today. I would venture to guess, that popularity, has a lot to do with creating a standard. If my prediction, comes to pass, Bob Dylan, would join a select group of musicians and composers, who took hundreds of years to become standards in music and would have done so in half the time.

In closing, this "Rock and Roll" is really still an infant. This genre of music has only been around for forty-three years and shows no signs of disappearing, due to it's being a fad, or for lack of interest. It's roots lie in rythm and blues, which always touches the heart and the soul. This is not to say, that other genres of music have not done the same. Bob Dylan's music has not only spoken to a generation, very dis-illusioned with their state of affairs, but also was targeted toward anyone with a heart and a soul. To ignore Dylan, was to head for an area, in this writers opinion, that most people would not want to be in.

It seems, looking back, (hindsight of course is always easier) that Bob Dylan was standing alone at the eye of the storm and that may have been the key to his survival as a man and an artist.

The tradition of folk music has always endured the wrath of the power structure in America. Tremendous talents like Pete Seger, Woody Guthrie, Phil Ochs, Dave Van Ronk, Richie Havens and Peter, Paul and Mary, were recipients of constant surveillance of The FBI, (Federal Bureau of Investigation) and because the messages in their music, brought hope to the downtrodden, were further labeled, "socialists" by entities that strongly supported the "staus quo" which usually meant holding on to their own power bases. People were not supposed to listen and pay attenion to people like Bob Dylan, but, rather were supposed to be focusing on what The President of The United States had to say, at any given moment, Richard Nixon.

For some reason I cannot determine ,whether or not Bob Dylan, to the best of my knowledge was ever subjected to this type of dehumanizing scruntiny. If he was, it was certainly not done at the level that prior folk singers had suffered. Finally, it seems there has always been a problem in The United States with alternative messages being mass-marketed to the public although the First Amendment of The United States Constitution would have you think otherwise. A message could always be deseminated if one had the means to do so. The Internet and World Wide Web are addressing that problem, beautifully. currently.

Many people with excellent ideas, but without the resources to have those ideas heard now have the vechile with which to go forward. However, before this information, superhighway, there was Bob Dylan, and we were very fortunate to have him, at that time in our history as a nation.

Yes, Mom and Pop, it looks like "Rock and Roll" is here to stay. If what is written here seems a bit confusing and complex to the reader, it really is not! The heart, and soul and justice will always triumph above cold practicality and partisan politics which only serve induividual interests and not our nation as a whole. Bob Dylan spoke to that end, most eloquently and a lot of people are much better off as a result. Dylan, his message and music are "Like A Rolling Stone" and timeless masterpieces that will be around for a long, long time.. See Ya All Next Time. Your Comments Are Welcome In The Guestbook For This Page

.

Postscript:

On January 5th 1998, Bob Dylan was nominated for three Grammy Awards relating to his 1997 hit album.Dylan was nominated for Best Album of The Year, Best Male Rock Vocalist and Best Contemporary Folk Album. His son Jakob was nominated for three Grammy Awards also. The Grammy Awards are the music industries equivalent to The Academy Awards in the movie business. This years Grammy Awards will be telecast on CBS, Wednesday evening February 25th 1998.

Bernard Paul

VOL. 1 NO. 24

POLITICS AS YOU LIKE IT

POLICY OR THE LAW: A GOVERMENT AGENCY CONTINUES ITS MOVE TOWARDS CRIMINALITY: THE SOCIAL SECURITY ADMINISTRATION AND ITS HANDLING OF DISABILITY CLAIMS

Most people would like to believe when coming in contact with a United States government agency or entity that we are at the highest level of bureaucracy, in comparison to a state administered bureaucracy, or municipal, (local) bureaucracy

. To be fair here, I must point out that many Federal, State and Local angencies, do a tremendous job,and are very responsive to the public, when a member of the public comes to them for assistance.

On the other hand, a few months back, the horrible way The Internal Revenue Service had dealt with the public garnered national headlines and was the focus of a United States Senate hearing. Subsequent, to those hearings, improvements are currently being made in the abusive manner that The IRS had been dealing with the public. For an in-depth look at last years IRS hearings in Washington D.C.

(please refer to my Commentary Archives for Commentary for Week of October 6th 1997-Commentary Number 11-"The United States Senate Takes On The Internal Revenue Service" (IRS)

The Social Security Administration, is another ball of wax entirely, and has dealt and continues to serve the public, as though it were a loose cannon and outlaw of Federal Agency's. It should be remembered at all times, that employees and administrators of Federal agencies are paid their salaries with our tax dollars. When was the last time you paid someone money, and the service they gave you back was no service, just abuse?

Well, The Social Security Administration, currently has a nineteen year history, of abusing the public, and ignoring the law, and instead in its decision-making, process, involving claimants for benefits, making its own law and following policy, instead of mandated laws. Due to its own mismanagement, The Social Security Administration, (heretoafetr referred to as SSA) is facing bankrupcty. In the next sixteen years SSA will have to divert over $500 million dollars from its old age retirement fund, to keep the disability fund solvent. SSA, currently is in such a bad way financially, that in an attempt to cut costs, its attempting to break its promise to our countries most vulnerable citizens, those with profound disabilities.

71

For any readers who are hard-line conservatives, please note, that SSA's Disability Insurance Program, *is not* some convoluted welfare program. The requirments to qualify for SSA Disability benefits are the strictist of any disability benefit program, public or private in the country.

A claimant when filing a claim for benefits with SSA, must have been disabled for one year prior to filing the claim and the disability must be expected to last at least one year. All of this must be backed up by medical documentation both private and sometimes by SSA's own doctors. A claimant must have sufficient quarters of documented employment from which he or she has paid Social Security taxes. Often,the monthly benefit allocated is below $500 a month to those benificiaries who prevail on their initial claims. In 1995, SSA, denied 69 percent of all initial disability claims.

In a process that affords a claimant the right of appeal of an initial SSA adverse determination, 62.5 percent of those initial denials for SSA disability benifits in 1995, were overturned on appeal, by Administrative Law Judges, who are by the way are also employees of SSA.

A virtual war has been going on between SSA's administrators and the Administrative Law Judges, who work within the same agency since 1979. Usually, when an original jurisdiction's decision is overturned, the claimant at that time, has been attempting to obtain the SSA disability benefit for almost two years.

Just think what that means. The claimant has filed a claim, claiming disabiltiy and no income. In almost three out of four cases, that initial claim is denied. Then an appeal is filed, and another year goes by, and perhaps the claim will be allowed at that point. Now, just what is SSA doing here. Are they trying to expeditousely provide protection for those who need some kind of income, when they become disabled? Does it look that way to you, my reader? Does'nt look that way to me!

Certainly, ways could be found to make the entire process work in a timely way and provide an expeditious, safety net, to those truly deserving of one, the disabled.

At this point, a little history is necessary to put this entire mess in perspective and allow my reader to see SSA for what it is, an outlaw bureacracy, at war with itself and those that it is mandated by law to assist.

To begin with, (and you my reader might laugh at this) The Social Security system, when founded, in 1935, was based on the premise that most of the people paying into the syatem, would not live long enough to collect any benefits and that the government would realize a windfall as a result. So, initially, Social Security was supposed to be a cash cow for the govenment, not the people who paid into it. Medical advances and people living longer as a result of those advances, short-circuited Social Security's anticipated windfall, from benificiaries who would die before qualifying for Social Security Old Age Benefits.

Bernard Paul

Secondly, those who advance governmental conspiracy theories are usually dismissed as suffering from paranoid delusions. However, check out this well documented systematic procedual irregularity, (which amounted to a clandestine conspiracy within The Social Security Administration) to illegally deny thousands of people who were at that time, (1979 to early 1983) receiving SSA disability benefits, for psychiatric reasons.

At the time all this happened Margaret Heckler was The Secretary of Health and Human Services, (the agency that oversees the operations of SSA) and The President of The United States was Roland Reagan. Who was President at that time is important, for what I'm about to describe, could not have been implemented without the approval of the White House at that time. The illegal actions of SSA at that time were founded in denying an individual class of people, (those with psychiatric imparments) their right to receive disability benefits from SSA, a clear violation of Section 1985 of The Civil Rights Act which prohibits blanket discrimination against any particular group in the allocation of Federal benefits. Hold onto your seats, for now I'm going to tell you how this was done!

Through, secret, (at that time secret) internal memorandums, distributed to State Disability Determination offices in all 50 states, State Disability Office officials were told by SSA's top adminstrators to contract with doctors throughout their respective states and call in through those doctors all persons receiving Social Security Disability benefits for psychiatric disabilities. In New York State, this was over 50 thousand people and nationwide over 300 thousand people. The State Disability Determination Offices were further instructed by SSA officials that in contracting with doctors in their respective states, to order the examining doctors to certify everyone they would be examining as being capable of doing substantial and gainful work, regardless of the medical evidence in their files which indicated otherwise. To top these illegal acts off, SSA then threatened to terminate the jobs of its own Administrative Law Judges, if they did not deny at least 75 percent of the appeals that were filed as a result of its own illegal actions

The name of that review program was "The Bellamon Review Program". Thousands of innocent people lost their benefits, and a national homeless problem was created as a direct result of the actions of SSA's officials, from late 1979 to early 1983. On February 8th 1983, The City of New York, along with The New York City Health and Hospitals Corporation, The Commissioner of The New York State Deparment of Social Services, and The Acting Commissioner of The New York State Office of Mental Health filed suit against SSA in Federal Court in Brooklyn, New York on behalf of those who had been made victims by SSA's illegal actions. The Chief Judge of The United States District Court for The Eastern District of New York, Jack Weinstein, presided over the lawsuit, which sought to reinstate the benefits lost to all they had been illegally taken from, lasted over two years and SSA lost on all points.

SSA then appealed Chief Judge Weinstein's decision to The United States Court of Appeals for The 2nd Circuit of New York, (the Federal Court, right below The United States Supreme Court) and lost there also. For those interested in lookimg at the actual decision, the legal citation for the lawsuit is:

73

City of New York vs. Heckler 578 F.Supp. 1109 (E.D.N.Y. 1984) and on the appeals level:
City of New York vs. Heckler 742 F.2nd (1984)

These cases can be obtained by going to your area law school and looking up the case according to the aforementioned citation, and photocopying it or by contacting a State Law Library, which most states have. By mailing them the two citations, for a copying fee they will send you the cases. Below is a brief excerpt from the actual Federal lawsiut against SSA.

"The District Court rejected the Secretary's jurisdictional contentions. (whether or not The District Court had the right to hear the case) Chief Judge Weinstein ruled, "that from 1978 to at least the early months of 1983" SSA engaged in a covert policy to deny class members, (those with the psychiatric disabilities) an individualized assessment of each claimant's capacity to engage in substantial gainful activity in violation of the Social Security Act and regulations enacted thereafter. 578 F.Supp. at page 1115.

What occured here was the de-facto granting of due process, with the final outcome having already been determined, in all cases, and thus the complete denial of due process to the class of people affected here. Yes, this group was entitled to a hearing and to present facts contrary to the examining doctors, colored final adverse decision (in many, many cases, the medical files spoke for themselves as to the validity of the claim) and the final decisions of SSA's Administrative Law Judges.

But no due process could be had, for the entire process had been rigged. The one Federal, State or Local entity that did not join this conspiracy was our Federal Judiciary. and Thank God for them. This comentator has always felt, that the buck always stops, when a matter is before a Federal Judge. The Federal Judiciary came down very hard for what SSA did and SSA spent millions of dollars in legal fees and thousands of man hours attempting to defend themselves against a basically, indefensible lawsuit.

SSA's own internal memorandums pointed out their gross ad flagrant violations of the law. They were caught cold.

Millions more was spent, revising (under Court order) the manner in which those with psychiatric impairments were evaluated for SSA Disability benefits. By following its own self-serving and mean-spirited policy instead of the prevailing law at the time SSA, showed itself to be criminal and a sociopathic bureaucarcy out of control, in its total disregard of the law in dealing with thousands who had obtained their benefits legally and had legitimate disabilities.

Most all. working within SSA, at that time knew the policy, to be illegal and implemented it anyway.Perhaps they did that because they feared if they did not follow SSA directives that they would lose their jobs. Certainly, no one in that position would have lost any lawsuit they would have filed after losing their job, for not following SSA's illegal directives, once it came out in Court, that they were being forced to break the law as a condition of their continuing employmnet with SSA.

They did have a choice! They choose to knowenly break the law. To the best of my knowledge, none of the people working for SSA at that time, were ever prosecuted for what they did and many if not all, continue to be employed by SSA, some in senior policy making positions. So for all you non-conspiracy theorists, heres one in black and white.

Finally, you would think after what happened as described in the aforementioned that SSA would never try this again and had learned its lesson. Wrong, dead wrong! Today SSA is back to its old tricks, just using some different methods which <u>border</u> on being illegal. In an internal memorandum sent throughtout SSA in the middle part of 1996 former acting Social Security Commissioner Shirley Chater, wrote to all Administartive Law Judges within SSA, *"Forget the law, as it applies to Americans with diabilities, we are the law"*. The internal memorandum had been prepared by The General Counsel for SSA,(SSA's top lawyer) and was also distributed to SSA's executive staff. The report is entitled, "Legal Foundations of the Duty of Impartiality in the Hearing Process and its Applicability to Administrative Law Judges Within SSA" The report dated January 28th 1997, was attached to a letter signed by Acting SSA Commissioner Charter who resigned from her post at SSA, four weeks after the release of the internal memo, on February 28th 1997.

The memo had outlined the apparent intention of The Social Security Administration to require its Administrative Law Judges, who rule on appeals for disability benefits, to ignore Federal law and precedent and adhere to Social Security policy when issuing determinations of appeals. In a letter, to New York Times reporter, Robert Pear, (which was used as the basis for a New York Times article on this subject dated April 21st 1997) former Acting SSA Commissioner wrote,(parapharsed) "An Administrative Law Judge within SSA is bound to follow Agency policy even if in The ALJ's opinion, the policy is contrary to the law". Just what is all this is about? I really don't know. Its clear to me, a layman, that the laws the laws and that policy comes in a distant second in what must be followed with regulatons, coming in a clear third. Now if the law is contrary to an agency's internal goals, then you must go to Court to change the law, not ignore the law and follow policy, created by the agency, to serve it's own agenda or even to show itself as an effective agency.

Good performance evaluations should not come at the expense of the public who are supposed to benefit from SSA's programs. Not only are Admistrative Law Judges being scared to death by whom they work with, at SSA, they are currently being told by The Federal Judiciary that they better follow the law, and rightly so

Now the public, they have to come in front of this type of a person, who will make a decision as to whether or not, (in most cases) they will have a roof over their head and a little food to eat, to survive. This current situation must be clarified, so ALJ's can do their jobs according to the law, and the claimant public seeking a fair determination, is not put into this Catch-22 unfair state of affairs. The continuence of this lawlessness on SSA's part represents political suicide for those involved and will only further enrage and outrage many people in our country who are totally turned off by politics and the bureaucracies that represent government.

This type of behavior by SSA is just unacceptable and must not be tolerated. If zero-tolerance of crime is national priority, enforcement of that zero-tolerance agenda must include runaway government agency's whose actions are clearly criminal in nature. There is no excuse for SSA's current behavior, for they have been warned by our Federal Judiciary, many times in the early 1980's.

Policy is policy! Policy does not reinvent or circumvent the law. I find it very disturbing that this lesson is or definition is still not yet clear to those at the higher levels of The Social Security Administration who are responible for the day to day operations of The SSA.

Postscript:

A copy of this commentary will be E-Mailed To The Social Security Administration's Central Office in Baltimore, Maryland, inviting their comments or reply, in a separate E-Mail. Any reply from SSA will be published, two weeks after it's receipt, as a priority commentary. It should be clear to my readers that after a substantial period of time has passed and you don't see SSA's reply in a weekly commentary, that SSA has declined comment on this weeks column. Thank you for making note of this.

See Ya All Next Time

VOL. 1 NO. 25

POLITICS AS YOU LIKE IT

THE CRIMINALIZATION OF JAYWALKING IN NEW YORK CITY:A MATTER OF PRIORITIES

The choice of this weeks topic was not an easy one. Should any of my readers feel that I have let them down by choosing to write about jaywalkers and how their behavior has now become a priority for a newly re-elected Republican Mayor in New York City, please forgive me, and I ask you to accept my sincere apology.

In a week, where Pope John Paul will visit Cuba for five days, and President Clinton has become the first Prseident in American history to be a defendant and give his testimony in a deposition, (re: Paula Jone's lawsuit against President Clinton for sexual harrassment) involving a million dollar civil lawsuit against him, and we will celebrate the birthday of Dr. Martin Luther King Jr.; and The Spice Girls rock group have given their first American concert, I have chosen to write about jaywalking.

God please forgive me for my shift of focus, as this possible transgression may be seen by some of my readers. For those readers who may not know what "jaywalking" means, its the crossing of a street, avenue, intersection, ect. ect. ect.; when the traffic light is red, which means, don't walk or crossing a street in the middle of the block. In New York City, with it's very heavy traffic and pressured schedules, jaywalking has been considered to be an inalienable right for pedestrians for a very long time.

New York Cities newly re-elected Mayor, (and lame duck Mayor, due to the term limits law) Rudolph W. Giuliani gets paid one-hundred and thirty thousand dollars a year to do his job. His recent crackdown and criminalization of jaywalking in my opinion just represents further harrassment of the public, (who have more than enough to deal with in any given day) and Mayor Giuliani's disregard for the rights of the public and not the other way around.

Additionally, whats happened here is a distortion of the allocation of resources and priorities in the day to day governing of a city. This all started during the Christmas season when our Mayor, decided that the placing of pedestrain barriers in one of the most heavily traveled areas of New York City, 48th through 51st street, on Fifith Avenue, right near Rockeffler Center and major retaliers was a good idea. The rationale behind the Mayor's idea was to have more efficient facillatation of vehicular and pedestrain traffic in a very congested area of New York City.

What happened turned out to be an embarassment for City Hall. The day after the experiment went into effect a large protest group dressed as "cattle" further congested the area where the experiment was taking place. Many retailers lost business, because of the now convoluted way pedestrains had to cross the street. Some people to get to the Northeast corner of a street, instead of directly crossing the street to get there had to navigate three traffic lights to eventually wind up on the Northeast corner of the block they wanted to go to.People were literally walking in circles! Within a week, the barriers were being ignored by the majority of pedestrains in the area. Some summons were given out,but for the most part the police felt ridiculous hassling shoppers during Christmas, in an area of New York City that is considered to be a showcase for the entire City of New York, and ignored violators. With tremendous opposition to the barrier experiment, which reached almost a total consensus against, Mayor Giuliani's reaction was to allow the experiment to continue, until January 5th and then he would decide whether the barrier policy was worth continuing. So much for responsive government, considering that most people felt the barrier expriment to be a failure.

January 5th came and went with Mayor Giuliani, not suspending the barrier experiment, but saying an indefinite period of time was further required to study the situation. Obviously, the dis-satisfaction of the majority of the people affected by the Mayor's experiment, meant little, to the Mayor in influencing him to disband the experiment, and who cares that the majority of the public does'nt like it! What do they know, seemed to be the Mayor's attitude. Onward!

On Monday, January 12th, a week after his barrier experiment was to receive a green light or a red light, the Mayor jaywalked, and issued his jaywalking decree. Some of the first violaters caught jaywalking were various aides to Mayor Giuliani who were then chased by reporters and asked why they had jaywalked, near the Mayors office. One administration official replied that he had jaywalked because, "no cars had been coming down the street". The official felt his trip into lawlessness should be forgiven because no cars could be seen, that somehow he had not violated the spirit of his boss's recent edict. Two dollars fines for jaywalking should be raised to seventy-five dollars. declared Mayor Giuliani and he further noted at a press conference held that day, that in just five minutes, on Fifth Avenue and 42nd Street, (a very heavily traveled area) that 52 people crossed against the traffic light or in the middle of the block and in that same five minute period a cab had hit one man.

On Tuesday January 13th, a major metropolitan daily newspaper with a daily circulation to readers of almost two million, (The New York Daily News) put this story on its front page, with the screaming headline:

WATCH OUT! Rudy targets jaywalkers for next major crackdown

On Wednesday, January 14th, over 100 uniformed police officers were dispatched to the midtown area of New York City to give pedestrains lessons on how to cross the street. On that very same day at 11 O' clock in the morning, three armed gunmen robbed The Bank of America's World Trade Center branch, (on the 11th floor of The World Trade Cenetr) as Brinks security guards were delivering two million dollars in cash. The robbers left the building, making their getaway by the regular passenegr elevator. The three were caught in less than a week, due to their own supidity, which included getting themselves photographed with their masks off, by some 300 security cameras at The World Trade Center Building.

Since the 1993 terrorist bombing of The World Trade Center, security there was supposed to be very tight there. Whatever police that may have been at The World Trade Center when the robbery occured certainly were'nt effective enough to stop the robbery from occuring or preventing the clean getaway.

Perhaps keen observation of people coming and going at The World Trade Center by more uniformed and plainclothes police could have prevented this robbery from happening.

It may not sound fair, but I'm going to write it here. Where were the police? Why they were about eighty-five blocks north of The World Trade Center, in force, uptown, teaching people to cross the street. Police officers in New York City, earn thirty-one thousand dollars a year as uniformed officers. Thats $610.00 a week or $15.25 an hour before taxes. This comes to $122.00 a day before taxes. For 100 police officers to teach pedestrains how to cross the street for one day, comes to one-hundred and twenty-two thousand dollars of taxpayers money.

The City of New York could create five jobs for a hundred and twenty-two grand and get five years worth of work out of their five new employees.

Am I to believe this, that this is going on while Brinks guards somewhere else in New York City are being robbed of two million dollars? In closing here, (I know, you my reader are probably saying, Thank God this commentary is finally coming to an end-but remember I opened this commentary by writing that I had severe reservations writing about this topic to begin with.

I warned you!

This whole situation about jaywalking being criminalized here in New York City, represents overkill. Certainly Mayor Giuliani can find better ways to make use of law enforcement and the taxpayers money. This situation continiues to be an ongoing one, with the Mayor, not having moved back from his original position in mid-December of last year, one bit.

Perhaps the final outcome will not be a news story, but will end up in the comics section of some Sunday newspaper in the future and that is where I refer my reader for the conclusion to this sorry mess.

Somewhere between Charlie Brown and Dick Tracy, thats where you'll probably find it. No editor in his right mind would dare put this story on the front page of his or her newspaper again, including me. Give me a break!

People walking in circles to cross the street. Police Officers giving adults lessons on how to cross the street. This Mayor wants to run for President of The United States? You wanna fight crime, Mr. Mayor, beautiful, however, how about going after some real criminals. See Ya All Next Time.

Bernard Paul

VOL. 1 NO. 26

REVISED EDITION:WITH POSTSCRIPT

POLITICS AS YOU LIKE IT

THE APPEALING PSYCHOLOGY OF TRADITION: THE PACK IS BACK: SUPER BOWL XXXII: SUPER BOWL SUNDAY 1998

This Weeks Commentary Is Being Released One Day Earlier Than Usual Due To Playing Of The Super Bowl This Evening

No Gennifer Flowers, Paula Jones, or Monica Lewinsky and the problems with President Clinton's alledged extra-marital affairs, here this week. You'll have to go to the conventional press, print and broadcast, with their individual political agendas to get this weeks top story in the political world.

So big is that story that it has even eclipsed The Popes trip to the island of Cuba, with all major news organizations going back to Washington D.C. at the speed of light at the beginning of last week to cover The Clinton scandal.

Today is Super Bowl Sunday, an event that could probably upstage the Pope and President Clintons current problems, for the one day, this event takes center stage.

Over one-hundred-million people watch The Super Bowl all over the world. The event is broadcast to some thirty-two countries. A football contest between two teams, second to none, in the football sports world. Maybe the yearly European soccer matches create an equal amount of interest and frenzy. Professional sports has become very, very big business.

The National Football Leauge recently signed a contract worth eighteen billion dollars, with three broadcast networks, for the rights to broadcast their games. Moreso, than ever before professional sports is being dominated by the players and their agents, who make Al Capone and John Gotti, look like paupers and nice guys.

Last week, in the baseball world, star centerfielder for The New York Yankees, Bernie Williams, (while vacationing in Puerto Rico) through his agent, informed Yankee team owner George Steinbrenner, that he would accept no less than nine million dollars a year, to play with The Yankees. In response to this "stick-up" without a gun, Steinbrenner, dispatched two top team excutives to speak with Bernie Williams about his demand to Puerto Rico. Williams refused to speak with the executives. What ever happened to the day that sports was just a game and was enjoyed for the thrill of the contest and the skill of the participants? Well, it looks like that day is long gone.

The average fan of professional sports is being left far behind in the ruthless race for the dollar bill in sports. Not only is the average fan being left behind, but most fans are being frozen out at the box office, and cannot even afford to go and see their favorite team, once in a while. Higher player salaries, has translated into much higher ticket prices. The baseball World Champions for 1997, The Florida Marlins, are trying to sell off half their players, just in an attempt to recoup some fifity million dollars they spent to put their five year old baseball expansion team on the map. The stories go on!

Thats why this weeks Super Bowl and one of the two teams participating, The Green Bay Packers, offer a bright light to the fan, who is being overun by the money-men of professional sports. Unless we are to believe that professional sports will be able to go on with lucrative broadcast contracts alone, or fill the seats of their areanas and stadiums, primarily with freinds and cronies from the corporate world, then the average fan, who helped make professional sports what it is today, counts very much.

The Green Bay Packers are a football team steeped in fan tradition. Going back to the beginning of this Super Bowl mania, in the mid-1960's was a maverick National Football Leauge Commissioner, Pete Rozelle and The Green Bay Packers,(one of the first participants in The Super Bowl) and their legendary coach Vince Lombardi.Coach Lombardi was quite a man. He once said; (parapharsed) "Winnng is'nt everything; _it's the only thing"._ The Super Bowl trophy that goes to the winnng team, is named after Vince Lombardi. Wisconsin, and Green Bay, home to the Packers is for the most part, a working class, blue collar city and state. Wisconsin's other claim to fame is that it produces most of the domestically manufactured cheese in The United States. It's other distinction and pride is The Green Bay packers football team, the only National Football Leauge team, in the leauges history _to be owned by its fans._

From its great games in The Super Bowl, some thirty years ago, with quarterback Bart Starr leading the Pack, up to todays game, with mega-quarterback Brett Farve, leading the Pack, once again, this franchise has never let its fans down. Today they are a rough and tumble football team, lead by coach Mike Holmgren, who coaches as though he were a direct protege of Vince Lombardi. The Green Bay Packers are probably the last professional sports team, that the average fan can call his or her own. They embody the pride and honor and spirit of the work ethic, (virtues fast disappeaing from the American landscape) in consistancey with the city and state they are based in. You can't help but smile, watching Green Bays, 6.75 million dollar a year quarterback, Bret Farve, do his job. He's a master play caller, having become such with no short cuts, just some very hard work. Green Bay comes to their second consecutive Super Bowl, appearence today, after easily dispatching of The New England Patriots in last years game. Their opponent this time around, is a team that has made it a regular event of losing Super Bowls, The Denver Broncos.

I pick Green Bay to win this years Super Bowl, (the oddsmakers put Green Bay at a 13 point favorite) not so much because Denver does'nt have a great team, but due to the fact that Green Bay is so much better and the average fan needs this boost to what they have stood for, for so long. It's nice to know too, that the average fan in Green Bay, is part of the profit margin too with this team. Hate to write it here, but I speculate that the most exciting part of this Super Bowl, may once again, be the half-time show, only because of the tremendous dominance of Green Bay, which I predict, in the first half of the game. Green Bay all the way, later today, and more power to the, The Pack, which is is truly back.

Finally, the fact that President Clinton may not be in office by the end of next week, or the process may have begun by next week to have him removed from office, due to the current circus going on in Washington, will not have me taking up too much space in my weekly commentaries in the future, or as my readers have seen, today.

To me, this is old hat, just another politician, (crook) caught with his hand in the cookie jar. This is not a story to me, but, sadly, has become an ongoing state of affairs, in American politics which has me totally turned off! The fact that all this is happening inside The Office of The President of The United

States is depressing, just as it was over twenty years ago, when it was Richard Nixon, who was caught cold.

Nixon said, (parapharsed) "I want the American people to know their President is not a crook". History and the facts have proven otherwise. This man is my leader? (President Clinton) No rush to judgement here, but I think this time, President Clinton is gone. Slick Willie, has out-slicked himself. A poll taken yesterday, said that 67 percent of the American people now feel President Clinton is unfit to continue as President. Sorry to end this commentary on such a downside. I don't create the events. I just write about them. Enjoy The Super Bowl Green Bay 31 Denver 13. See Ya All Next Time. Your Comments Are Welcome In The Guestbook For This Page

Postscript: Sunday Evening-January 25th 1998-10:20 P.M. E,S.T.-For the second time in Super Bowl history a wild card team has won The Super Bowl. The final score was Denver 31 and Green Bay 24. The result of this game now has the Editor & Publisher of this page, two for two in predicting a winner in a sports contest. Last September I predicted in a column here, that The New York Yankees baseball team were likely to repeat as World Champions for 1997.

(Politics As You Like It Commentary No. 10-September 29th 1997)

I am now batting a thousand on the loss side. Congrads to The Denver Broncos-Super Bowl Champs

Bernard Paul

VOL. 1 NO. 27

POLITICS AS YOU LIKE IT

KARLA FAYE TUCKER: SHOULD GENDER AND RELIGIOUS CONVERSION MITIGATE A DEATH SENTENCE FOR MURDER?

REVISED EDITION WITH POSTSCRIPT

This week we once again address the issue of the death penalty, doing so from a different venue, (The State of Texas) and a different set of facts.

(See Past Commentary for Week of October 13th 1997-The Death Penalty In New York State-Vol. 1 No. 12)

Forty-eight hours from now

The State of Texas is set to execute 38 year old Karla Faye Tucker, by lethal injection, for the June 1983 slaying of a Houston couple, Jerry Lynn Dean and Deborah Thorton. Carried out with an accomplice, the murders were very grusome, with the victims being beaten to death with a hammer and a pick ax. Karla Faye Tucker was totally intoxicated and under the influence of drugs at the time of the crime.

At the age of ten she was addicted to herion. The accomplice, David Garet, died in prison of liver disease in 1993. Shortly before his death, he had been granted a re-trail. During Mrs. Tuckers trial, her defense attorney neglected to tell the jury of her intoxicated condition at the time of the crime.

This may have mitigated the juries decision to sentence Mrs. Tucker to death instead of life in prison The two prosecutors that obtained Mrs. Tuckers conviction have come out currently, in support of clemency in this case. Two of the victims relatives also favor clemency and one of the victims brothers feels Mrs. Tucker should die.

On December 8th of last year, The United States Supreme Court refused to hear Mrs. Tuckers appeal, which set in motion, this Tuesday's execution date. The death penalty has always had strong political overtones surrounding its application. I have written in my past column that I support the death penalty in selective cases such as the pre-mediated killing of a police officer and in crimes so disturbing, as to shock the conscience. The example I used in my

October 13th 1997, commentary, was of Colin Fergerson, a man who opened fire on a rush hour train going out to Long Island, New York, killing several innocent people in Decemebr of 1993.

Karla Faye Tuckers case is seen as being different by many observers, currently. The first thing we are faced with is that she is a woman. Texas has not executed a woman since they hung Chipita Rodriguiz in 1863, for murdering a horse trader. Since, The Supreme Court re-instated the death penalty in 1976, only one woman, has been put to death. In 1984, North Carolina executed Velam Barfield.

Texas leads the nation in executions. Since 1982, 107 have been executed by lethal injection. From 1924 to 1964, 361 have been executed in Texas's electric chair. The United States is the last civilized nation on earth to have a death penalty. Karla Faye Tucker is currently being held awaiting her fate, at The Mountain View Unit of The Texas Department of Corrections near Gainesville, Texas.

Enter, stage left, Pat Robertson, the founder of The Christian Coalition and head of The Christian Broadcasting Network, home of the reknown, "700 Club". The "700 Club" is seen every day on ninety percent of the cable stations in The United States. Mr.Robertson, was also a former candidate for President of The United States.

Pat Robertson, a strong supporter of the death penalty,has come out against the execution of Karla Faye Tucker, saying, "let compassion prevail". As the prime basis of his support of Tucker, Robertson, further says, "I am convinced that Tucker has found Jesus and turned her life over to God". In simpler terms, Tucker has become a born-again Christian. In addition while in prison she has married a minister. Karla Faye is no longer anything that resembles the violent world of illegal drugs, petty crime and prostitution, that had brought her to prison, her supporters say. Karla Faye Tucker has strong support for the commutation of her death sentence, throughout America's fundamentalist and evangelical community.

The legal apparatus to obatin clemency in Texas is difficult. Enter, stage right, the current Governor of The State of Texas, George W. Bush. He is the son of former President George Bush and is seen as a contender for The Presidency himself in the year 2000. He is also a very strong supporter of the death penalty. **Governor Bush cannot grant clemency in this case without the full recomendation of The Texas Board of Pardons and Paroles. The Texas Board of Pardons and Paroles rarely consider a clemency petition. Without that recomendation, his options are restricted to granting a thirty day stay of execution. Many observors feel Governor Bush is in a catch-22, no win situaton here.If he declines to intercede on behalf of Ms. Tucker he will be seen as the Governor who did not do anything to prevent the execution of a woman, and did not bow to the pressure of The Christian Coalition.**

Additionally, Governor Bush will be seen as doing nothing to stop the first execution of a woman in Texas, in 137 years, or since the days of The Civil War. If Governor Bush does try to stop the execution he will be seen as being soft on crime, by his constituencey, who are strong supporters of the death penalty. Either way, Governor Bush steps into a political minefiled and will suffer political damage to his future with this matter

Then comes the issue of gender politics. Some would ask, why should she be spared? Because she's a woman? The religious implications also confuse. So, she's a born-again Chrsitian. There are hundreds of male death row inmates in The United States who have become born again Christians also. Should their executions be called off too? What about the religious conversions to other faiths, like Islam, for instance? Why should'nt those conversions be the basis for granting clemency in death sentences?

I feel it is noteworthy, that Karla Faye Tucker is the benificiary of support from a man, who strongly supports the death penalty, Pat Robertson. To say that a human being who has turned ther life over to God, is not capable of making a contribution to society, as she would spend the rest of her life in prison, were her death sentence commuted, is something I cannot believe.

I further believe, that this matter comes down to a question of faith. Are we as a society, in punishing criminal behavior, seeking justice? If its justice we seek, there are many ways of obtaining justice. It is my opinion that justice should always be tempered with mercy and compassion. Not to do so makes us no better than the criminal we seek to execute. Murder, killing, the taking of another human life, whether by The State or by another person, to me represents the same thing, When this is done in the name of the law and the state, it still amounts to the taking of a life. At that point, it no longer represents justice, but retribution. We here in The United States are governed

by the laws of man and God. Many would agree that the laws of God would and should supercede the laws of man. Both, clearly indicate, "thou shalt not kill"! Who are we as human beings, to, in making law, to dictate exceptions to Gods word. I find most executions insulting to humanity. In addition, I find the murder of the victims in death penalty cases, to be moreso, very disturbing. With the exceptions I have outlined in my past column, I cannot support the death penalty, on moral, religious and philosophical grounds. The fact that we would execute a woman, the basis and foundation for all human life, is something that further disturbs me. We should remember, that our country, The United States, has in the past, rejected pleas for clemency in death sentences from The Pope, himself, and the late beloved Mother Theresa. We must also recognize in a case recently which involved a clearly retarded man who did not know right from wrong, that The United States Supreme Court refused to grant a stay of execution. Their refusal to do so, was not justice, but complicity in the murder of an innocent man, who should not have been held accountable for his actions, because he lacked the requisite intelligence to be responible for his crime.

A dangerous line is crossed when as a society we seek retribution rather than justice. For those who would ask what about justice for the victims, I ask, must justice for a murder victim be met with the execution of the offender in all cases. Retribution to the best of my knowledge equals vengence. The exercise of vengence is supposed to be confined to God according to the Scriptures.

In closing, it has been proven time and time again, that the death penalty does not serve as a detterent to future crimes of the same nature. Matter of factly, so, in jurisdictions where the death penalty has been imposed, it has caused an incraese in murders after its imposition. I must side with Pat Robertson in this case. Certainly the life of a woman who has turned her life over to God, could be spared. Finally, I find it equally disturbing, that the decision to spare Karla Faye Tuckers life, will hinge, on whether a Governor of The State of Texas, feels he can get re-elected, or become a strong candidate for President in the year 2000. Thats not justice, just politics.It is my opinion, that if this execution proceeds, that we all go down one notch, as human beings. If you would like to contact Governor Bush and help save Karla Faye Tuckers life, his address is below: Additionally below is the E-Mail address

for The State of Texas. Governor Bush's Office is currently not accepting any E-Mail communications.

Hon. George W. Bush-Office of The Governor-Box 12428-Austin, Texas, 78711 <u>or</u> webmaster@www.state.tx.us

———————————————————————

<u>Postscrpt:</u> Karla Faye Tucker was executed by The State of Texas at 6:45 P.M. Central Standard Time On Tuesday, February 3rd 1998. Two additional appeals to The United States Supreme Court were filed on the day of her execution, and were denied. <u>United States Supreme Court Associate Justices Sandra Day O'Connor and Anthony Kennedy could not be located to have their vote taken.</u> Joining the plea for clemency were Pope John Paul II and Jerry Farwell along with Binaca Jagger of Amnesty International.Karla Faye Tucker went to her death with a smle on face saying she loved everyone. She apologized for her crime to the family members present at the execution and hoped that her execution would bring them peace. Texas Governor George W, Bush refused to grant a thirty day stay of the execution. As I wrote in my above column,

"I think we will all go down one notch in life if this execution proceeds"

It is a sad day when the death penalty represents revenge and retribution and rehabilitative efforts are totally ignored. Thats just politics, not justice. Those actions are reserved for God and not human beings. We become no better than the convicted criminal and lower ourselves to the level of the criminal when we take a life, in the name of the law. Few exceptions exist in my mind for imposing the death penalty.

I think further that The Texas Board of Pardons and Paroles, who have never granted clemency to anyone, should be examined and that a clear uniform criteria should be established in the future for all death penalty cases, for the granting of clemency. This was not an ordinary case. The aggorance with which The Texas Board of Paroles and Pardons along with Texas Governor George W. Bush and Justices of The United States Supreme Court acted, in the face of millions of people pleas from all the world to save this person from execution, will not be forgotton.

It is my sincere opinion, that this was a genuine case where mercy and clemency was warrented. Shame on The State of Texas, for having the dubious distinction as the death penalty capital of the world.

In the twenty-two years since the death penalty was re-instated, Texas has executed 144 people, more than any other jurisdiction in The United States-Tuesday February 3rd 1998-9:10 P.M. Eastern Standard Time-Editor & Publisher of "Politics As You Like It"-Bernard Paul

VOL. 1 NO. 28

POLITICS AS YOU LIKE IT

JOHN GRISHAM: NUMBER ONE BEST SELLING AUTHOR-NOVELIST CONTINUES TO SET THE BOOK WORLD ON ITS EAR:AN AMERICAN MASTER

With pleasure this week I write of one of America's most interesting and best selling authors of fiction, John Grisham. Personally, I am not one for reading fiction, preferring the reality non-fiction can offer. However, with John Grisham, I have again begun to enjoy fiction.

The last writer of fiction I felt this way about was horror master Stephen King. The old adage, that this is a book, that once you pick it up, you won't put it down, applies to all nine of Mr. Grisham's books, some of which have been made into also very spell-binding and provocative movies. The series of movies based on Grisham' books have also achieved great popularity.

If you are not familiar with just who John Grisham is, you probably will be when you view the titles below of his work in the past eight years. Mr. Grisham's literary genre is the legal thriller. Much of what he has written is drawn from his experiences as a criminal defense attorney, in the deep South.

A Time To Kill (1989)

The Firm (1991)

The Pelican Brief (1992)

The Client (1993)

The Chamber (1994)

The Rainmaker (1995)

Runaway Jury (1996)

The Partner (1997)

The Street Lawyer (1998)

Mr. Grisham has also written the original screenplay for "The Gingerbread Man" which is currently playing in theaters. All tolled his books have sold close to twenty-five million copies since his first book in 1989.

That first book, "A Time To Kill" was rejected by twenty-five publishers and was written while Mr. Grisham was serving as an elected state legislator from his home State of Mississippi. The publishing company that finally did publish his first book. Wynwood Press, was a small publishing company based in New York City, that was famous for publishing the religious monthly magazine, "Guideposts".

Grisham recieved six millon dollars for the movie rights, to "A Time To Kill"

John Grisham was born in Jonesboro, Arkansas, in 1955. He attended Mississippi State University and earned his Bachelors Degree in Accounting there in 1978. His choice of accounting as a major was based on his desire to work in his families business.

Mr. Grisham went on to attend The University of Mississippi Law School and earned his law degree from there in 1981. His speciality was tax law. Fresh out of law school he opened a storefront crimnal defense practice in his home town. In 1983 he ran for the Mississippi State Legislature and won. He served as a Mississippi State Legislator for seven years. During this period he also published a magazine, entitled "Oxford American". Mr. Grisham lives and works in Oxford, Mississippi.

Essentially, according to Mr. Grisham, to break the boredom of being a legislator, he began work on his first book in 1986, "A Time To Kill". Grisham would get up at five in the morning and write for about three hours before going to work at the Legislature. In later years, Mr. Grisham remarked, (parapharsed) "that I had been reduced to introducing a bill in the Legislaure honoring Tiny Tim and there was just not enough work to do, to keep me busy"

Most readers of Grisham's books have been impressed by his style of writing. Mr. Grisham says he has recieved many compliments from his readers over the years with the main compliment being that his books "flow".

This is no accident. Grisham's two favorite authors, (both also from the deep South) are the lengendary John Stienbeck, (The author of "the Grapes of Wrath") and William Faulkner, who many call the last great American novelist.

Grisham attempts to write in the same style of John Stienbeck. In all Grisham books, the events, plot and characters, story line, become evident in the first few chapters of the book. Writing a book so it "flows" is not an easy thing to do. Each chapter must unflod into the next very smoothly. When finished, that kind of a book. is a pleasure for the reader to read and rarely boring.

Grisham's genuis further shines when it is take into account that in school, (high school through law school) he had never taken one course in creative writing of any kind.

Mr. Grisham has commented in the past that he did not feel that a reader of fictional books should have to read the first ten chapters of a twenty-five chapter book, before figuring out what the basic plot was about! In what many people feel is his best book, "A Time To Kill", Grisham deals with racial politics in the deep South. The book is based on an actual trial Grisham had observed, though written fictionally. The story deals with how the criminal justice system in Mississippi deals with a black man who has murdered the murderers and rapists of his daughter.

An all-white jury had gone easy on the murderers of his daughter. In his second book, "The Firm" (the one Grisham hit it really big with) we follow a brilliant law school graduate as he unknowenly begins his law career working for a law firm in Tennnesee, that he finds out is doing all of its work for The Mafia. The young lawyer barely escapes with his life after discovering whom he is actually working for.

In the movie, Tom Cruise, plays the young attorney, fresh out of law school. One great job of casting there. Grisham's next book, "The Pelican Brief", deals with the murder of two United States Supreme Court Justice's and what happens when a young law school student, discovers the reason they were murdered. Academy Award winning actor Denzel Washington,(won for best actor in 1989 for the movie "Glory") along with Julia Roberts as the law student play the leads in the movie version.

Next comes "The Client" the story of a young man, who stumbles upon some very important information and must go into hiding to protect himself from harm. He is befriended by a tough female attorney, played in the movie, by another Academy Award winner, Susan Sarandon, who played Sister Helen Prejean, in "Dead Man Walking" a movie about the different sides to the death penalty.

John Grisham's fifth book, (also made into a movie) "The Chamber" addresses the murder of a Jewish civil rights attorney and his family, by a bombing, in the deep South, and his son, who is an attorney and attempts to save him from the death penalty.

Next, my favorite Grisham book, "The Rainmaker" which I could not put down.

In "The Rainmaker" we have a young law school graduate, whose first case out of law school is an attempt to obtain the proceeds of an insurance policy for a mother's son who has died. The insurance company had put an ad on the back of a matchbook cover and geared most of its business toward poor people, whom they felt, could do little, when the insurance company would arbitrarily and capaciously deny whatever claims they would file with the insurance company. The young law school graduate takes the distraught mothers case, after the insurance company refuses to pay the claim filed by the mother. despite the fact that all premium payments had been made on time and the terms of the insurance policy had been met to the letter of the law by the grieving mother.

The young attorney comes upon an insurance company not only bent on refusing to pay the claim but ruining the young lawyers law career before it even gets off the ground.

The first Judge the case appears before is totally corrupt. He dies and the second Judge is a personal friend of the young attorney. To even things out, the second Judge, even though a close friend of the young lawyer, does not rescuse himself, (remove himself) from the case.

Suddenly, the four insurance company lawyers, in their Brooks Brothers suits and hourly fees of three-hundred dollars an hour and more, can't even get a motion granted for a two day delay in the proceedings. In the end the young lawyer wins the insurance settlement and additional lawsuit monies and in doing so puts the insurance company out of business, due to the flood of other lawsuits that then were filed against the insurance company and the publicity which his case had generated in the media. Nice twist.

I'll now leave my reader to his or her own devices to discover the plots of Grisham's next two books, "Runaway Jury" and "The Partner" and jump to John Grisham's newest book, which was released last week entitled, "The Street Lawyer"

In "The Street Lawyer" Grisham sticks to his winning formula; and that is, a white male lawyer undergos a crisis of conscience and takes on a social cause.

The story in "The Street Lawyer" centers around a greedy Washington attorney who is held hostage in his office by a homeless man. The homeless man is shot and killed by a police swat team sniper. The greedy attorney spurned on by this incident quits his high-paying job as a corporate lawyer and and helps sue his former law firm on behalf of a group of homeless squatters.One of the squatters dies with her young daughter, after a lawyer from "The Street Lawyers" former law firm, has her illegally evicted from the squat. She had been paying rent while living there and therefore was not a squatter but a legal tennant. The illegal evicition winds up costing her and her daughter their lives. They are found dead in the middle of the winter, in an abandoned car.

This new book is expected to do very well too. Grisham and his current publisher, Doubleday Books, are also breaking new ground, in using The Internet to promote his recent books.

The hardcover run for "The Street Lawyer" matches last years run for "The Partner", 2.8 million copies. This is a record run for any author that Doubleday Books has published in the past. Doubleday Books is considered to be one of the the top publshing houses in the world. Last year Doubleday, through America On-Line excerpted the first two chapters of "The Partner". Eighty-Thousand people visited the Internet site promoting, "The Partner" on the first day the site went up. Wow! The first chapter of "The Street Lawyer" is also being offered on The Internet. If you are interested in looking it all you have to do is type in the URL below and when you get to the site, just type in your E-Mail address and the chapter will be sent to your E-Mail address.

http://www.bdd.com/grisham/

In closing here, John Grisham's novels are an excellent read. At a time when lawyers and the legal profession, are at an all-time low with those in the public who are not lawyers,

John Grisham continues to ride a wave of success, writing of the more ideal and nobler part of lawyering in The United States. Perhaps this is why he has been so successful, for he writes of lawyers and the legal profession, in a way most of the general public would like to see them portrayed, helping the underdog, in life.

How does Grisham himself feel about his enormeous success and popularity.

"ten years from now, I plan to be sitting here looking out over my land. I hope I'll be writing books, but if not, I'll be on my pond fishing with my kids. I feel like the luckiest guy I know"

Pretty humble statement from a guy who has 100 million copies of his books being distributed and read in 38 countries around the world. Good man and a great writer who offers idealistic role models in his book, that the legal profession here in The United States should aspire to.

I highly recomend any of his books to my readers, so you can breath some fresh air, and escape from today's American politics and politicans, who have become the laughing stock of the world and anyone with a brain between their ears.

Choose a healthy escape and renew your faith, in politics, as it should be, read John Grisham. See Ya All Next Time.

Bernard Paul

VOL. 1 NO. 29

POLITICS AS YOU LIKE IT

MUST WAR EQUAL GENOCIDE: A GRAVE SITUATION IN IRAQ: IS USE OF FORCE THE ONLY ANSWER?: THE EFFECT OF UN/US SPONSORED SANCTIONS AGAISNT IRAQ

This Tuesday evening President Clinton, in a televised address to our nation, will take his case for further military action against Iraq, directly to the American people. President Clinton's wish to bomb Iraq for the second time in seven years has been rebuked by The Congress, (whose consent he requires to declare war) the Soviet Union and China. He has the full support of Great Britain in proceeding against Iraq.

Can a resolution of this matter, at this time be obtained without the further use of force? I doubt so, seriously! Can we as a nation that is looked up to by many other nations as a leader on the world stage, stand by and allow Iraq to stockpile chemical weapons and weapons of mass destruction? I would hope not! Is the use of force the only answer? Yes, however we possess the military capability, to limit that use of force and confine such, to specific military targets and areas where the weapons of mass destruction are located. Further mass bombings of the entire country of Iraq will just result in massive civilian casualities, against a population, who in my opinion has lost the ability and resolve to get rid of Saddam Hussein and the group of insane people around him, that have brought all these problems to Iraq.

I don't buy, the line that the people of Iraq are one-hundred percent behind the leaders of their country and there is a lot of propoganda flowing here, from both sides, The United States and Iraq. I could support a selective bombing campaign, to knock out, military bases and chemical weapon stockpiles and communication cenetrs.

We, (The United States) certainly have the satillite intelligence to know where those targets are and even if those targets are moved around, our electronic intelligence can give us up-dates within two hours of any change in location of the weapons of mass destruction. To use stauration bombing of the entire country of Iraq at this time, would not be consistant with the purpose of such bombings and just represent an attempt to obatin genocide against the entire country of Iraq and innocent civilians.

Granted, war is war and war is hell and very dirty business, but even war, has it's rules and limitations. An end by any means in a war, history, has shown, was confined to people, (if I can call them people) like Hitler and Stalin, who murdered millions of people to achieve personal political goals.

The basic mission of any war, is to seek out and destroy. However, our military technology has reached such a high degree of sophistication, that the saturation bombing of Iraq, could be abandoned for the most effective surgical strikes which would achieve our objectives. What President Clinton, won't be talking about, Tuesday evening is the current state of Iraq's population, who we here in The United States automatically assume are one-hundred percent behind Saddam Hussein and the leaders of the government of Iraq.

In an effort to show, just whom we would be bombing, (if our miltary opted for mass bombings, instead of selective strikes confined to actual military targets) I am reprinting the article below by Rick McDowell, who belongs to the Chicago-based organization, Voices In The Wilderness, whose goal it is to end the US-led, UN sanctions against the people of Iraq.

The mebership of Voices In The Wilderness has been threatned by Federal prosecutors with twelve years in prison if they continue to make their fact finding missions to Iraq.

Obviously, the information Voices In The Wilderness members obtain on their trips to Iraq, is not information that our government would want people in our country to know, otherwise, why would members of the group gathering the information be threatned with long prison sentences?

The purpose of reprinting this article is to show the current state of the people of Iraq and to ask, must people in this state be bombed again? Is there another way?

Bernard Paul

Iraq:As The People Suffer

by

Rick McDowell

When I returned to Iraq in late May of 1997, nearly six months since the implementation of UN resolution 986 ("Oil for Food") I expected to see improvements in the availability of food and medicine. I found, instead, a deterioration of all conditions necessary for the sustenance of life.

Traveling to Iraq for the third time in nine months, I encountered a resigned hopelessness amongst the people, a population historically known for its resilience. Seven years of the most compehensive sanctions in modern history have reduced Iraq and its people to utter destitution. The United Nations Security Council's economic sanctions, invoked only ten times since the inception of The United Nations. and applied eight times since the end of The Cold War, constitute an extension of the devastating Allied bombing campaign of 1991. For the sixth time since January of 1996,a delagation from Voices In The Wilderness,, a campaign to end US-supported UN economic sanctions against Iraq, traveled to Iraq in public volation of US law.

The delagation visited hospitals in Baghdad, and the southern port city of Basra. Members met with UN and relief officials, doctors, government workers, religious leaders and Iraqis from all walks of life. Our findings of increasing suffering, death and desperation throughout Iraq are confirmed by recent UN reports.

The UN Food and Agriculture Organization reported in December of 1995 that more than one million Iraqis have died--- <u>567,000 of them chlidren---as a direct consequence of economic sanctions.</u> UNICIF,(The United Nations Childrens Fund) reports that 4500 children under the age of five are dying each month from hunger and disease. An April 1997 nutritional survey, carried out by UNICEF, wih the paticipation of The World Food Program (WFP) and Iraq's Minister of Health, indicates that in Central/Southern Iraq,

27.5 percent of Iraq's three million children are at risk, due to acute malnutrition. *<u>To date, more children have died in Iraq than the combined toll of two atomic bombs on Japan and the ethnic cleansing of former Yugoslavia,</u>*

The UN's Department of Humanitarian Affairs reprots that Iraq's public health services are nearing a total breakdown from a lack of basic medicines, life-saving drugs and essential medical supplies. The lack of clean water---50% of all rural people have no access to portable water---and a collaspe or waste-water treatment facilities in most urban areas are contributing to the rapidly deteriorating state of public health.

Airborne and waterborne diseases are on the rise, while deaths related to diarrhea diseases have tripled in an increasingly unhealthy environment. The World Health Organization (WHO) reports a six-fold increase in the mortality rate for children under five, an explosive rise in the incidence of endemic infections, such as cholera, and typhoid,, and a markedly elevated incidence of measles, poliomyelitis and tetanus. Malaria has reached epidemic levels.

The WHO further states that the majority of Iraqis have subsisited on a semi-starvation diet for the past several years. The use of depleted uranium during The Gulf War in 1991---which may be a contributing factor of Gulf War syndrome---may also be linked to increases in childhood cancers, including lukemia, Hodgkin's disease, lymphomas, congenital diseases and deformities in fetuses, along with limb reductional abnormalities and increases in genetic abnormalities throughout Iraq,

The vaunted "Oil For Food" resolution is a failure, its promise of food and medicine having been proved to be too little, too late. According to WFP by the end of May, 1997, Iraq had exported 120 million barrels of oil and received 692,000 metric tons of food, 29% of what had been expected under the deal. Of the 574 contracts submitted to The Sanctions Commitee for exports of humanitarian supplies to Iraq, 331 were approved, 191 placed on hold, 14 blocked and 38 were awaiting clarification. Of the $2 billion in Iraqi oil revenue authorized for a six-month period, 30% is designated for war reparations, 5 to 10% for UN operations, 5 to 10% covers maintenance and repair of the oil pipeline ad 15% is earmarked for humanitarian supplies for the Kurdish population in northern Iraq.

About, $800,000 is available for Central/Southern Iraq or approximately 25 cents per person, per day for food and medicine, Regardless, UN Resoluion 986, does not provide for critically needed parts to repair Iraq's water, sanitation and medical infrastructure, which was devastated during The Gulf

War in 1991. The importation of such basic items as chlorine, fertilizers and pencils is prohibited. Lacking spare parts and minerals needed to repair their water and sewage treatment facilities, the condition of many Iraqis, is scarcely improved by the food they receive. The utreated water is contributing to disease and death. Without hard currency, the economy of Iraq, estimated to have the second largest oil reserves in the world,, has collapsed.

Average public sector wages, for the few who have employment, have fallen to less than $5 a month, while hyper-inflation has caused the price of goods to rise astronomically.The Iraqi dinar, worth $3 pror to sanctions, was worth .000625 in May of 1997. Skilled workers, including docors and engineers, have deserted their jobs to become taxi drivers, or cigarette salesmen.

Iraqi professionals are leaving the country in increasing numbers. With an estimated 80% of Iraqis, affected by the sanctions, families are selling household and personal possessions to purchase food and medicine. As the population struggles for survival, the social fabric of Iraq is disintergrating, as witnessed by the wide-spread rise in begging, street children, crime and prostitution. The people of Iraq have been on a roller coaster of hope and despair for seven years and seemed to have settled into despair.

For example, Frail, the manager of a small hotel, asked us to go home and tell our govenment to bomb Iraq for 42 more days, and get it over with, for she says, "We are dying a slow and painful death under sanctions".

A young doctor at a Baghdad hospital said, "Our life is over". Another doctor who has practiced for eight years and is forced to play God, with the few life-saving drugs available, makes 3,000 dinars a month, or $2, while a bottle of milk for his children costs 3, 500 dinar. He asked "What does your country gain from our suffering?". An Iraqi reporter despairingly stated, "The world is upside down, nothing makes sense anymore, it's all gone mad."

Most horrific is the pain in the eyes of mothers who wait in hospitals--with their children---for far too many mothers it is a death watch. _The children, born since the Gulf War and hardly involved in the politics of sanctions, suffer in silence, often without access to painkillers, drugs, antibiotics or hope._ Some childhood cancers realized an 80% cure rate prior to the sanctions.

Now, without cancer-fighting drugs, the survival rate for children with these same cancers is 0%. The United Nations chartered to protect civilain

populations from the ravages of war, is, instead, engaged in a war of collective punishment,, a war of mass destruction, directed at the civilian population of Iraq. The UN at the insistance of The United States, and contrary to international conventions and treaties, has created in Iraq, a zone of misery and death--with no end in sight. Considering the horrific suffering and death of children and families in Iraq, the lack of public debate over UN/Us participation in *this massive violation of human rights* is astonishing.

The toll of these sanctions on an entire generation of Iraqi children is incalculable. What are the implications of Iraqi children growing up traumatized by hunger and disease, if they survive at all? How can the deeds of one leader or even an entire government be used *to justify this unprecedented, internationally sanctioned violation of human rights?*

The scourge of sanctions on the people of Iraq must come to an immeadiate and unqualified end.

At a conference held in Detriot, Michigan, last Novemebr, by US Catholic Bishops, Bishop Thomas Gumbleton, had this to say:

"The hidden nature of the war being waged against Iraq is tragic. Editorials seldom appear, and we see no front page stories, even though these sanctions have caused the death of more than one million people, consituting one of the greatest human rights abuses of our time"

President Clinton, Tuesday evening will attempt to convince our nation, (where most people are not aware of what has been brought out in this commentary) that the people of Iraq, must have unleashed upon them, the most awesome military strike short of nuclear weapons, that a world power can use for the second time in seven years.

As noted earlier in this commentary, I doubt whether the people of Iraq, have the wherewithall to remove Saddam Hussein from power. The depth of suffering, due to a leader who did not hesitate to use chemical warfare on his own people, has reached an unacceptable level among many innocent Iraqi people. We as an honorable nation, and a shining example to the world, owe it to ourselves, to find a way to reslove the current crisis in Iraq, without the further use of force, or if we must use force again, to restrict that force to getting rid of the weapons of mass destruction and militay installations.

To do otherwise I fear, would produce another holocaust. The author of the aforementioned article and his address, phone number are below:

Mr. Rick McDowell

c/o-Voices In The Wilderness

1460 West Carmen Avenue

Chicago, Il 60640

1-(773) 784-8065

This commentary is dedicated to commentator and writer Bill Moyers and his wife Judith Moyers who produce documentaries for The Public Broadcasting Service. (PBS) Mr. and Mrs. Moyers were the only American journalists, to the best of my knowledge to have the courage to report the aftermath of what went on at the end of the Iraqi war, in 1991 in a doccumentary aired by (PBS) shortly after The Gulf War concluded..

A short quote from Mr.and Mrs. Moyers doccumentary appears below:

(parapharsed) "There are no winners in war". "Both sides lose" At the conclusion of The Gulf War, American ground troops were seen shooting fleeing Iraqi soldiers in the back, as they had their hands up, and were trying to surrender"

Bill Moyers has been honored in recent years with two Golden Baton Awards by Columbia University's Graduate School of Jounalism, the highest honor that school can bestow upon a working journalist.

It is in the tradition of Bill Moyers work as a journalist for over twenty-five years that I have written this weeks commentary. There is usually more than one side to most stories and for an informed, fair decision to be made about courses of action, one should know both sides of any given issue, before deciding how to proceed

Usually, the side being hidden, does not serve the interests, of where the message is coming from. You are not being informed when you receive a message like that, only mis-led and thats not informing you, only playing politics with your mind. See Ya All Next Time!

VOL. 1 NO. 30

POLITICS AS YOU LIKE IT

OHIO STAE UNIVERSITY: THE IRAQI CRISIS: THE FIRST ADMENDMENT VS. NATIONAL SECURITY: SHOULD THE PUBLICS RIGHT TO SPEAK OVERSHADOW THE NATIONAL SECURITY OF THE UNITED STATES?

This weeks commentary is a little late, because I've been running around trying to buy a gas mask for the good part of this Sunday afternoon. All stores in my town were sold out, however I did find a licensed street peddler who had one left to sell. As I was handing the peddler my money for a state-of-the art gas mask, he was arrested for jaywalking and I was told by the police officer doing so, to take a walk. I weakly protested to the cop, noting that my life might be in danger, without the gas mask. He told me, my life meant little, when it came to the law and told me if I did not go on my way, I would be arrested for obstruction of justice. I guess the fifty dollar fine (raised from two dollars by executive order of our Mayor two weeks ago) The City of New York will collect for the jaywalking fine is more important than my life. Oh yes, the peddler was arrested, because he had no ID with him, despite the fact, that he had his peddlers license with a big picture of himself dangling from his neck.

If any of my readers know where I can buy a gas mask, pease contact me immeadiatly. Thank you! Before I begin this weeks commentary, consistant to the above headline I wish to make this point. *I don't consider it to be responible journalism, when every major news organization in the space of three days, has reported, how, when and where, one may obtain, poison gases, or the instructions to manufacture gases such as Anthrax and VX. There are enough unbalanced people in The United States, to make the release of such information, dangerous, to the public at large.*

Now, I move from under my bed, (where I have been for the good part of this week) to attempt to write this commentary, before another screaming, breaking story or banner headline scares me half to death.

Hats off to the conventional media this week, for creating a near panic across our country. If that gas, or this gas were to be used here or there, millions would perish in a scant few hours.Thre are no plans to defend against this on a mass scale. Thank you! I don't have enough problems without the media telling me this. Is'nt the possibility of biological warfare, fun? I got more exercise this week, jumping up and down, from under my bed, than I've had in years and maybe lost a few pounds doing it. The last time I had this much fun, was with the fallout shelter crap, in the 1950's. Then we were going to have nuclear weapons used against us!

This week I returned from Mars after viewing a Cable News Network, (CNN) sponsored town meeting, broadcast live around he world from the campus of Ohio State University.

Now, CNN, is a great news organization, however, many people for years have questioned the sanity of its founder and current co-chief Ted Turner. This event broastcast in mid-afternoon, was the brianchild of Rick Kaplan, the former executice producer of ABC World News Tonight with Peter Jennings. Mr. Kaplan had been executive producer of World News Tonight, twice during its some 156 weeks as the top-rated national evening news broadcast. (Currently, World News Tonight is ranked third, behind, The CBS Evening News with Dan Rather and NBC Nightly News with Tom Brokaw)

Rick Kaplan, became part of Ted Turner's on-going raid on, ABC, NBC, and CBS News to spirit away top talent to CNN. Through a close friendship, developed over the years with President Clinton, Rick Kaplan was able to obatin the exclusive broadcast rights to last weeks town meeting. Participating, in the town meeting, were Clinton administration officials, Defense Secretary William Cohen, Secetary of State Madiline Albright and National Security advsior Sandy Berger. The event was anchored by esteemed CNN reporters, Bernard Shaw, (who reported directly from Badhdad, Iraq, at the beginning of the 1991 Iraqi war) and Judy Woodruff.

This meeting was an attempt by The Clinton Administration, to bring their current case for bombing Iraq to The American people. What transpired was nothing short of incredible. In what may have been originally produced to be a staged event where the responses of those in attendance at Ohio State University, would compliment Clinton Administration foriegn policy in Iraq, turned into anything but that. A quick point of information, staging of any kind in the reporting of a news story, will usually be strong grounds to get a reporter fired from most news orgaizations.

Staging, means, that the story is being manipulated in such a way, to produce a result desired by the news organization. This type of news coverage is not news, but a fraudulent way of presenting an event to the public and is looked down on in the field of jounalism by those who maintain high standards. I must note, that after watching this town meeting, that I felt bad for the participants, Defense Secretary William Cohen, Secretary of State Madiline Albright and National Security Advsior Sandy Berger, who endured the wrath of shouting protesters in the audience and downright insulting questions, which I felt went beyond how we are currently or will be dealing with our foriegn policy in Iraq.

I was further dismayed when I learned that later in the same week that The Ohio State University matter occured, that Senior Clinton Administration official Bill Richardson, was shouted off the stage at The University of Minnesota afetr trying to present a case for the further bombing of Iraq. It seems that a lot of people in the heartland of America, where people are usually pro-United States anything, at any given moment, have taken the same position I wrote of in my commentary last week. That being, the further loss of Iraqi civilians is just unacceptable. Now, just where does the right to be critical of US foriegn policy interfere with the effective implementation of US foregn policy? Well, I must admit, thats a tough question.

I feel, that if Clinton Adminstration officials had listened or cared about what people had to say or think about Iraq,(people outside The Beltway in Washington D.C.) for a long time, they would not be subjected to people shouting at their Senior Administration officials, in Middle America. On the other hand, I feel it is disgusting, what Cohen, Albright and Berger had to endure, in defending Clinton's curent policy against Iraq. There must be respect for the Office's they represent, even if it be proven, that nothing but a pack of lies come from those offices.

I would further note, that if the reaction obtained from Middle-America last week is an indicator of how normally loyal Americans currently feel about their country <u>then we are in big trouble.</u>

My personal opinion, for whatever it is worth, tends to believe that everything going on in the Middle East, currently, represents our countries wish to dominate the regions oil supplies, and has little to do with weapons of mass destruction. An excellent point brought out during The CNN Town

Meeting was how The United States has bankrolled and sold all kinds of weapons to the Indonesians, who have murdered thousands of people in East Timor. A story that is rarely written about with, the exception being The New Yok Times sporadic coverage of that story.

Finally, I feel The CNN attempt to present a staged event to the world, was insulting to the average persons intelligence and should act as a wake-up call to Washington. However. Washington, has been in a deep sleep, for a long, long time. So I doubt, the lesson to be learned from The CNN Town meeting will have any effect on Washington, that has a track record of only responding to special interests and the money those special interests can bring to the table, or to The Lincoln Bedroom recently. If the people who run the government in Washington wanted to kow how the average person felt this week, they found out! I think it will be a long time before we see another town meeting of this type.

Politicians don't take kindly to winding up with egg on their faces, or for that matter, anyone else. Wall Street may be doing well, but the majority of the rest of the country is not, despite what we are being told. People's level of tolerance for bull these days is at an all time low. Wake up, Washington! The alarm clock is ringing. Don't throw the alarm clock out the window to shut it off. Reach over, shut the alarm off, and listen to what the people are saying. It might help to do so. See ya All Next Time!

VOL.1 NO. 31

POLITICS AS YOU LIKE IT

FRONT PAGE NEWS: THE MAYOR OF NEW YORK CITY IS CAUGHT BREAKING THE LAW:EDITORIAL PRIORITIES

This weeks commentary will be brief while I continue to recover from that the latest bout of insanity that masks itself as public policy from The Mayor of The City of New York's Office. Mayor Rudolph Guillani,(aka to many New York City residents as Rudolph Mussolini) in recent weeks has renewed his campaign to improve the quality of life in New York City. As part of this campaign, our Mayor has mandated that all vehicles in New York City will now follow the speed limit of 30 miles per hour. that noise will be kept down, rude cabdrivers will have their licensees suspended and that New York Cities two-hundred and thirty thousand public employees will overnight have manners and be nice when dealing with the public in their everyday various jobs.

I expect in a few months our current Mayor will pass a law that will indicate, in New York City, you will need The Mayor's permission to walk one step backward or one step forward.

The Mayor's recent campaign is not law and order but harrassment of the law abiding public with a capital H. Within three days of his current speed limit proclamation, our Mayor was caught going twenty miles over the speed limit on his way to a meeting in Staten Island, an outer area of New York City.

Followed by a crew of New York Daily News reporters who metered his speed, The Mayor was one of the first victims of his speeding declaration. More disturbing, (considering all that is going on these days, including the shooting of another police officer several days ago in New York City) is that the editors of New York Cities largest newspaper, The New York Daily News, choose this story for the front page, of the Sunday edition of that paper.

The New York Daily News has a daily circulation of over two million readers. I find it insulting to most peoples intelligence that an editor of a large metropolitan newspaer would decide that this speeding story was something the public would need to know about and give it front page treatment, considering all else that could have received front page status for a Sunday newspaper.

As a matter of fact I don't even know why I have written about this topic, except to highlight what I feel is the absurdity of the current state of affairs in what used to be called "Fun City".

Finally, a noteworthy point. In past commentaries I have written about the state of the economy. This week, I read that New York State, (the State that is on the way back) is ranked 48th out of 50 states in the creation of new jobs. New York City, continues to have a double-digit unemployment rate, twice that of the national average.

However, our politicians and media hand us stuff that has nothing to do with quality of life. The creation of new jobs, both locally, and nationally, would improve the quality of life! No, we're fed stories about how a sitting President may have been fooling around with a 24 year old intern, in his office, how a Mayor has broken the law by speeding, and how a variety of chemical weapons can and will kill me.

Thanks, this I really need to know about. Don't believe the hype! Focus, my friends, focus!

Take a close look at your government and tell me if you can believe what you see and hear. After that, project what you see and hear to five years from now and tell me what you think.

My passport is vaild and does'nt expire until the year 2002. What I see going on is an insult to The United States Consitution and those who wrote it. See Ya All Next Time!

VOL. 1 NO. 32

POLITICS AS YOU LIKE IT

CBS BROADCAST NEWS PIONEER PASSES AWAY IN NEW YORK: FRED W. FRIENDLY:1915-1998

This past week one of broadcast journalism's pioneers, died at the age of 82. The cause of his death was multiple strokes. At the funeral held last Friday, in Riverdale, New York, current CBS Evening News anchorman, Dan Rather, and 60 Minutes (another CBS News program) commentator, Andy Rooney, were part of a large group of friends and colleauges paying their respects to Mr. Friendly.

Together, with another broadcast news pioneer, Edward R. Murrow, Mr. Friendly, helped set the standard against which quality news programming is measured, to this day at CBS News and the entire broadcast journalism industry. An extraordinary, brilliant, and insightful man, Fred Friendly, came over to CBS television news from CBS Radio News, with a manadte from CBS Television Network founder William Paley in 1951.

That mandate being to develop and produce CBS News documentaries for television, a very new medium at that time. Friendly had been part of a group of CBS radio broadcast journalists, like Ed Murrow, Robert Trout and Charles Collingwood, who had reported the action in World War II from Europe, and part of a group of broadcast journalists who had reported the liberation of the Nazi's concentration death camps in Germany by Allied Forces at the end of World War II.

I had the pleasure of meeting Mr. Friendly and talking with him, at a tribute that was held in his honor at my alma mater, Fordham University in 1993. To give you an idea of the tremendous respect this man had in the field of broadcast journalism, present at that tribute also, was Walter Cronkite and Bill Moyers, two giants in the field of broadcast news.

In a distinguished and controversial career with CBS Television News, Fred Friendly, often bumped haeds with William Paley and network executive Frank Stanton, over the subject matter of various documentaries he would produce.

In the early 1950's when Republican U.S. Senator Joseph McCarthy from Wisconsin, was scaring everyone in United States to death, and The House Committee On Un-American Activities (HUAC) was doing the same,There were Comunists coming out of the woodwork as far as Sen. McCarthy and HUAC were concerned.

Fred Friendly and Ed Murrow, came up with the idea to do a program, which would show Sen. McCarthy for what they thought he was, a very mean-spirited, demagouge, looking everywhere for Communists and far exceeding his authority. As a result of the McCarthy hearings, thousands of innocent people had their lives and careers destroyed by "the blacklist". McCarthy, assisted by staff attorneys, Robert F. Kennedy and Roy Cohn, had conducted what many felt was nothing more than a glorified "witch hunt"

Basically, it was guilt by association. If you were called before Sen. McCarthy's committee, you had to name other people, even if you were not a Communist. Sen. McCarthy had CBS Television founder William Paley terrorized too.

Fred Friendly and Ed Murrow, pressured Paley to do the program, and finally, Paley gave the green light. In one of broadcast news televisions finest hours, Ed Murrow, on a program created and produced by Fred Friendly, called, "See It Now" held McCarthy up to a "mirror" for the American people to take a close look at him.

The subsequent reaction to the program, contributed to the downfall of Senator Joseph McCarthy and Ed Murrows career in televsion news came to an end shortly after the report was done.

In another "See It Now", Friendly-Murrow effort, the case of U.S. Air Force Lt. Milo Rudoulvich was the focus. The military wanted to boot Lt. Rudoulvich out of The Air Force, because they had discovered that his parents were members of The Communist party. Lt. Rudulovich, vowed to fight his discharge, and as a direct result of the "See It Now" program, which told his story, Lt. Rudoulvich, was re-instated in The Air Force and served honorably for the rest of his tour of duty in The Air Force.

In another "See It Now" program, Friendly and Murrow, focused on the plight of migrant farm workers in California. Called, "Harvest of Shame" the program exposed the horrid conditions under which the farm workers toiled and the very low pay they received for their work.

The program improved conditions for the farm workers and led to their organizing with Cesar Chavez of The United Farm Wokers Union, which fought for better conditions for the farm workers.

Ed Murrow and Fred Friendly also worked together on a program called, "Person To Person" which brought Americans into the homes of celebraties for live interviews. Edward R. Murrow went on to head The USIA, (The United States Information Agency) and died at too young an age of lung cancer at his farm in Pawling, New York. Murrow had been a heavy smoker and the pressure from his years at CBS News did'nt help his overall state of health either.

In 1964, Fred Friendly was named President of CBS News. Two years later he resigned after James Aubery (the head of CBS Television entertainment) and William Paley had decided that broadcasting "I Love Lucy" reruns in mid-afternoon was more important than doing live broadcasts of congressional hearings, looking into The Vietnam War.

Paley, had insisted that the reruns, of "I Love Lucy" were more profitable for CBS than the congressional hearings about Vietnam. Fred Friendly, felt, that CBS had an obligation to inform the American people about what was going on in Vietnam, and the money be dammed. This was Fred Friendly! Hard driven, and with a purpose to present the public with the facts and the truth, no matter what the cost. During his long career with CBS News, Fred Friendly had honored his employer and his craft by winning ten Peabody Awards.the equivalent to an Academy Award in motion pictures, for broadcast journalists.

After leaving CBS News in 1966, at the age of 50, Fred Friendly went on to teach broadcast journalism, at Columbia Universiity's prestigious School of Jouranlism, up to his death last week.

Mr. Friendly also helped develop and put together the concept for The Public Broadcasting System, (PBS) which presents some of the finest television programming to be seen. Mr. Friendly additionally produced and moderated a series of programs in the 1990's for The Public Broadcasting

System, on The First Amendment and free speech focusing on the constitutional legal implications of that area of the law.

One of Mr. Friendly's enduring quotes, talks of what he felt his mission was as an educator and broadcast journalist. "My job is to make the decision making process so agonizing that the only way out, *is by thinking"*.

Fred Friendly did'nt feel broadacst journalism was entertainment, rather he felt what it should be is an important public trust, that must be handled with care.

Today's tabloid journalism is not what Mr. Friendly stood for. He stood for excellence, in informing the public, and felt that television should represent much more than a cash cow, without a conscience.

Sadly, in the race for ratings and money, television has become just that. However, for those who would aspire to the lecacy of Fred Friendly, the yardstcik is there to all our benefits. What passes for news these days is an outright insult to the foundation of broadcast and print journalism.

The way the media is handling the current matter involving President Clinton and former White House intern Monica Lewinsky is a good example of that. Unless, we soon return to responsible reporting from the media, we will no longer be able to separate, fact from fiction.

If that be the case, then we all, might as well be reading comic books, to get our news, for the news we'd be getting would represent the same level of information that a comic book provides, which is not very much. Thats not news, but just another rip-off of the public at large.

Fred Friendly will be missed by many and long remembered for his contributions to the world of broadacst journalism. Rest In Peace to a fine man and educator. See Ya All Next Time

VOL. 1 NO. 33

POLITICS AS YOU LIKE IT

IF OUR ECONOMY IS SO GOOD:THEN PLEASE EXPLAIN THE FOLLOWING

This week I am reprinting three separate articles on the state of the economy that are in direct variance with what we have been told about the economy in the past six weeks. The best economy in some twenty-five years? The lowest unemployment rate in a long time? The best cilmate for college grdauates seeking entry-level jobs in years? Sounds real good, right?

After reading the next three articles, all by New York Daily News Staff Reporters, I leave you to make your own judgment, or to make any sense out of the aforementioned questions. The New York Daily News is a newspaper published in New York City, with a daily readership of over two million people.

The New York Daily News is part of The Chicago Tribune syndicate of nationwide newspapers. It's current owner and publisher is Mortimor Zuckerman, the owner and publisher of the magazine, U.S. News and World Reports which competes with Time Magazine and Newsweek magazine every week, for its share of the newsmagazine weekly reader market.

Poll:We Struggle To Stay Afloat by Corky Siemaszko-Wednesdy-March 4th 1998-New York, New York

Nearly two-thirds of Americans say they're having trouble making ends meet despite he Wall Street boom and a roboust economy according to a poll released yesterday.

We're working longer hours, dipping into savings to keep afloat and racking up credit card debt, a Marist College poll of 917 adults across the country found. "People are struggling despite low inflation, low interest rates, low levels of unempoyment," said pollster Lee Miringoff.

"We're hearing glowing reports, about the economy from the politicians, but that does'nt reconcile with **fact** that people are struggling in their daily lives. That struggle apppears to be taking its toll. Sixty-three percent of those surveyed reported they have difficulty meeting their monthly bills, and 25% "always" worry they'll come up short, pollsters found.

To stay afloat, 72% of those polled said they put off making major purchases, 54% said they work longer hours, 52% admitted they've been tapping their savings and 36% said they wwere cutting back on basics like food and clothing. They're also buying on credit-those surveyed said their family's average credit card balance was $3,058.00 in December 1997. Forty percent reported they were working harder now than they did two years ago-just to keep up with expenses.

And the struggle is eating away at family life, the pollsters found. Families facing the financial crunch are three times more likely to spend less time with one another and four times more likely to have quarrels, pollsters found. "Purchasing power is down," Miringoff said.

"So families have to cut corners. People are finding ways to cope." The poll which was conducted bt telephone on January 26th and January 27th of this year, has a margin of error of plus or minus, 3.5 percentage points.

Food Pantries Feel Pinch-by Raphael A. Olmeda-Wednesday-March 11th 1998-New York, New York

A booming local economy is having little effect on easing the burdens faced by soup kitchens and food pantries around the city, according to a report released yesterday. Last year, (1997) more than 425,000 New Yorkers relied on emergency food providers, according to a survey by Food For Survival, the food bank that distributed 31 million pounds of food to nearly 1,200 programs in the city. "In the midst of a historic economic boom, thousands of New Yorkers are still dependent on receiving emergency food assistance," said Lucy Caberra, president of Food For Survival.

She noted that some food pantries and soup kitchens are even having to turn people away. "This shows, that we as neighboors, need to help,and we are not doing enough to help those that don't have enough to eat," Cabrera said. The study does not address whether the hunger problem in New York City has gotten better or worse over the last few years.

Kayode Vann, who coordinated the study, said the 1997 report will be ued as a baseline for futue comparisons."There's close to a half a million people that are clients of the Emergency Food Program Network" he said. New York, however, still does better than the rest of the nation, whwre food donations have decresaed 5%, to 10% in the last few years Cabrera said.

The study, called, "Hunger:The Faces and the Facts," was released as part of a national survey by Second Harvest, the parent agency of Food For Survival. The national report announced in Washington D.C., yesterday, found those looking for emergency help are often not homeless but the working poor--families with wage-earners who still need extra help making ends meet.

"The national results and the results in New York are similiar in many respects," said Vann. Both show the homeless make up roughly 16% ot those served by emergency providers and that almost 80% of the families of four seeking help had a household income of less than $15,000 a year. Locally, in New York City, 47% of the seeking assistance were unemployed.

Children under 17,made up 20% of those served, while senior citizens, (over 65) made up 30%. "A big reason for the growth in hunger is the decline in welfare and food atamp rolls," said Judith Walker, executive director of New York City Coalition Against Hunger.

Fighting To Fill A Need-by Raphael A. Olmeda-March 11th 1998-New York, New York

The Rev. Mary Thompson, had little time to talk yesterday, but much to say. Preparing to serve anywhere from 80 to 100 hot meals at the We Care program in Soundview, (located in The Bronx, New York) Thompson said she had a rough time keeping up with the neighboorhood's needs.

"Some of the people move on," They get jobs. They get rehabilitated..Their siuation improves. But let me tell you right now, no matter how many people move on, there are more people waiting to get in." It has gotten so bad, Thompson said, she has had to turn people away-a situation that is all too common in the city's emergency food pantries and soup kitchens.

According to the survey released yesterday by the Food For Survuval network, nearly a third of the city's food pantries report having to turn clients away for a lack of food. On top of serving hot meals, We Care, also gives away 1,500 bags of groceries every week from its food pantry. That number is just a fraction of the groceries given away at Love Gospel Assembly, a Food For Survival Provider on The Grand Concourse and East 183rd Street in The Bronx section of New York City. "Each bag is prayed for" said volunteer, Brian

Draper, 40. "We put in 10 to 12 grocery items per bag, and I'll fill up 75 to 100 bags a day," Draper, who once turend to Love Gospel for his own needs, now volunteers 40 hours a week to meet the needs of others.

Love Gospel also provides more than 700 hot meals a day to adults and children. I'm only here once a month" said Monica Hernandez, 42, as she waited on the food pantry line with her son, Michael, 6. "This is the week that food stamps run out." Eddie Santiago, 32, an unemployed chef, said he dislikes the idea of turning to a food pantry. But he was on line yeaterday too. "The politicians say everything is good," he said. *"Meanwhile people here, are eating macaroni and beans while the politicians enjoy their steak."*

This sad state of affairs was also brought to us by President Clinton, and his signing of The Welfare Reform Act of 1996, which he signed to get himself re-elected and to look tough to Republican Party supporters of then Presidential candiadate Bob Dole. In otherwords, President Clinton, literally took the food out of peoples mouths to get himself re-elected, not to mention the food away from almost five hundred thousand children, also, who lost their food stamp benefits due to Clinton's Welfare Reform, legislation.

Meanwhile, First Lady Hillary Clinton, gives speechs about how much she wants to do in helping improvished children in our country.

My prediction for Welfare Reform can be read in my previous commentary at my commentary archives which can be accessed on the main page for this website.

Please refer to:

Welafre Reform:An Experiment Programmed To Run Amok:Commentary for Week of August 25th 1997-Commentray Number 5

See ya All Next Time. Your

VOL. 1 NO. 34

POLITICS AS YOU LIKE IT

THE WAGONS BEGIN TO CIRCLE AROUND PRESIDENT CLINTON: IMPEACHMENT SEEMS TO BE A REAL POSSIBILITY:ZIPPERGATE

In the past month and a half, I have declined to write anything related to events in Washington D.C. that have turned our current President into a potential convicted felon.

The reason for such being, that I have felt from its inception, that "Zippergate" has been a politically motivated partisan attack on President Clinton. In keeping however with the priorities of this website, which promise that readers suggestions for topics will be written about, I am going to try and make some kind of sense out of this circus that has insulted and stained The Office of The President of The United States in the recent past.

The suggestion for this weeks topic comes from Jim McIntyre who resides in Northern Weschester County, New York. Mr. McIntyre maintains a website called "Jimboslim's" which offers a variety of humorous entertainment. His site was designed with a Web Tv Terminal.

There are several issues about "Zippergate" that disturb me. One, no one seems to be bothered with the possibility that The President of The United States may be a man with no loyalty to his current marriage. In otherwords everyone seems to be saying its okay to fool around. After all, all men do this, to some degree, right?

The problem though with President Clinton, is that if he did fool around a lot, he should'nt lie about it. I find this line of thinking annoying.

It is my feeling that there is something wrong with cheating on your wife and family and any attempt to legitimize such behavior should be frowned upon. The way this situation has been portrayed, is to say, if President Clinton cheated on his wife, it's okay, if he'd only fess up. I could just see Betty Friedan and Gloria Steinem dealing with that feeling, coming from "the good old boy network" of chauvinistic thought.

Second, while many would caution against a "rush to judgement" in this series of matters involving our President, I would venture to speculate at this time, that an old axiom could safely be applied, currently. That being, (parapharsed)

<u>"If it smels like a rat, then it probably is a rat."</u> There just seems to be much too much that President Clinton is accused of here, for him to be totally innocent of everything. If the standard for an individual holding, The Office of President of The United States and presiding as President of The United States, is that he or she be totally beyond reproach without the slightest degree of impropriety. then I'm afraid only God could be President of The United States. Certainly one would expect The President of The United States, to have a high degree of morality and integrity in his personal life and not having such does affect the image and effectiveness of that office, in my opinion.

A leader of the free world should be held to a higher standard just by what that office should represent to the world and the American people. If a President has a seedy personal life, that can carry into the way that President would conduct the affairs of state. The nature of politics by itself does not allow for perfection, granted.

Too many people have come out of the woodwork, and while, many would say, innocent till proven guilty, <u>an avalanche of accusers and accusations in this matter, would have the perponderance of evidence standard, kick in which is all that is required to prevail in a civil matter.</u> The beyond a reasonable doubt standard is confined to criminal matters. President Clinton has been called "Slick Willie" for a long time. I think he has "outslicked" himself at this point. The United States Supreme Court pretty much threw out the double-standard a President had, when it said in a recent decision that President Clinton must face justice, while he is in office, with the Paula Jones matter, which is set to go to trial in late May, if Clinton's lawyers can not get the case dismissed for lack of evidence.

Finally, what I feel is the partisan nature of the on-going investigations in this matter, can lead only to the impeachment of President Clinton. The Office of The Independent Counsel headed by Republican Kenneth Starr is under the gun to come up with evidence. I feel the very survival of that office is at stake here.

Grand Juries have been convened in three states and thousands of pages of testimony have been taken. Independent Prosecutor Kenneth Starr has aleady indicated that all evidence obtained against President Clinton, at the conclusion of his investigation will go to Congress,who will then have to decide whether to commence impeachment proceedings against President Clinton. I doubt after all the witnesses and testimony given in this matter, that Ken Starr will come up with nothing.

Given the Republican majority in The Congress and The United States Senate, <u>I see President Clinton as history, by October 1st of this year, if not before that.</u>

Whether or not, The Office of The President of The United States and the manner in which the running of our country could be undermined with this matter, should be a bi-partisan issue, I doubt when the vote to impeach is taken, that many Republicans will vote not to, if this is a truly partisan "witch hunt".

While The Republican Party has it good points too, be reminded that they had no problem wih closing down the entire Federal government for three weeks, while engaging in political in-fighting with President Clinton.

It should also be considered that on President Clinton's watch, Wall Street has enjoyed record and historic gains. Big business could very well, short-circuit any impeachment proceedings, doing so, from behind the scenes, just as they control elections, by donating huge sums of money to both major political parties, in national elections.

The result of that intervention, should it occur, would have a lot of Republican's in The House and The Senate, voting against the impeachment, and have President Clinton retaining his office. Money, is the fuel that runs politics and Wall Street has more money now, than ever before in history.

If you ask, well what are you saying? The facts mean little here. Yes, I'm saying that. The ultimate determinant as to whether or not Bill Clinton remains President, in my opinion has very little to do with what he's accused of and more to do with a variety of poltical behind the scenes senarios. I predict President Clinton's impeachment as a certainty, because not much more can fall on him, before Wall Street says, money or not, he's, got to go. Wall Street pretty much runs The United States, not Wshington D.C.

Bernard Paul

The best spin-doctors, and media manipulators in the world cannot clean this mess up, in my opinion.

Finally, the recent invocation of "executive privilge" in this matter, by President Clinton, is not the act of an innocent man. Of course only time will tell, if my subjective feelings here will come true. See ya All Next Time.

VOL. 1 NO. 35

POLITICS AS YOU LIKE IT

VETERANS DIE AS A RESULT OF DEPARTMENT OF VETERANS AFFAIRS HOSPITAL CUTBACKS: IS THIS THE TYPE OF MEDICAL CARE YOU CAN EXPECT AFTER YOU FIGHT FOR YOUR COUNTRY?

This weeks topic was suggested by Jeffery Gersten who resides in Monticello, New York. Mr. Gersten had also suggested a topic on public education which was written about in a commentary for the week of September 22nd 1997, entitled, Public Education Or De-Education.

In what can be described as nothing less than a royal mess, The Department of Veterans Affairs, it seems, has really fumbled the ball with this situation. The Department of Veternas Affairs, (heretoafter referred to as The VA) is a cabinet level federal agency that provides a variety of services for honorably discharged veterans from The United States Military. The VA's annual budget allocation from Congress to run it's agency, is 41 billion dollars.

Within this massive bureaucracy, also resides our nations largest hospital system, which exclusively treats veterans of the military for a variety of ailments, on an in-patient and out-patient basis. As with all other federal agency's in the recent past, The VA has been under the gun to cut costs and in doing so, become a more efficient streamlined operation. On May 13th of last year, the lid came off the kettle, as one of the ways The VA had decided to cut costs, became public knowledge.

A small newspaper, in Orange County, New York, (The Middletown Times Herald Record) broke a story about how the death rate had doubled at two local VA Hospitals, from October 1996 through March of 1997. The newspaper article went on to atribute the increased death rate, directly to the cutbacks in funding to the two hospitals, which produced understaffing at both facilities. The two hospitals under investigation are The Franklin D. Rossevelt Veterans Hospital in Montrose, New York, and The Veterans Affaris Hospital in Castle Point, New York.

The two hospitals comprise what is called <u>The VA Hudson Valley Health Care System.</u> In 1996. these two hospitals cared for a combined total of eighteen thousand veterans. Both hospitals have undergone staff reductions of 17 percent of their total work force. Castle Point lost 117 employess's and The FDR VA Hospital lost 263 employees. These losses were due to layoffs, buyouts, retirements and attrition. Attrition is a process, where an employee leaves, for whatever reason, however the open position is just not filled.

The Department of Veterans Affairs used the following to justify the cuts at the two VA hospitals.

A Significant Shift of Veterans Residing In The Northeast Now Residing In The South And The West

An Emphasis In Providing Most All VA Medical Care In The Northeast On An Out-Patient Basis Instead Of An In-Patient Basis

To Achieve Compliance With The Veterans Equitable Resource Allocation Program (VERA) Being Administered From VA In Washington D.C.

On the same day that The Times Herald Record story was publsihed, Congresswoman Sue Kelly, a Republican represenative from the area the two affected VA hopitals were in along with 18 other Congresspersons from New York State wrote The Secretary of The Department of Veterans Affairs demanding an investigation of The VA Hospital situation.

On May 20th 1997, seven days after the article appeared, The Secretary of The Department of Veterans Affairs and other officials of The VA, met with The New York Congressional Delagation in Washington D.C. <u>Rep. Sue Kelly (R) who represents the area the two VA hospitals are located in, had voted for the VA hospital cuts, as part of Newt Gingrich's. "Contract With America", (Many called it "The Contract On America") several years ago.</u>

<u>When the story broke, she went the other way, arguing against the cutbacks.</u> Typical politician, right?

. When I learned of this matter in late January of this year, I wrote Congresswoman Kelly's office asking why she had flip-flopped on her position regarding the cuts at the two VA hospitals and whether she had indeed voted for the cuts. I received no response to several E-mails that were sent to her office.

The meeting that was held with The New York State Congressional delagation and The Secretary of The Department of Veterans Affairs, promised an in-depth investigation of the delivery of services by the two hospitals and the effect of the cutbacks on the mortality rate at the two facilities. The results of that investigation were released on December 1st 1997 and noted no direct relation between the cutbacks at the two hospitals and a doubling of the patient death rate.

The report was conducted by The Office of The Medical Inspector for The Department of Veterans Affairs, and is quite extensive. Should you wish to look at it, it can be obtained by writing a letter to the following address:

FOICA Officer-Freedom of Information Act Requests

The U.S. Department of Veterans Affairs

810 Vermont Avenue N.W.

Washington D.C. 20420

Additionally, if you would like a complete copy of The VA Medical Inspectors Report sent to you by E-Mail, please E-Mail me at Bernard007@webtv.net and I will sent you a copy of the report within 48 hours of the time I receive your request.

I feel like most Americans, that we owe a great debt to those who have fought in the defense of freedom on behalf of our country all over the world, in countless campaigns.

Most certainly,, The Department of Veterans Affairs could have forsaw the consequences of the cutbacks on the mortality rate at the two hospitals involved here. No veteran after fighting for his or her country should once again be subjected to being in harms way, by a hospital system being run by a bunch of bean counters or care only about monetary expenditures and little about the delivery of quality health care to a group of human beings who have more than, earned that right.

To add insult to injury here, recently the administrator of one of the two hospitals being investigated returned 20 million dollars in funding to The VA in Washington. Now, he may think that will earn him a big promotion.

However, what it will earn him, is the loss of his job, as veterans advocates in the affected region are currently intensely lobbying for his expeditious termination. This situation is an on-going one.

I feel its an absolute shame, that something like this can go on. The Department of Veterans Affairs should clean its own house, here, and issue a public apology, for knowenly causing the deaths of the veterans in the two hospitals, involved. I call this murder by bureaucracy, or *bureaucratic terrorism.*<> *Under the law, in our legal system, it is called, misfeascence which means if you can prove in a court of law, that the party or parties, knew their actions would or could cause the death of a person, and did nothing to prevent that, they would and could be held responible and have to pay monetary damages to those hurt by their actions.*

Can anyone say, honestly after reading this commentary that VA officials had no idea that their actions resulting in significant cutbacks at the two hospitals, would not result in the deaths of more patients than usual? I, doubt so seriously. At a meeting between doctors and VA officials at one of the two hospitals, several months ago, to discuss this situation, something happened that is represenative of the entire matter written of here.

The doctors participating in the conference, deliberately left the beepers that they could be called on in case of emergency, out of the meeting room. During the meeting, an emergency occured and because no doctor could be reached, the patient died.

In conclusion here, it is my opinion, that unless this us against them attitude adopted by most Federal Agencies, against the public they are paid to serve comes to a halt, and quickly, more innocent people will suffer.

On the good side, I must commend The Department of Veterans Affairs for looking into this matter, in an expeditous manner, even though VA investigators found nothing wrong. The original Times Herald Record newspaper article had used Department of Veterans Affairs documentation to present to the public emphrical evidence of the correlation between the doubling of patients deaths and staff cutbacks at the two hospitals.

Whether or not that will improve the situation, or whether the investigation is all show, and back to status quo, once the pressure dies down, remains to be seen, in the future.

Our veterans deserve nothing but the best and I hope the aforementioned is just an abberation and not the beginning of a national trend of indifference and lack of compassion, which has affected other areas of our society in the recent past.

Postscript:

The conclusion of The Medical Inspector's Report and Investigation By The Department of Veterans Affairs, was that the mortality rate at the two hospitals in question was no greater than before the cutbacks.

This finding was issued by The VA, despite the extensive article which appeared in The Middletown Times Herald Record, showing otherwise, on May 13th 1997.

In otherwords The Department of Veterans Affairs, stonewalled the entire investigation and denied all allegations made against them.

Great Show! At the count of three lets all applaud our dilligent public servents.

See Ya All Next Time

VOL. 1 NO. 36

POLITICS AS YOU LIKE IT

THE TRAGEDY IN JONESBORO ARKANSAS: TWO YOUNG CHILDREN CHARGED WITH MURDER:BACK TO BASICS

This weeks commentary will be brief because I like the rest of the nation, remain in a state of shock over the horrific events that took place in Jonesboro, Arkansas several weeks ago.

What can one say or write, when confronted with a matter, where two boys, aged 11 and 13, decided one day to open fire on their fellow school children. What kind of atmosphere may be present in our society that would produce this tragic event?

In my generation; (I was born in the Mid-1940's) if you broke up with your girl friend, it wasn't an excuse to shoot other people. You just forgot about it and went on with life. Additionally, if you had a fight with another boy, you'd fight, shake hands after the fight, and it was over. Life went on.

It is difficult for me to understand how a young boy after breaking up with his girlfriend, uses this as an excuse to pick up a rifle and fire it indiscriminately into a group of his fellow classmates, killing and injuring many of them. One of the teachers at the school was also killed, while trying to shield her students from the gunfire.

Some, have come out and said in the aftermath of this tragedy, that bad influences, such as various movies from Hollywood, which glorify violence, should be blamed for an event like this.

While I doubt, children at the ages of 11 and 13, have yet learned the difference between right and wrong, and therefore could be held fully accountable for their acts, I don't buy into the Hollywood excuse. Rather, I strongly feel, <u>that good parenting, almost in all cases produces good kids.</u> Why a child would require lessons from his father in how to use firearms, is beyond me.

Perhaps The NRA, (National Rifle Association) could justify the use of firearms by children, but I cannot. Responsibility, on the way most children turn out, or how they conduct themselves as children lie with the parents and what examples they give to their children. The proper about of love, discipline, (not abuse) and guidance, usually produces, decent children and responsible decent adults. In other words, you have to care for and about your kids and want the best in life for them. I remember when I was much younger and played a lot of baseball, one of my favorite games. The positions I played were first base and centerfield. When things were not going well, our manager and coaches, always went, *"back to the basics"*. Doing such, produced better results nine out of ten times.

Without the effort of my coaches and manager to take us back to basics, we probably would have played a lot worse. In New York City, where I live, for the past thirty years, a massive entrenched bureaucracy called "The Board of Education" is another example of what I'm trying to bring out here

The New York City Board of Education is responible for the administration of New York City's public school system and the education of over one million children at the elementary, junior high school and high school levels.

You would think in a system like that, that the childrens interests would come first. However, for too many years, the people who work for The Board of Education and their interests came first along with teachers unions. These days, the same people that helped create this mess in New York City our politicians, are trying to fix it.

Now children are not stupid. They take a look at this and the way they are being treated and whatever respect they have for other people, and in some cases goes down one notch.

How many notches does a childs negative opinion of adults have to go down before we produce more sociopaths? There will always be consequences for irresponible actions in a variety of situations. Our children are the future of this country.

I find it reprehensible, that children could be looked upon as criminals. While it may sound too simple, the answer to this madness is back to basics and a little old-fashioned love.

My heart and sincere condoleneces go out to the victims of this senseless tragedy and I hope something is learned by others as a result of the events in

128

this case. An uncaring, non-compassionate, immoral, unethical, self-centered, society has its consequences. I for one do not wish to be made into a victim of those who do not care and wish to remain a human being, so I choose to care and hope for better days for my country and the world. How do you feel? See Ya All Next Time.

VOL. 1 NO. 37

POLITICS AS YOU LIKE IT

OLIVE BRANCHES AND DOVES: A REAL POSSIBILITY OF PEACE IN NORTHERN IRELAND: AT LAST

This Easter Sunday, hope springs eternal, after many, many years of conflict, between Great Britain and Ireland, for peace. In what can be seen as nothing less than a miracle, the announcement to the world, about the peace agreement was made last Friday, on Good Friday. Good Friday is seen by the world's Catholics as the highest holy day of their religious calander.

The historic agreement was reached shortly after President Bill Clinton of The United States intervened by telephone, to keep the peace talks from collapsing. Those talks were held in Belfast, Northern Ireland, and had gone on for 32 hours without interruption. The prime portion of the agreement between Britain and Ireland is the return of the right of self-government to Northern Ireland after 26 years of direct rule by The British government. Hostilities between the two parties, date back to 1916 when Irish separatists staged The Easter Monday Rebellion, in an attempt to form an Irish Republic. That rebellion was defeated by The British.

Since, that time, thousands have lost their lives, and thousands more have been injured in fighting between the two factions. The peace accord agreed to is subject to a May 22nd voter referendum by the people of Northern Ireland and the people of The Irish Republic in Southern Ireland. <u>The key provisions of the peace agreement would allow for the following if approved on May 22nd:</u>

Allow Catholics and Protestants in Northern Ireland to govern themselves by establsihing a 108 seat Assembly, after 26 years of British rule. To make sure that The Catholics, who are in the minority, have a real voice under this new system key decisions would require a 60 percent majority or a majority of unionists and nationalists.

A council would be set up between Northern and Southern Ireland which would promote joint policy making decsions on a variety of domestic and international issues. Any recomendations of the all-Ireland council would require the approval of the Protestant-majority Assembly and the Irish

Parliament. Great Britain would be allowed to retain the current system if no consenus is reached by the fall of this year and the new Assembly would be abolished if such consenus was not reached.

The release from prison, (parole) within the next two years of several hundred members of The Irish Republican Army, (IRA) and two pro-British paramilitary groups, who were convicted for a variety of violent and non-violent offenses.

To allow Northern Ireland to unite with Southern Ireland if a majority agree to that unification.

The right of dual citizenship for the people of Northern Ireland. They would be allowed to call themselves either Irish or British.

Call for a referendum on The Irish Republic's consitution which currently claims ownership of Northern Ireland.

The negotiation team for this agreement was led by former United States Senator George Mitchell from Maine, British Prime Minister Tony Blair and Irish Prime Minister Bertie Ahern. Comments on the peace accord have been made from all over the world. Some of those comments appear below.

<u>President Bill Clinton of The United States</u> "After a 30 year winter of sectarian violence, Northern Ireland today has the promise of a springtime of peace. The agreement...opens the way for the peole there to build a society based on eduring peace, justice and equality."

<u>British Prime Minister Tony Blair</u> "We have carried out what we believe to be the will of the overwhelming majority of the peope of Northern Ireland:the chance to live in peace, the chance to raise children out of the ahadows of fear"

<u>Irish Prime Minister Bertie Ahern</u> "Today's agreement is a victory for peace and democratic politics.We have seized the initiative from the men of violence. Let's not relinquish it, now or ever."

<u>Former British Prime Minister John Major</u> "It is a wonderful Easter present."

Sinn Fein Leader Gerry Adams "There is still not peace. The agreement is not a settlement. There are good things in it that people will have to get their heads around. The words 'historic day' and 'defining moment'and all of that have been overworked. The real historic day is when we will have peace. Let's build for that."

Former United States Senator George Mitchell-Chairman of The Peace Talks "The people of Northern Ireland will make the difference. If you support this agreement and if you reject the merchants of death and the purveyors of hate, if you make it clear to your political leaders that you want them to work, then t will. The choice is yours."

There seems to be a cautious amount of optimism and pessimism on both sides here, and it will take a lot of work to finally achieve peace for both sides. I would venture to say, that the rudiments for the peace are on the table and everything must work from that to achieve the peace so sorely neeeded here.

In my opinion, I find it incredibly amazing that either side was even willing to talk about peace considering the horrendus atrocities committed against each other in the past.In the 29 years of bloodshed over three-thousand four hunderd people have died in Northern Ireland, The Irish Republic and England.

Included in those killed were the cousin of Queen Elizabeth, Lord Mountbatten, who was assasinated by The IRA, on August 27th 1972. Former Prime Minister of Great Britain, Margaret Thatcher barely escaped death at the hands of IRA terrorists on October 12th 1984 while attending a British Conservative Party Conference, at The Grand Hotel in Brigton, England. Four people were killed in that bombing.

The methods of how The IRA had decided to obatin its political objectives for Northern Ireland, (bombings in Britisn civilan population areas) put many innocent people in harms way and shifted a lot of the worlds opinion and support away from The IRA.

Their bombing campaigns were very vicious. Howver, it has been said in the past, "that one mans terrorist is another mans freedom fighter". If that axiom is acceptable, then what are the limits to the methods one would use to achieve freedom on a micro or macro level?. From, what I've seen in news reports on television and radio and read in various newspapers, it would seem to me that The IRA, was trying to achieve its goals by any means neccesary.

Then again, what are the paramaters for an unofficial war be waged for freedom? Is everyone saying The IRA, should have been governed by the rules of war put forth by The Geneva Convention. (World War II, The Korean, Vietnam and Gulf wars were all fought under the rules of The Geneva Convention)

Finally, whatever peace can be achieved here between Ireland and Great Britain, its really about the childen of both lands, who hopefully will not have to grow up in a war zone and as a result of such, will be able to live normal lives. hopefully in the future. Blessed be the peacemakers. If this attempt at peace works out in the future, then the world has been blessed this Easter and Passover week. We should all pray and hope for that peace to materialize and be an enduring one. There must be real change in Northern Ireland, or the peace will be very superficial. See Ya All Next Time.

VOL. 1 NO. 38

POLITICS AS YOU LIKE IT

A MODERN DAY MURDERER PASSES ON WITH NO JUSTICE FOR HIS OVER TWO MILLON VICTIMS:CAMBODIA'S POL POT:ARCHITECT OF THE KILLING FIELDS

Just days before his current captors were considering turning him over to an international genocide tribunal, to face justice, Pol Pot, billed as one of this century's last Communist revolutionaries, died in his sleep at the age of 73, last Wednesday .

Pot died while being held prisoner in a rebel camp in Northern Cambodia near the border with Thailand. The unofficial cause of death was heart failure. Rumors are circulating that Pol Pot was actually murdered, however, no one will ever know if he was because no autospy was held, and his body was cremated.

In 1975, Pol Pot took over the leadership of Cambodia, while overthrowing a United States backed Cambodian government. He was assisted in the takeover by an army of guerrillas called, The "Kemer Rouge" Kermer Rouge was not a fancy term for some exotic cosmetic, but a very effective killing apparatus for Pol Pot. The Kermer Rouge became Pol Pot's instrument of mass deatn and genocide of over two million people in Cambodia.

This was accomplished through mass executions, stravation and disease. According to Pol Pot at the time this was happening, he was seeking to institute a more agrarian society, based on Red China's Maoist political philosphy, which Mao Tse Tung, had put in place in Red China. The purpose of Pol Pot's re-education campaign, (as it was called) was to get rid of Western influences in Cambodia.

The mass killings took place over a period of four years. Most of those murdered by Pol Pot and his Kermer Rouge thugs, were from the intellectual and educated part of Cambodian society. (Doctor's, Lawyers, ect. ect) An entire generation of Cambodia's educated class of people died in the genocide.

How someone like this man could take power, or not be quickly overhrown himself is beyond me. The Kemer Rouge to whom Pol Pot became captive, held a mock war crimes trial of him. Pol Pot was overthrown by an army of his comrades last year. Piles of his countryman and womens skulls became the trademark of Pol Pots regime.

The 1984, Acadeny Award winning motion picture, "The Killing Fields" told the story of what had happened, through the eyes of a New York Times reporter, who barely escaped with his life in covering the events of that era. The degree of evil that this man, Pol Pot represented is just incomprehensible.

The re-building of Cambodia into a civilized nation will take several generations, as a result of this mans actions. Meanwhile, the friends and family's who were made victims of Pol Pot's re-education campaign, recieve absolutely no justice whatsoever except his reported death, which could have been staged to apaese the many, many people in Cambodia, including The Kermer Rouge, who wanted him brought to justice.

Then, many people did not want the truth about what happened to be told by Pol Pot at any international trial that might have been held. The only redeeming legacy of Pol Pot's regime to the world, is to show what happens when a Maoist-inspired leader takes over a country and sees Western culture, as being an obstacle to the kind of government he or she would want to institute. Millions must die, for that type of government to be successful.

Certainly, from a laymans point of view, something is very wrong with a government that must commit genocide against a certain group in their country, to achieve or maintain political power.

We have seen this many times before in history and the repeated world-wide condemnations of political genocide, does'nt seem to prevent it from happening, even in modern times.

The situations, currently in East Timor and Indonesia, along with what has occured in Bosnia, says to the world, that genocide is an acceptable way to achieve a political end.

So, if a certain groups of people don't go along with the program, killing them for their political beliefs, is no problem. It does'nt seem like strong United Nations or United States condemnation of these practices change anything.

I would very rarely wish someone dead! However, good riddens to this mass murderer and purveyor of evil, Pol Pot. May history show, that our country, The United States, did everything in its power, to stop Pol Pot.

In the 1960's there were a lot of American kids protesting against the goings on in Vietnam and Cambodia. If they knew that one of the prices to be paid, for our country withdrawing from Vietnam, was Pol Pot, and the aftermath of his regime, I wonder if they would still have protested so strongly.

Certainly, the saving of of two million lives, would have been worth our further involvement. though you could find very few youngsters at that time in The United States who would agree with that.

We had covertly bombed Cambodia, incessantly,(in a secret and illegal campaign during Richard Nixon's Presidency) but that did'nt seem to prevent Pol Pot from achieving power or doing what he did.

Finally, as always, hindsight allows for 20/20 acuity and is a very easy perch to observe events from. It is events like this mass murder that happened in Cambodia that make me Thank God, I live in and was born in The United States every day.

However, that does not mean that The United States, my native land, does not use mass genocide, within it's own country, without the violence to eradicate certain portions or groups in The United States.

It should be remembered that The United States is not absent from Amnesty Internationals, human rights violators list in its own country, and contrary to popular belief does have many political prisioners incarcerated in The United States.

The methods may be different, but the ends are the same, Depending on the methodology used, you can create many political climates which would have the effect of a mass genocide without firing one bullet at anyone.

That's an entirely different topic, best saved for another time. See Ya All Next Time

Bernard Paul

VOL. 2 NO. 1

POLITICS AS YOU LIKE IT

A NEW SULTAN OF SWAT:AT LAST WE HAVE A BONA FIDE HERO:MARK MCGWIRE OF THE ST. LOUIS CARDINALS BASEBALL CLUB:(AND SAMMY SOSA OF THE CHICAGO CUBS TOO)

WELCOME TO THE SECOND SEASON OF "POLITICS AS YOU LIKE IT" GOOD TO BE BACK!

The game of professional baseball has enjoyed a banner year in 1998. After suffering several yaers of declining fan interest due to a players strike and higher prices for tickets, (which put out of reach, the average baseball fan being able to attend a game) baseball as America's premier sport is back big time.

Leading the resurgence in what has been called for a long time our "national pastime" is a man of LL'Abner sorts. (For those readers who do not know who LL'Abner is,he was a cartoon charcater of gigantic proportions, who lived in a place called Briarpatch, and was a very big fella, with not too much upstairs. His girl loved him anyway. She was a knockout blonde who was called Daisy Mae)

In our country, we have been sadly lacking in genuine hero's for thirty or so years. What hero's we have been fortunate enough to have had in the past, for the most part turned out to be tragic figures torn apart by a so-called adoring public. Few stand the test of time. Perhaps in baseball, Joe Dimaggio, the star centerfielder of The New York Yankees in the 1940's, would an exception to the aforementioned. As an adoring public we tend to idolize our heros, and maybe due to our own insecurities we then try to make them less than they are, no matter what the accomplishment.

The home run in major leauge baseball is as if not more majastic than the slam dunk in basketball, a player running 100 yards, (the entire playing field) for a score, (touchdown) in football, or the hat trick in the game of hockey. (A hat trick is three goals, "scores" in one hockey game) When a baseball player hits a home run, the ball is hit so far, no player on the field can catch the ball and the team that the player hits the home run for scores a run <u>and runs win ballgames.</u> Some home runs hit in major leauge baseball travel as little as 275 feet and some have traveled as far as 650 feet. The home run brings most fans to their feet cheering, for to hit a homer, is usually a display of raw batting power by the player who accomplishs this. Baseball fans love to see home runs soaring far distances into the seats of ballparks. The guys in baseball who hit home runs frequently have mass followings and are adored by the fans, and the media. In recent modern days Reggie Jackson, (who hit three long distance home runs in The World Series against The Los Angeles Dodgers a while back) is a good example of what I write of here.

Prior to this baseball season the home run record for a single season was held by Roger Maris. In 1961 he hit 61 home runs for The New York Yankees, breaking former New York Yankees, (the lengendary) Babe Ruth's 1927 home run record of 60 home runs in a season. (just a side-note here, in the year Roger Maris broke the home run record he was paid thrity-five thousand dollars by his employer) Roger Maris was a tragic figure at that time, due to the fact that most New York Yankee fans, (incuding myself) wanted to see Maris's teamate and very popular ballplayer, Mickey Mantle break the home run record. The M & M boys they were called.(Mantle and Maris)

This commentary highlights and salutes major leauge baseball's new "King Of Swing"; Mark McGwire who plays first base for The National Leauge's St. Louis Cardinals. On Septemebr 8th of this year Mark McGwire hit his 62nd home run of the season,a line drive to left field, off of Chicago Cubs pitcher, Steve Trachsel, breaking a record which had stood for thirty-seven years. Fifty-One of McGwire's 65 home runs have been hit off of right handed pitchers. This is notable because it is usually more difficult for a right handed batter, (McGwire bats right handed) to get a hit off of a right handed pitcher. *It should be noted that the focus of this commentary is on Mark McGwire and not Sammy Sosa of the Chicago Cubs,* (who has also broken the record, and as of the day this commentary is being put up is only two home runs behind McGwire) because this writer truly feels that Mark McGwire's overall performance in his thriteen years as a major leauge baseball player fairly allows him to make a distinction. So, for you Sammy Sosa fans, I acknowledge that Mr. Sosa of The Chicago Cubs has also had an outstanding season, home run wise. It should become apparent as this commentary unfolds why I have chosen to focus on Mark McGwire, the holder of 41 major leauge baseball and team records.

Mark McGwire, was born on October 1st 1963 in Pomona, California. He is 6ft. 5 inches tall and weighs 250 pounds and plays first base an infield

138

position. He was selected as an eighth round free agent draft choice by The Montreal Expos's on June 8th 1981 but did not sign a contract with The Expo's. The reason McGwire choose not to sign with The Expo's is because he wanted to attend The University of Southern California, (USC) a top baseball college. He set USC's home run record, which still stands while a student there. Shortly before he became a member of The 1984 Silver Medal winning, Olympic baseball team, he was selected in the first round, (10th pick) of the free agent draft, in June 1984 by The Okaland Athletics. He played with Oakland until the end of the 1992 season and was granted free agency staus on October 26th 1992. (Free agency gives a baseball player the right to sell his services to any other team in major leauge baseball) On December 24th 1992, McGwire resigned with The Oakland Athletics for five years. On July 31s 1997, McGwire was traded by Oakland to The St.Louis Cardinals for pitcher T.J. Mathews and minor leauge pitchers Eric Ludwick and Blake Stein. Ironically, McGwire's manager with Oakland, would become his manager with The St. Louis Cardinals, Tony LaRussa. (LaRussa is a praticing attorney in the off-season) The St. Louis Cardinals are as traditional a baseball club, as they come. They have been owned for generations by the Busch family, the manufactuers of world famous Budweiser beer.

Mark McGwire has been tearing the cover off of the baseball for the thirteen seasons he has played major leauge baseball. On May 16th of this year he hit a home run that traveled 545 feet. In the old days of baseball, these type of home runs were called tape measure jobs because of the long distances they went. Below are some of the awards mark McGwire has won, which will in all probability include this seasons, MVP award, (Most Valuable Player) home run, rbi, (runs batted in) and slugging percenatge awards along with The James J. Hickcock Belt Award for professional athlete of the year. As this commentary is being written, McGwire leads the major leauges with an incredible .793 slugging percentage. (1000 is perfect)

American Leauge Rookie of The Year 1987

American Leauge Home Run Champion (49) 1987

American Leauge Gold Glove at first base-1990

American Leauge Silver Slugger at first base-1992 American Leauge Comeback Payer of The Year-1992

American Leauge Home Run Champion (52) 1996

American Leauge Silver Slugger at first base-1996

And the band plays on for this remarkable baseball star, as it should! Hold on to your hats my readers, because you don't get the true picture of Mark McGwire until you see the whole story below of this future baseball Hall of Famer and he's still got four or five great seasons left in him. It's a long ride, so hold on:

Editors Note: ***Please take notice that some of the records below are subject to change due to the fact that the baseball season for 1998 still has 7 days to go before it ends. The statistics below represent those of Mark McGwire up to 7 P.M. Eastern Standard Time, September 20th 1998, when this commentary was put up on The Internet for reader consumption by the editor and publisher for this page.

McGwire Is The Only Player In Major Leauge History To Hit Over 50 Home Runs In Three Consecutive Seasons-1996 1997 and 1998

He holds the major leauge record for home runs in two consecutive seasons (123)

Holds the major leauge record for home runs in three consecutive seasons (175) 1996 1997 1998

Holds major record for home runs in four consecutive seasons (215) 1995 1996 1997 1998

Holds major leauge record for home runs per at bat in a single season (every 8.13 at bats) 1995 1996

Holds major leauge record for the highest RBI(runs batted in) per hit ratio in 200+ at bats (1.03) 1995

Holds the major leauge record for the most home runs in a consecutive series (20) 1996

Holds major leauge record for hitting a home run in 17 different major leauge ball parks 1987

Holds major leauge record for fewest at bats to 50 home runs (390) 1996 1998

Holds major leauge record for home runs through the end of July (42)

Holds major leauge record for fewest at bats to 400 home runs (4,726 at bats) 1998

Holds major leauge record for fastest to 40 home runs (90th game-281st at bat) 1998

Holds major leauge record for fastest to 50 home runs (125 games) 1998

There are currently 162 games played in a Major Leauge baseball season.

Holds major leauge record for home runs by a right handed batter in a single season (65) 1998

Holds major leauge rookie season home run record (49)

Imagine hitting 49 home runs in your first year playing major leauge baseball. WOW!

Holds major leauge rookie season record for extra bases for long hits (183) 1987

Shares major leauge record for fastest to 20 home runs (41st game) 1998

Shares major leauge record for most home runs in two consecutive games (5) June 27th 1987 (3) June 28th 1987 (2) June 10th 1995 (2) June 11th 1995

Shares major leauge record for most runs scored in two consecutive games (9) June 27th 28th 1987

Shares major leauge record for home runs in one inning (2) September 22nd 1996-5th innning

Shares major leauge record for walks in a nine inning game (5) April 23rd 1997

Holds American Leauge rookie season slugging percenatge record (.618) 1987

Holds National Leauge record for home runs in a season (63) 1998

Holds National Leauge record for home runs by a first baseman in one season (63) 1998

Hold National Leauge record for longest home run streak to start the season (4 in 4 games)

Holds Oakland Athletics home run record for 30 home run seasons (7 times) 1987 1988 1989 1990 1992 1995 1996

Okaland Athletics team record for career home runs (363)

Oakland Athletics team record for career runs batted in (RBI's) (941)

Oakland Athletics career team record for extra base hits (563)

Oakland Athletics team career record for slugging percenatge (.563)

Oakland Athletics season record for home runs (52) 1996

Oakland Athletic team record for slugging percentage in a single season (.730) 1996

Oakland Athletics record for on base percenatge in a single season (.467) 1996

Shares Oakland Athletics team record for scoring runs in a single game (5) June 27th 1987

Shares Oakland Athletics team record for home runs in a single game (3) June 11th 1995, June 27th 1987

Shares Oakland Athletics team record for walks in a single game (5) April 26th 1997

Holds St. Louis Cardinals team record for home runs in the month of September (15) 1997

Holds St. Louis Cardinals record for home runs in a single month (17) 1998

Holds St. Louis Cardinals record for home runs in a season (65) 1998

Holds St. Louis Cardinals record for home runs in consecutive seasons (87) 1997 1998

Holds St. Louis Cardinals record for home runs at Busch Stadium in a season (63) 1998

There you have it! Whew! 41 one major leauge records and I'm sure Mark McGwire will set quite a few more records before he retires. As things stand now, he will go down as one of if not the greatest player to have ever played the game.

In addition to being very good at what he does, Mark McGwire is reported to be a really nice and decent fair man. In these times of declining morality in our country, McGwire becomes a breath of fresh air, to those of us who would like to have someone to admire and look up too.He has been as accomedating as his rare situation would call for with the fans and the media throughout this historic season. A few weeks ago, (before he broke the home run record) Big Mac, (as he is affectionately called by his hometown fans in St. Louis) was thrown out of a game for arguing a called third strike which is automatic grounds for being asked to leave the game in baseball. When asked how he felt about being ejected from the game by the press after the game, McGwire replied,(parapharsed quote) "I deserved to be tossed from the game". In the "tear down our heros department, they'll have to go a long way to do it to this guy. Not that there was not an attempt to do so. Approximately five weeks ago, the press reported that McGwire had been taking some over the counter drug which made him Superman. That story, and rightly so, disappeared from the press. _You don't do what Mark McGwire has done in thirteen seasons of major leauge baseball being stoned out on drugs._ McGwire's secret to his success can be attributed to several things, hard work, and an incredible amount of discipline and talent. Of course the conventional media will print or broadcast almost anything and this is why they have for the most part lost the trust of the public.

Finally, I wish to point out that Mark McGwire was not scouted by Major Leauge Baseball, nor was he the product of a baseball farm system. He was a free agent when the Montreal Expo's offered him a contract in June of 1981. An unknown entity at that time, he went on to be selected to play in The All-Star Baseball game, 10 times in 12 years. This year he was the highest vote getter for The All-Star Team in The National Leauge with three-million, three-hundred seventy-seven thousand, one-hundred forty five votes. I feel Mark McGwire is a good example of someone making it outside,"the good old boy network" and way of doing things in our country, which is usually corrupt and falls into "the who you know sysndrome". This type of system excludes millions of people in our country who are very talented in a variety of fields, and thus never realize their potential and then are told they did'nt work hard enough and it was their fault they did'nt make it! Free agents usually do not get professional sports opportunities. Big Mac is one of the rare exceptions to the aforementioned. We should all salute this man and enjoy his work while he's playing baseball. Definitely a future Hall Of Famer, and a man for the ages. Hats off to Mark McGwire and congraulations on an exceptional year. "Politics As You Like IT" will return with more commentary on Sunday, October 4th 1998. See Ya All Then

Bernard Paul

VOL. 2 NO. 2

POLITICS AS YOU LIKE IT

LEE STRINGER'S "GRAND CENTRAL WINTER":STORIES FROM THE STREET

This week I return to a problem that continues to shame America in our so-called booming economy, homelessness.This includes currently, two-hundred and fifty thousand Veterans of The United States military.

After, millions of dollars raised privately, and millions more committed by our government to make this problem go away, it just has not. I wil go out on a limb here and venture to speculate that the problem is not that enough money and time have been directed toward solving homelessness, but rather the huge sums of money, as usual have not reached those whom it was meant to help to begin with.

Pretty uniformly, <u>eighty percent</u> of every dollar directed toward most all poverty programs, gets siphoned off by those who run the programs or work for them.

That does'nt leave very much for the clients of the programs who seem to be used just to obtain huge sums of money, in the name of whatever affliction they may have. Given this, it becomes obvious that the main bar to progress in homelessness, substance abuse, ect. ect. is the bureaucrat and his or her partners in crime, (yes it is a crime to mis-direct funds meant to help the poor climb out of poverty) who just ignore the mandates and missions of their programs. This is why the probelms of the poor refuse to go away. Self interest. Not becuase the poor are too lazy, uneducated, or not competitive enough or without skills or the ability to obtain skills required for the workplace.

Over the years, (since 1980) I've grown very tired of the "poverty pimps hustle". With the publication and release of Lee Stringer's new book on being homeless, by someone who was actually homeless, my faith has been renewed a little. Finally we have the story from someone who was actually homeless, not some Hollywood version, written by someone who vacations in Malibu, California,, and would'nt be seen driving anything cheaper than a Ferrrari. A person like that thinks being homeless is sleeping on a beach overnight.

"Grand Central Winter", "Stories From The Street" by Lee Stringer, is published by Seven Stories Press a small publishing house located in The SoHo area of New York City. (The SoHo area of New York City is a very artsy, trendy part of Manhattan, a part of New York City) The forward to the book, is by world-reknown writer of fiction, Kurt Vonnegut and is reprinted below:

His name is Lee Stringer. Like Jack London, he is a self-educated storyteller of the first rank, and an uembittered survivor of extreme poverty, long-term homelessness and addiction.

Lee Stringer's tales are grimly entertaining. They are about how the most useless and rootless and endlessly harried of New York City's outcasts manage to stay alive day after day. They are reportage, not fiction. The author himself a character in every story, was for years and years as bereft of dignity and self-respect as are his subjects.

Even when a crack addict, though, gathering cans redeemable for a nickel apiece, being chased off subways for hawking *Street News,* a weekly newspaper about and by pariahs like himself, Lee Stringer, discovered a new high. It was writing for that paper. He wrote so interestingly and well that he became editor. He gained a purpose in life beyond getting the next crack fix. On the paper's office couch, he at least found a place to sleep where police could not improve the quality of life in the city by rousting him.

He kicked his drug habit. That makes him worthy of our attention, however fleeting, as a small-time hero. But this man can write! His stories are deliberately unsentimental. He might have made himself and his wretched characters from real life seem lovable or cute or raffish, or at least pitiable, and thus established himself as a sort of Dammon Runyon <u>Editors Note:</u>Damon Runyon, was a 1930's 1940's writer whose work focused on street types in post-depression New York City. Runyon, wrote about gamblers, prostitutes, numbers runners and other assorted marginal types who he felt had interesting lives mainstream America should know about. For his work, Runyon won many writing awards including a Pulitzer Prize, the most pretigious writing award)

Nowhere in all his first-rate writing has Lee Stringer concealed the hook of collective guilt should we dare to bite. But those who do bite will find resonant new demensions, as have I.

What is to be done?

Kurt Vonnegut

New York City

May 13th 1998

146

In 1984, author, Lee Stringer shared a rent-stablized two bedroom apartment with a friend on The Upper West Side of New York City. His friend's name was on the lease and subsequently when his friend became sick, and Lee had been downsized out of his job as an executive for a small company, his landlord who wanted to cash in on the higher rents a two-bedroom apartment could command, threw Lee out in the gutter. What transpired for the next thirteen years to Lee, as he navigated the streets, abusive city shelters, and a very huge and cavernous, gothic transportation terminal in New York City, called "Grand Central", where he slept two levels underground, near train tracks, is his story.

He takes the reader into a world few of us have first-hand knowledge of and few would want to experience, even for a short while. I watched Lee Stringer being interviewed by Tom Snyder on his late night CBS television program, a few months ago. I was very impressed with the lack of bitterness that Mr. Stringer displayed during the interview and came away from the interview feeling Mr. Stringer was a very nice man, who had been propelled into unfortunate circumstances.

He esacped from his dire situation not through the help of the "poverty pimps" or a city that has committed millons of dollars to making homelessness disappear, but rather, through his own skills and efforts, discovered by the publisher of "Street News"; (a weeekly newspaper sold by homeless people in New York City) The 1980's was an era where a lot of people did not really become what they knew they should be in terms of treating those less fortunate than themselves. While, the Michael Miliken's and Ivan Boesky's stole millions by peddling wothless junk bonds on Wall Street, the era's conspicuous consumption and blatant greed, lent to the lack of compassion, as something that was okay. This atmosphere also helped create a lot of innocent victims among the ranks of poor and lower middle class. Many, today, still suffer from what was created, during that era. Lee Stringer's story is an inspiration and we are fortunate to have his views on being homeless in print. His survival is incredible considering that the system had sought to crush this innocent man, into oblvion for no other reason than it's own greed and for Lee's crime of being down on his luck and poor. I highly recommend that you pick up a copy of "Grand Central Winter" to read a story, long over-due. The book is 239 pages long and costs $21.95. Lee Stringer's essays have also appeared in The Nation,, The New York Times and

New York Newsday. Mr. Stringer plans to continue writing and currently resides, (not homeless anymore, Thank God) in Mamaroneck, New York about forty miles from New York City, in Weschester County, New York. "Politics as You Like IT" will return with more Commentary On Sunday, October 18th 1998. See Ya All Then

VOL. 2 NO. 3

POLITICS AS YOU LIKE IT

IRON MIKE:THE REAL DEAL: <u>(SURE RIGHT!)</u> A JUMPING BEAN NAMED VAUGHN AND OF COURSE DON KING TOO

A few weeks back as part of a special cable television promotion that gave a premium cable channel for free, for a couple of days, I tuned into a boxing match. The name of the cable channel was Showtime. What I saw was not a show, but a joke and an insult to my intelligence. I tuned in to a boxing match. This was'nt supposed to be any boxing match. One of the two fighters was the current heavyweight champion of the world, Evander "The Real Deal" Holyfield. Broadcast live from Holyfield's hometown, Atlanta, Georgia, I was delighted to have this heavyweight championship fight being beamed into my living room for free.

In the past I had paid up to fifty dollars for boxing matches similiar to this one on the Pay-Per-View channel. The fact that this fight was <u>another Don King promoted fight</u> should have tipped me off, that the match was'nt even worth watching for free. Holyfield's opponent in this fight was a journeyman fighter by the name of Vaughn Bean. The fight went the distance, (a full twelve rounds) and Holyfield retained his heavyweight championship with a unanimous decision. This means he had more points than Bean on all three ringside judges scoring cards, thus a unanimous decision. Now scoring in boxing adheres to a ten point must system. In otherwords, the winner of a round of boxing receives ten points and the loser of a round, depending on how badly he does in the round, receives nine points or less. If one of the fighters in a round gets knocked down, he usually, as a result of geting knocked down, gets only two points for the round.

Now a lot has been said and written about how Evander Holyfield is a paragon of virtue in the boxing game, in comparison to Mike Tyson, who is seen as the bad boy of boxing by many, many, sports fans. Tyson, (the former two-time heavyweight champion of the world) was suspeneded from working as a boxer, a little over a year ago, for biting a piece of Evander Holyfield's ear off during a championship fight in Las Vegas, Neveda. Tyson currently has an aplication pending before The Las Vegas State Athletic Commission to get his boxing license back. His recent aplication to The New Jersey Athletic Commission was withdrawen. The return of his license is to be based on the reports of doctors who will decide if he is psychologically fit to return to boxing Tyson has also had some out-of-the ring incidents which don't really make him a shining example to the youth of America, or a tower of morality and virtiue. This has included a conviction for rape for which he served six years in prison and many run-ins with his former wife, Robin Givens and a very recent situation where he had to be restrained from punching someone who had rear-eneded his car. only to point out a few of Tyson's problems in the past. The fact that Don King has been promoting Tyson's fights since he was released from prison six years ago, does'nt help matters for Tyson either. Tyson, who earns upwards of forty to fifty million dollars a fight, and is currently close to being broke, recently terminated Don King as his promoter. There is a long history of fighetrs in boxing crying, *"I wuz robbed"* when they were involved with Don King.

Now, the purpose of this commentary is not to dump on Evander Holyfield, Mike Tyson or Don King, but rather to point out that Evander Holyfield is really not the saint that boxings image makers have made him out to be. What seems to be lost in all this is just how dirty and underhanded a fighter Holyfield is. This sweaky clean Olympic medal winning, I'm a nice guy image, that Holyfield has been given by the sports media, is bunk in my opinion. Futhermore, I'm also of the opinion that "The Real Deal" is really "The Raw Deal, and here's some reasons for the way I feel.

Nothing I can think of would justify what Mike Tyson did to Holyfield last year, when he bite a piece of Holyfield's ear off during a championship fight with Holyfield. I wish to point out though, that before Tyson displayed this bizzare behavior which led to his immediate disqualification and loss of the fight with Holyfield and the subsequent suspension from boxing, (rightly so) that Holyfield had viciously head-butted Tyson for at least three rounds prior to what Tyson had did. Head butting in boxing is illegal and can be devestating to the fighter that is head butted. Many fighters careers have been ended with intentional head butts which can cause permanent head injuries in a fighter and serious irreversible brain damage.

I seriously doubt that the veteran referee in the ring during the fight, Mills Lane, did not see Holyfield's intentional head butting of Tyson. Referee Mills Lane, never warned Holyfield, once about his dirty fighting, which can and has put many fighters in hospitals and ended the only job they knew or had, boxing. A fair, clean, Olympic champion, does'nt intentionally head butt his

150

opponents into technical knockouts. (technical kockouts occur in a fight when one fighter cannot continue due to very serious injury) Head butts have also been known to cause deep cuts above fighters eyes that have caused fights to be stopped. Was Holyfield's head-butting of Tyson supposed to be excused by Referee Mills Lane, because Tyson, was the bad, bad boy of boxing? If Tyson's career was to be ended by these vicious head butts of Holyfield, was that okay, becuase of who Tyson was according to the media's image that had been crafted for him? Actually, with the exception of the ear biting incident, I can't recall of any Mike Tyson's fights where he had fought dirty.

If anything, Tyson, has always had the raw talent to knock out an opponent with one punch very early in a fight. Not an animal, as some people would label him, but an extremely disciplined talented, powerful fighter. I submit that the actual, "Real Deal" has always been Mike Tyson and not Evander Holyfield.

Now, to the Vaughn Bean, fight, which took place a few weeks ago and another example of Holyfield's antics in the ring, which might make Mike Tyson look like a saint. Now in this championship boxing match Holyfield was supposed to be a heavy favorite to win. Vaughn Bean was a virtually unknown boxer who was ranked in the top ten of the heavyweight division of boxing. Don't ask me how a fighter can be ranked in the top ten and be unknown. In today's boxing world, anything is possible. What occured during the twelve rounds of boxing was a superb fight which Bean should have won, were it not for Holyfield's dirty fighting, as I saw it, once again.

The fight went the first eight rounds with Bean and Holyfield trading blows and running all over the ring. Holyfield looked far from the heavyweight champion he was. Actually, Vaughn Bean was looking a lot better than champion Holyfield in the first eight rounds of the fight. The fight was even on all referees scoring cards going into the ninth round of the fight. Midway into the ninth round Holyfiled had Bean in the corner of the ring, hit him with a left hook, which stunned Bean. Bean leaned towards the ropes of the ring reacting to the hard punch Holyfield had unloaded on him. As Bean leaned toward the ropes, (he had not gone down from Holyfields punch, nor was he going down) Holyfield pushed Bean, with both hamds causing Bean to fall down on one knee to the canvas of the ring. While on one knee, (and still no knockdown signaled by the referee) Holyfiled hit Bean with a right, left combination which knocked him totally down. *THE REAL DEAL?*

The mandatory eight count for a knockdown began by the referee and Bean got up and continued on to finish the fight. Holyfield, received a 10 to 2 for Bean score for the round of his so-called knock down of Bean on all three referee scoring cards. At the end of the fight Holyfield won the fight by four points on one judges scoring card, and by less than six points on the other two judges scoring cards. In the post fight interviews, Vaughn Bean was so upset he was unable to talk to "Showtimes" commentator, Jim Gray. Beans manager, Butch Lewis, was so upset, he had to be physically removed from the ring so "Showtime" could continue with its post fight coverage in the ring. The referee when asked for his comments on the controversial Bean knockdown, by Jim Gray of "Showtime" said, "it did'nt really matter", (the knockdown) because Holyfield would have won the fight anyway.

I guess the referee, Showtime, Don King, everyone involved with bringing the public this fight, figured no one knew how to count, and even if we did, so what! It is beyond me, how the bogus knockdown of Bean by Holyfield, did'nt matter, in the overall outcome of the fight. For without the knockdown, Vaughn Bean winds up having enough points on all three judges scoring cards to win the fight and championship from Holyfield, by a very close margin.

Don King, when asked for his post-fight comments, with his usual big smile all over his huckster, face, complimeted both fighters on a great fight, but did not address the so-called knock-down round of the fight. Typical, for Don King!

In summing up here, I feel that boxing has become such a joke, that any respect that is given to a competitive sports contest should no longer be given to the boxing game. Holyfield, as a boxer, in my opinion is no better than Tyson, if not much worse. inside the ring. Outside, the ring, I of course must give the nod to Holyfield. When asked after the fight, why he hit Vaughn Bean, while he was down on one knee, Holyfiled replied, (parapharsed) "a fighter must protect himself at all times". This from "The Real Deal", an Olympic champion, and heavyweigt champion of the world. What happened to the "fair fight"? Is it just, the ends justify the means? Is that the message sent to our youth by Mr. Holyfield Do what you gotta do to win at all costs. Well, clearly, I feel this is the wrong message, period. Disgusting, is the best adjective I can come up with to describe the attitude of all involved with this fight. Is what I think and feel as a member of the viewing public and a sports fan so inconsequential that I can be told anything even when it goes beyond

Bernard Paul

common sense and logic? In this case I'm afraid so! This is all my fault. The night of the fight, I had a choice. On another channel they were showing some old Woody Woodpecker cartoons In hindsight, I might have been a lot better off tuning into Woody Woodpecker. Shame on Don King and the so-called "Real DeaL"! I will never watch another Don King promoted boxing match. I've had enough! For another "Politics As You Like It" boxing commentaery, please refer to a commentary I wrote during December of 1997 below:

<u>THE JOKER IS WILD:PRINCE HASEEM HAMED:FEATHERWEIGHT BOXING CHAMPION OF THE WORLD AND HOME BOX OFFICE (HBO)</u>

"Politics As Yo Like IT" will return with more commentary on Sunday, November 1st 1998. See Ya All Then.

153

VOL. 2 NO. 4

POLITICS AS YOU LIKE IT

WOW! IT'S ALMOST LIKE RIDING A ROLLER COASTER:A NASA PIONEER RETURNS TO SPACE:77 YEAR OLD UNITED STATES SENATOR JOHN GLENN:A COLD WAR HERO AND LIVING LEGEND GOES FOR ANOTHER RIDE

In a feat that can be seen as nothing short of a miracle for a man his age, seventy-seven year old pioneer astronaut and living legend John Glenn has returned to space. He is the oldest person to have done so. Thirty-Six years ago on February 20th 1962, Glenn became the first American to orbit the earth as part of The National Aeronautic and Space Administrations, (heretoafter refered to as NASA) Mercury Space Program.

At that time our country was locked in a Cold War with the Russian government, and both country's were vying for supremacy in outer space. Space was one of the battlegrounds for the Cold War. Either sides successes were seen as victories for Communism, (Russia's political ideology in The Cold War post World War II era) or Capitalism. (the United States political ideology) At the time of his first flight, John Glenn was 40 years old and a Marine pilot in the military. He was one of our country's first seven astronauts. Glenn remains a symbol of hope and progress to a generation of baby boomers and senior citizens who highly admire his achievements.

John Glenn was prevented from making further space flights after his initial flight, first due to then President John Kennedy's insistence that Glenn was a national treasure that needed to be protected from the risks of further space travel and second when he developed serious bouts of vertigo. It's rather ironic that a man who had traveled thousands of miles above the earth, had deveoped an afflication, for a time, that was is characterized by a fear of heights.

Last Thursady afternoon, at 2:18 P.M. Eastern Standard Time, Glenn joined six other astronauts blasting off from The Kennedy Space Center in Florida.This Discovery mission is planned for nine days in space and will cover three and a half million miles. The projected final cost of the trip is four hundred and twenty-two million dollars. The launch which went flawlessly was delayed by several holds in the countdown for eighteen minutes. Last

Bernard Paul

minute system checks, which were caused by three alarms on the spacecraft going off and the unauthorized entry of a private plane in the rockets air space were the reasons for the brief delay. The launch had been originally scheduled for 2 P.M. Eastern Standard Time.

There is tremendous interest in this flight. A crowd of some two-hundred fifity-thousand people, which included President Clinton and First Lady Hillary Clinton watched the blast off, along with millions more watching in The United States and around the world on television. President Clinton remarked that he "was thrilled" with the mission and complemented Glenn's "bravery" in deciding to participate in the flight. The purpose of John Glenn's participation in this Discovery mission, will be to collect data on the psysiological effects of space flight on aging. Since Glenn is 77 years old, he is the perfect person to assume this role of expeimentation as essentially a human guinea pig.

Unlike his first space flight, when he rode alone at the top of a rocket called, Friendship 7, this current mission on a STS-95 rocket will have him riding below the flight deck in the cargo bay and he will perform his work of conducting tests on the six other crew members in a pressurized Spacelab module. The tests Glenn will perform will be on the blood and urine specimens of the rest of the crew flying with him.

This Discovery mission will be the last (the current mission being the 24th Discovery Space mission) before efforts towards the placement and construction of an international space station begin in 1999. The Discovery flight commander, Lt. Col Curtis Brown Jr.; said, "we are overwhelmed by the curiosity and the excitement about our flight." Many memebers of the Discovery crew including Glenn have complained about all the media attention. However, this is a bona fide media event if there ever was one and once again John Glenn is in a position to raise the spirits of his country, which is currently mired in political chaos, for a different set of reasons than were not present in early 1962.

For people who were not yet born or too young at the time of John Glenn's first space flight, last Thursday's trip held little appeal. Most in that group have visions and relate to our space program in terms of the tragic Challenger explosion and accident which killed seven people.

155

Critics of this current mission feel John Glenn is just going on a glorified space ride and is the recipient of this perk, because as a United States Senator from the state of Ohio, he has strongly defended President Clinton, in the congessional campaign finance scandal. investigations. Glenn is the most popular United States Senator in Ohio's history and will have served four terms, (24 years) when he retires at the end of this year. This commentator has long been a critic of space program expenditures. The reason being, the huge sums of money it has taken to keep the space program going, which could be diverted to a host of social programs in our country. I've conteneded for a long time, that NASA's missions and programs should not recieve funding priorities, especially, now that the Cold War is over. NASA has been a cash cow for our defense industries, and our military industrial complex for a long time only slowed by The Challenger disaster. Glenn's return to space will renew interest in the space program, and the cash will begin to flow once again into NASA'S coffers while children go hungry in our country and families in all four branches of our military (enlisted career personnel) must use food stamps to feed thenselves and their families. Their military pay is not high enough to afford food for a wife and several children.

Last Thursday's flight and John Glenn's involvement in it was initially Glenn's brainchild. In 1996, Glenn proposed the idea to Daniel Goldin, a NASA administrator. Goldin accepted Glenn's proposal under the conditions that scientists would determine his participation would be of value and that he pass a strict physical examination. There was serious concern over Glenn's age, as to his participation in the flight. However he passed all medical tests with flying colors. Scientific advisers to NASA also signed off on the medical tests and resaerch value of the data which would be obtained by Glenn's involvement in the Discovery flight.

Once in space Glenn will be connected to 21 different body sensors which will monitor his balance, bone density, heart rate and blood pressure. By the end of the mission he will have given 24 urine and blood samples which then be analyzed to determine the effects of space travel on the aging process. Space travel has been known to accelerate the process of aging and weaken the immune system of human beings. The results of the tests on Glenn during this flight will help to further verify the aging process while in space and perhaps assist in devloping some solutions to it.The effects of weightlessness in space in the aging process will also be studied.

The risk to John Glenn during this flight is not as grave as most people would think, because of his advanced age. flight director, Phil Enngelauf, noted, a, "slight increased risk" to Glenn, because of his age. His reaction time in any emergencies that might develop during the flight, was cited by Engelauf, as one of the reasons for the "slight increased risk" of having Glenn on board No special emergency procedures have been instituted for this flight, nor has any new training been given for emergency procedures, as a result of Glenns partcipation in this mission.

John Glenn's on-board doctor for this flight is Dr. Scott Parazynski who was seven months old when Glenn went on his first space flight in 1962. Dr. Parazynski said, "I'm really thrilled and honored to be flying the skies with my boyhood hero"

In closing here I venture to guess that most Americans who were around for the first flight can't help but get a little misty-eyed by Glenn's return to space. In a time when our nation is searching for role models of significance and hero's, John Glenn has reminded us all, the limitness of purpose and determination a man can have. Our nation is fortunate to have him. I consider it a cheap shot, that our conventional media tried to undermine Glenn's achievements in recent weeks by claiming this flight was a "political perk" and that Glenn's support of Savings and Loan convicted felon Charles Keating in 1990, should diminish Glenn in the eyes of the public. Leave it to the conventional media, our networks and news media to always find sometime bad. If they would do this to John Glenn, imagine for a minute what they would do, and have done to the average citizen, given the opportunity. The first casualty of war is the truth. We'll leave that for another commentary though. "Politics As You Like IT" will return with more commentary on Sunday, Novemebr 15th 1998.See Ya All Then!

VOL. 2 NO. 5

POLITICS AS YOU LIKE IT

IS FEMA AUTHORIZED TO DO ALL THIS? YEP! THE FEDERAL EMERGENCY MANAGEMENT AGENCY IS A LITTLE MORE THAN YOU MIGHT THINK IT IS

Additional Links Regarding This Commentary Are Available At The End Of This Commentary

Have you ever wondered what might happen if The President of The United States declared a national emergency? Well if you have visions of a benevolent Uncle Sam helping you in every way possible to survive a national emergency, think again! In 1989, then President George Bush signed an Executive Order which gives The Federal Emergency Management Agency, (heretoafter referred to as FEMA) awesome broad-sweeping powers. In the Bush authorized order, (still in effect) FEMA was told to build 43 holding camps with a capacity of thirty-five to forty-five thousand people for each camp. There are also hundreds of secondary facilities, some with capacities to hold a hundred thousand people.

According to The Director of Communicatios for FEMA, Milton Goodman, "all FEMA does is respond to floods and other disasters". However, when FEMA's broad powers are examined (which include their right to suspend The United States Consitution in time of national emergency) FEMA actually in it's role, becomes the strong arm agency of our federal government.

Why would holding camps be built to hold hundreds of thousands in case of national emergency, ask yourselves? Are the camps required to hold prisoners of the state, or huge amounts of American born political dissidents who would dare oppose a new political order in The United States? Is this The X-Files in reality, in the not too distant future? Interesting questions which perhaps can be dismissed as paranoid poppycock, right? Well maybe! However there is cause for legitimate concern when one takes a close look at the variety of executive orders in place, and the powers those executive orders give FEMA. Below are those executive orders in detail.

Executive Order # 12148 stipulates that FEMA is in charge during national emergencies, such as national disasters, social unrest, insurrection, or a national financial crisis.

Executive Order # 11051 emowers FEMA with the complete authorization to put the following orders into effect in time of increased international or domestic tension

Executive Order # 10995 states that FEMA if neccesary to accomplish it's goals may sieze all communications media ihe United States

Executive Order # 10997 provides for the seizure of all electric power, petroleum, gas, fuels and minerals, public and private

Executive Order # 10998allows the seizure of all food supplies and resources, public and private- and farms lands and equipment.

Executive Order # 10999 provides for the seizure of all means of transportation, including personal cars, trucks, or vechicles of any kind and total control over all highways, seaports and waterways.

Executive Order # 11003 allows the government to take over all airports, and aircraft, commercial public and private.

Executive Order # 11005 allows the government to take over all and seize all railroads and inland waterways and public storage facilities.

Executive Order # 11000 allows the government to seize all American people for federally supervised work forces. If the government deems it as necessary, they may even split up families to enforce this order.

Executive Order # 11002 empowers the postmaster general to conduct a national registration of all persons. Under this order all U.S. citizens must report to their local post office to be registered. It is at this time, that families might be separated and individual members assigned to a new area.

Executive Order # 11004allows The Housing and Finance Authority to relocate entire communities and to designate new areas to be abandoned and new locations to be repopulated.

Executive Order # 11001 permits the govenment to seize all functions of health, education and welfare.

There you have it and these are only the orders which are public record in The Federal Register. Who knows what other orders are in place that we don't know about that are secret in the name of national security. Hey, wait Uncle Sam, I'm your nephew! Family! *Just what is all this about?* All these orders make me a little nervous and I think rightly so. Sounds to me like the implementation of martial law or even something worse than that. I'm sure former President George Bush, who spent twelve years in Washington as President and Vice-President of The United States and several more years as Director of The Central Intelligence Agency, (CIA) had The United States of America's best interests at heart when he signed these executive orders, right?

Some might think and feel that George Bush, in retirement is doing a lot more than spending time on his yacht up in Kenebunkport, Maine. Interesting! Very interesting, considering, in just about twenty-five months from now, strong contender for the office of President of The United States, Republican Governor George Bush Jr.from the state of Texas may be sitting in The Oval Office running our country. In a supposed Bush Jr. cabinet, all kinds of appointees from the extreme right wing of The Republican Party would be welcome. Given, that we were fortunate to see one nut-case resign in the past two weeks, (Newt Gingrich (R). Ga.) they would be coming out of the woodwork in a Bush Jr. presidency, in my opinion and former President George Bush Sr. would certainly have enornmous imput were his son to be elected President in the year 2000.

So, I don't know exactly where we are going as a country, for no one can accurately predict the future. However, I do wonder why it would be necessary to implement all of the aforementioned executive orders in case of a national emergency. Does'nt our goverment trust it's own people? Just because they lie to us on a regualr basis in Washington is no reason for the people not to trust their government and then a lot of people lie when they come in contact with the goverment too! These days we are being told a President can be a proven liar and be trusted to handle international and domestic affairs at he same time. One has nothing to do with the other, right? I guess for people with IQ's below 25, that proposition makes sense and peole in Washington figure most of us can't figure out what they are doing or talking about anyway, so we can be told anything at any given time. Wonderful! Just Wonderful! I must now trust and also agree with a bunch of systematic sociopathic liars in Washington, these days and if I don't I'm percieved as being anti-goverment by the powers that be. This is more than absurd. With me it just does'nt fly, period. Perhaps the readers of this commentary can cite to me with their comments in my guestbook, under what premise of common sense and logic, that a proven liar should be trusted? Two and Two here, equals One, Washington would tell me also with a straight face. Man, Oh Man, God help us, please. The aforementioned is the reason over 119 million people eligible to vote in our elections twelve days ago, (64 percent of the electorate in our country) did not exercise their right to vote. That's almost 2 out of 3 eligible voters who did not vote. Incredible! Just Incredible! Oh, by the way,I did vote, even though in my opinion my vote means very little until true and fair campaign finance reform becomes law. That can of worms is best left for another commentary in the future. In the meantime, I'm calling The White House tomorrow, because I think I've saved enough money to sleep in The Lincoln Bedroom. God Bless America. "Politics As You Like IT" will return with more commentray on Sunday. November 29th 1998. See You All Then and _Happy Thanksgiving To All Of My Readers_

Bernard Paul

VOL. 2 NO. 6

POLITICS AS YOU LIKE IT

CAMPAIGN FINANCE REFORM:TAKING BIG MONEY OUT OF THE PROCESS:IS ANYTHING FOR SALE IN WASHINGTON:CITY HALLS AND STATE HOUSES ACROSS THE UNITED STATES?:WELL, YES!:HOW MUCH IS THAT DOGGIE IN THE WINDOW?

In two weeks, (December 13th 1998) the bi-weekly commentary that appears here will be written by guest Internet columnist Jeff Gersten who hails from Monticello, New York. Mr. Gersten is currently a regular columnist for the Internet Zine, Net4 TV Voice. His columns appear every two weeks and he has been writing for Net4 TV Voice since April of this year. It is my pleasure to highlight this excellent columinist here in two weeks.Thank you Jeff for offering to appear here as a guest commentator.

This week I attempt to make sense out of a system that has essentially robbed most Americans of the representation that The United States Constitution guarantees them. Government for the people by the people. Nowhere in our Constitution does it say, Government for those who pay the most money and as a citizen without huge resources, you wind up with virtually no representation.

I think think the framers of our Constitution meant the system to be a fair one where everyone would have reasonable access to our represenatives. It should be remembered that the original signatories of The United States Consitution, were people of substantial means at that time, lawyers, land owners, and in some cases, slave owners, or the propertied class of that era. Still, the question remains, (with some common sense and logic applied, something rarely used today by far too many people) would a group of propertied people write a document, (The Consitution of The United States) which went against their own business interests?

Most historians, professors of American history and secondary school educators would probably answer yes to that question. History as we all know, is what those who write about it, claim it to be. All too often, history, when examined closely, proves to be distorted and misrepresenated in many areas regarding a variety of topics.

The book and the ability to read and write well were pretty much the exclusive purview of the propertied classes in the late 1770's in the United

States. So down the road we got history written by money, published through interests with money, pushing the interests of money and power for the good part. Only very recently has the truth started to come out about this period in American history.

Campaign finance reform is long overdue. The key question, is whether we will all wind up with <u>meaningful</u> campaign finance reform, or just the same old stuff with a whole new set of laws and regulations, that leave the same people manipulating and benefiting from our elected represenatives To get an idea of what I write of here, please take a minute and go to the Federal Election Commission link below, to see just who contributed what sums of money in 1997 and 1998.

<u>Federal Election Commission Statistics For 1997-1998 Contributors Of Soft Money To Candidates For Office In 50 States-United States Of America</u>

After looking at the above FEC link, the question remains, can Mr. Mrs. or Ms. Joe Average American citizen expect to get as much from his or her Congressperson, United States Senator, or local and state represenatives, as Phillip Morris Inc. who contributed over one million dollars in New York State to various candidates in the 1997 and 1998 election year?

If not, then is this a level playing field or is this a field most Americans can even play on? Should I take the field to play a game, thats rigged against me from day one by big money?

Well, with over 119.5 million Americans registered to vote in the most recent election who declined to vote, the answer to the above questions should be quite obvious. That's over sixty-percent of all eligible voters who did not vote in the last election.

Recent scandels in Washington, have just added insult upon insult on the intelligence of the average American. Sale of cemetery space to a non-veteran in Arlington National Cemetery. Acceptance of money from foriegn interests in direct violation of our laws. Offers to sleep in The White House if the money contributed is substantial.A Presdent who feels cheating on his wife on government time, in The Oval office and then lying about it is oaky. What all this means to me, is for the little I could contribute, perhaps, maybe, I'll be allowed to stand 2000 yards away from the White House and take a picture of the place, if I contribute fifty bucks to The Presidents campaign.

This is not represenative goverment. Those who claim it is are just as corrupt as those who benefit from this perversion of "government by the people for the people". I don't think, as an American citizen, that I'm asking too much, that government be fair. Of course many would tell me I'm insane to expect anything close to fairness in goverment. To those people, I would say, there's enough in the pie for everyone.

What is our younger generation supposed to think about our <u>so-called leaders</u> when they take a look at what is going on today in politics. Finally, I feel campaign finance reform will be fought very vigoriously, by those who control our political institutions today, our corporations. If the results of their involvement in the past, in the political process are taken into account, campaign finance reform, at best will be an uphill fight all the way. Happy Holidays everyone. I'll return with more commentary on Sunday, Decemebr 27th 1998. See You All Then. Your comments are welcome in the guestbook for this page. Net4 TV Internet Voice Columnist Jeffery Gersetn will be here with his commentary, on Sunday, December 13th 1998

VOL. 2 NO. 7

POLITICS AS YOU LIKE IT

AUGUSTO PINOCHET:WILL A DICTATOR BE FORCED TO PAY FOR CRIMES AGAINST HUMANITY?

GUEST COMMENTARY BY JEFFREY GERSTEN

Click Here To Read Other Columns By Guest Columnist Jeffrey Gersten For Net4 TV Voice:An Internet Zine:(Magazine On-Line)

I probably should introduce myself. I am Jeff Gersten and Bernard has invited me to write a guest commentary for him. If you read Bernard's guestbook, you will see my name come up regularly. There is also a link to my regular column at Net4TV Voice in Bernard's favorite links, link on the mainpage of this website. I also wrote the review of Bernard's website linked on his mainpage also. That review can also be found in Net4TV Voice.

I do not normally write a "political column" and have been struggling with what topic to write about for this venture. I first considered writing about how legislators in my home state, New York, are about to go back in a lame duck session to give themselves a 38% raise. (Actually they have now done this) I decided that though all of you might understand what I was outraged about, it was not a topic worthy of the international audience that this website has. I then considered writing about the NBA lockout in the world of professional basketball, a sort of millionaires versus the billionaires column.. But no, there have been too many sports commentaries on Bernard's site recently and after all who really cares if they settle.

Then I discovered a topic that seemed worthy of a Politics As You Like It commentary. Presently the government of Great Britain is struggling with the issue of complying with an extradition request for Augusto Pinochet, the former leader of Chile. The concepts of human rights and diplomatic immunity are pitted against one another.

A little background is in order. Pinochet became the leader of Chile in 1973 after a bloody coup (probably with CIA assistance) overthrew the democratically elected socialist government of Salvador Allende. During Pinochet's rule thousands died, thousands fled into exile and others were "disappeared" or tortured. Here is an example of what was done by that government. In 1976, Allende's former ambassador to the US as killed by a car bomb in our nation's capitol. The government of Chile refused to extradite the accused killers.

Baltazar Garzon, a Spanish magistrate, signed a warrent for Pinochet's arrest. He was originally working on an investigation of abuses in Argentina, but his investigation led him to the Chilean situation. Garzon has charged Pinochet with genocide, torture, and terrorism in what he says was a systematic effort to rid Chile of dissent during his 17 year rule. The Spanish government took the position that it could not interfere with an independent magistrate and sent on his extadition request to the British.

Pinochet was in England on a visit. He is a noted Anglophile. He also has always felt welcome in England. Dame Margaret Thatcher has been a big suporter of his and gratful for the help Chile extended to Britain in the war over the Falklands. At the time of the extradition request, Pinochet was laid up in a hospital with a back problem.

The problem for the British governemnt is whether to honor or not honor the request. On the one hand, it seems obvious that crimes against humanity should not go unpunished. On the other hand, the government of Chile claims that Pinochet has diplomatic immunity. Diplomatic immunity is a time honored tradition. Without diplomatic immunity any country could act like Iran did in 1979, when they grabbed those in the US Embassy as hosatges, during the Carter years.

Maybe a little backtracking is in order at this point. Pinochet stepped down after losing an election in 1990. He did remain leader of the Chilean armed forces until earlier this year. He was granted the title Senator-for-life by the Chilean government. Chile has put forward the position that as a Senator and the fact the deeds in question were done in his capacity as a government leader should bestow diplomatic immunity on Pinochet.

In a dramatic 3-2 vote the British Lords Court voted to honor the request for extadition. If they had turned down the request, that would have been the end of the matter. Because they voted to allow extradition to go forward, British Home Secretary Jack Straw now has the job of making a decision of honoring the deportation order or not honoring it.

To not honor it would in effect be saying that any acts by a government leader, no matter how abhorent, are immune from international law. If Hitler were found today, could he claim diplomatic immunity because his acts were those of a government leader in his official capacity? In a more realistic analogy, what about all the atrocities committed recently in the former Yugoslavia? Should those responible be immune from prosecution if they were acting in the capacity of a governemnt official? Or what about Idi Amin?

To honor the request, on the other hand would set a precedent, at least in Great Britain, that diplomatic immunity could be overrode by an extradition request. Could Argentina send an extradition order for Margaret Thacther for sinking ships during The Falklands War and expect it to be honored? If Bill Clinton was visiting Great Britain, could the government of Sudan demand his extradition for bombing a factory? The list of these examples is endless.

So, what is my opinion on the matter? What do I believe the government of Great Britain should do? I am going to be somewhat ambiguous. Real problems do not have simple solutions. If they did they would not really be problems. I think the crimes against humanity part to this should be paramount. I do think that Pinochet should be extradited and face his accusers. I would hope through negotiations a way is found to do this without setting a precedent that we may all come to regret in the future. Where I live the qualifications to be a justice of the peace do not even include having received a law degree. Can you imagine the mischief that could be done if every judge in any jurisdiction could just demand the extradition of any foreign leader?

It is well known that extreme cases make bad precedents. That is my worry with doing what I believe would be the right thing and turning Augusto Pinochet over to his accusers.

We can see the kind of consequences I am referring to right now in our country. There was not a lot of opposition to the idea of a special prosecutor law after the abuse of power during the Nixon years. There later was some oposition in a dissent concerning its constitutionality written by Associate United States Supreme Court Atonin Scalia, concerning the separation of powers and the possibility of the abuse of power. How right he turned out to be! For example we just saw Independent Prosecutor Donald Smaltz spend seventeen million dollars of our tax money to bring a 38 count indictment against former Secretary of Agriculture Mike Espy. The judge threw out eight counts, the jury, despite 70 prosecution witnesses and <u>ZERO</u> defense witnesses said not guilty thirty times to take care of the other counts in the indictment. And we all know there are much worse examples out there of people who have turned themselves in to an obsessed prosecutor with an unlimited budget of your tax dollars to spend. I will not demean myself enough to name him, but you know to whom I am referring. (This is not to be taken as a defense of some of the moronic things done by the elected leader he is pursuing.)

But I have strayed off the topic. One of the interesting things that I have discovered in my research on this topic is that they do not imprison anyone in Spain over the age of 75. Since Augusto Pinochet was born on November 25 1915, he is 83 years old. I am not quite sure what punishment that they have in mind; nor have I come across what proposed punishment would be in any of my readings.

British Home Secretary Jack Straw has made his decision. He has allowed the extradition process to continue. Pinochet's lawyers are expected to appeal the decision, so it is not final yet. The Chilean government has withdrawn its ambassador to Great Britain. Only time will tell whether the positive outcomes from this precedent will outweigh the negatives. I do believe that this was the right first step; a message has been sent to governments that in the future there will not be immunity from crimes against humanity.

Bernard, thank you for this space and I hope my effort have been worthy of "Politics As You Like IT"

Editors Note:

Jeff, an excellent job on this commentary and thank you very much for your interesting and informative insight on this topic. More than worthy of this website. I hope maybe sometime in the future you'll want to do it again. Just this postscript, I would like to know who will bring to justice the officers of Chase Inc, (A Rockefelelr family owned bank) who this past week, it was learned, assisted Adolph Hitler in his efforts in Germany during World War II. Is Chase Banks role in helping Hitler to be ignored because of The Rockefeller families vast holdings and power? Why should those who bankrolled Hitlers madness be immune from being brought to justice. Why should'nt Chase Bank of North America pay reparations to Holocaust survivors as the country of Germany has done? Not to do so would be a further slap in the face to the victims of The Holocaust and the

surviving family members of those victims. Imagine a top American bank guilty of this insulting transgression. If it were up to me I would'nt let Chase Inc. continue to do business in our country, as a result of this recent revelation.

VOL. 2 NO. 8

POLITICS AS YOU LIKE IT

THE INNOCENCE PROJECT AND CENTURIAN MINISTRIES:AN EXPANDING EFFORT TO FREE INNOCENT PEOPLE SENT TO PRISON:SOME JUSTICE FOR INJUSTICE:THE USE OF DNA TESTING TO FREE THE INNOCENT AND CONVICT THE GUILTY

Well, the end of the year 1998, is upon us, and what a year it has been. Boy does time fly! I hope 1998 has been a good year for all and that 1999 is a better one too. I would like to take this opportunity to thank all the readers and visitors who have come to this website in the past. Your support, interest and participation are appreciated by me. The comments and opinions that you've expressed in my guestbook are important and valuable as other visitors share them, as do I. Without you there would be no "Politics As You Like" Thank You For Sharing And Keep Coming.

A few weeks ago, while watching ABC News "Nightline", (yes, I still watch televsion) I was captivated by a rare group of people that were being interviewed by "Nightline" anchor, Ted Koppell. Assembled for the interview were twenty of a group of sixty-nine people who had been released from death row because they were innocent.

Now, before I go on here, for you ultra-conservatives, right wing "police state types" who wish to call me a "bleeding heart liberal", I don't think strong support for law enforcement and application of the death penalty in certain types of cases, (as is my stated position both past and present) should include the execution or imprisonment of innocent people. I have yet to hear from the ultra-conservatives any degree of outrage at this set of conditions in the criminal justice system, which may well be more than an aberration in our nation.

During the "Nightline" interview a prosecutor suggested that since the former death row inmates had been freed, "that the system had worked". Contrary to that statement of the freed people who were being interviewed, one stated, (parapharsed) "that they he been freed despite the system and not because of their efforts". All in the group agreed and noted that the investigations that culminated in their exonerations had their genesis from outside the criminal justice system.

The total freed from death rows across our nation in the past twenty-five years under the aforementioned circumstances is sixty-nine. I am a strong supporter of law enforcement and apauld the heroic efforts of police officers to make all our lives better, day to day. However, on the other hand. I cannot endorse, railroad jobs, or express trains to incarceration, or death row, that occur for a variety of reasons that are unique to the criminal justice system here in America.

The old axiom, that everyone who is arrested must be guilty, is just not true. Further, I would go out on a limb here and speculate that the people we know of that are imprisoned unjustly here in our nation just represent the tip of the iceberg.

Until, the same amount of attention is paid to the truly innocent as is now being given to the guilty, our justice system will be unworthy of universal respect. Consider the following fact. In our country only two states out of fifty have an apparatus in place to compensate those released who have been found innocent. This should be rectified if justice is the true aim in the application of criminal justice. When we replace justice with retribution, there is really no closure for victims of crime. An innocent person sent to prison for a crime they did not commit is as much a victim of crime as is a person that has had a crime committed against them. The degree of outrage we express as a society against a criminal offender should be equal to the degree of outrage expressed by the "railroad jobs" of innocent people. I find the lack of this outrage for the innocent sent to prison, or death row, insulting to my intelligence, at the very least. Part of the reasons for these cases of false imprisonment is the new attitude in law enforcement that the end justifies the means, or whatever it takes to convict and the facts along with the law be dammed. Prosecutorial excesses have become a major problem in our country of late and must be addressed if any degree of fairness is to be retained by the process. There are rules to be followed, and those rules include prosecutors on the Federal, State and Local level. Whatever credibilty the political process in The United States has left is at stake.

When the people who are responsible for enforcing and writing the law, don't follow the law, there is something very wrong. A system like that does not represent criminal justice, but political tyranny. When an FBI Crime labs methodology of evaluating evidence can be questioned with unquestioned success, (as was done last year) then we must all sit back and examine evidence that is being used to send people away for long periods of time. Not to do so, makes the law-abiding citizen as ripe for a conviction of any sort, as the truly guilty. It is not enough to reverse the process, once it is learned that an innocent man or woman has been unjustly convicted. The institutional rot which allows these miscarriages of justice to occur must be eliminated so true justice can be enjoyed by all in our country.

Gerald Lefcourt, the current President of The National Associaition of Criminal Defense Lawyers said in November of 1997:

"Countless innocent Americans are behind bars or on daeth row for crimes they did not commit. Law schools and journalism schools are often in the best position to correct these grave injustices, as we've seen in the State of Illinois where more people have been freed from death row than hve been executed"

Mr. Lefcourt made his remarks in an annoucement that a major effort was beginning to expand the exisiting *Innocence Project* to law and journalism schools nationwide. Mr. Lefcourt was at one time a staff attorney with The Legal Aid Society-Criminal Defense Division in New York City. He was fired by The Legal Aid Society in the early 1970's when he made the following statement:

(parapharsed)" I feel the level of representation that The Legal Aid Society gives to black defendants in criminal cases is a blueprint for black revolution in our society"

The Legal Aid Society at that time offered Mr. Lefcourt his job back if he would retract his statement. He refused to do so. Mr. Lefcourt through the years has become a nationally prominent attorney who in the recent past was an on-air consultant to CBS News and Court TV during the O.J. Simpson trial.

The level of attorney representation is at the heart of many of those wrongly convicted in our country. While the Sixth Admendment to The United States Consitution assures the <u>effective</u> representation of counsel to defendants in criminal proceedings, that is hardly what the good majority of indigent defendants receive. Public Defender offices throughtout The United States are without the resources to provide the proper representation. With staff shotages, high caseloads per attorney, and budget cuts, innocent people go to prison, only becuase they lack the money to pay for a decent attorney. So pretty much if your poor and charged with a crime, in The United States, your guilty, case closed. That's not criminal justice, but an absolute mockery of criminal justice. A mirage! An illusion! What one who is poor can be sure of, is that they will get a lawyer who represents, the ineffective and defective assistance of counsel, a clear constitutional violation. So not only do innocent people go to prison but they go after having an attorney, for the most part, who could not represent their interests even if they wanted too. This sham, of course is paid for by taxpayer dollars.Certainly, here in The United States, seen as the most progressive country in the world, this can be improved upon. However, it should also be remembered that our nation currently has the <u>highest incarceration rate in the world</u> and is the last <u>civilized?</u> nation on earth to impose the death penalty.Note additionally, that our nation is not absent from Amnesty International or Human Rights Watch list of major human rights violators right here in The United States. These are both disturbing and alarming facts that all decent citizens in our nation should be concerned with. How can we be a leader and light to the world when we treat our own people this way. Work must be done to correct this abhorent state of affairs.

In the past fifteen years a lot of the aforementioned has been brought to light. First, by an organization, based in Princeton, New Jersey called Centurian Ministries. Founded in 1983 by Jesuit lay minister James McCloskey, this non-profit organization has been successful in obtaining the release of more than 15 innocent people from prison. Rev. McCloskey, who left an executive position on Wall Street to earn a Masters of Divinity Degree from Princeton University notes the mission of Centurian Ministries as the liberation from prison of those who are completely innocent of the crimes they have been convicted and imprisoned for.

In 1992, at Benjamin N. Cardozo Law School, in New York City, the second organization, dedicated to freeing the innocent, The Innocence Project was founded, by attoneys, Barry Scheck and Peter Nuefeld. Cardozo Law School is a part of Yeshiva University. Barry Scheck is called an All-Star litigator by many in the law profession. He was part of O.J. Simpson's dream team of lawyers which won his acquital on murder charges and he also successfully defended British nanny, au pair, Louise Woodward on murder charges. Mr. Scheck is also the world's recognized expert on the use of DNA evidence in criminal proceedings, an emerging area of law, at this time. Born, in Queens, New York, he attended Yale University as an undergraduate and earned his law degree at The University of Southern California at Berkeley's Boalt Hall School of Law. At the age of 49, Mr. Scheck, looks a lot younger. He is one of the most passionate and agressive attoneys, and advocates this writer has ever seen. Currently, he teaches ethics and criminal law at Cardozo Law School.

Barry Schecks own opinion of himself includes his feeling that he is basically a law reformer and a part of the law reform effort in The United States. He is also in the process of, (along with attorney Peter Neufeld) of rewriting the certfication requirments for crime labs in New York State. Scheck, despite heavy disapproval from many, is currently consulting with the prosecution on the JonBennet Ramsey murder investigation in Boulder, Colorado. While in law school in California, he spent a year assisting farm workers, also. However, of all he has accomplished to date, his Innocence Project is closest to his heart.

Barry Scheck, through the use of DNA testing has helped free 42 people, some who were exonerated while on death row. Scheck feels he has an extraordinary opportunity to help the innocent. Mr. Scheck was involved n the first DNA case in The United States during 1988. He had no scientfic background when he was involved in that case. Asked recently what the cases where DNA evidence led to innocent people being released from prison, represented to him, Scheck replied:

Bernard Paul

"the post-conviction DNA exoneration cases are telling us that there are more people being convicted for crimes in our criminal justice system who are innocent than any of us wanted to beleive. It's really that simple. And there are many causes for it"

One of the main causes Scheck goes on to say, is the lack of effective representation of criminal defendants as noted by this writer earlier in this commentary. Since 1996, The United States Department of Justice in it's report, *Convicted By Juries, Exonerated By Science:The Post-Conviction DNA Cases* noted that, 35 people have been found innocent by use of DNA testing and freed from prison. Below are some examples of The Innocence Project's successes:

New York NightmareA jury in Weschester County, New York convicted Terry Chaimers of rape, sodomy, robbery and two counts of grand larceny on June 9th 1987. He was sentenced to 12-24 years in prison.

After an unsuccessful appeal, at Chaimers uring, Innocence Project attorneys got blood samples from both Chaimers and the victim, as well as physical evidence from the original rape kit. The evidence was sent to the Forsenic Scienece Associates (FSA) for DNA testing. The FSA's two reports, released in July of 1994, resulted in the determination that Chaimers could be eliminated as the source of semen on the two swabs collected from the original rape kit. Chaimer's conviction was vacated and dismissed, and he was released from prison in April 1995, *after serving 8 years for a crime he did not commit.*

When "Unlikely" Is Unjust A Nelson County, Virginia, court convicted Edward Honaker of seven counts of sexual assault, sodomy and rape. He was sentenced to three life sentences plus 34 years even though the prosecution's case was suspect, featuring a forsenic expert's vauge testimony that hair found on the victims shorts "was *unlikely* to match anyone" other than Honaker.

It did match somebody else.After making several pleas for forsenic testing, Centurian Ministries and Innocence Project lawyers discovered that the trial testimony used to convict Honaker had been hyponotically induced and the fact that Honaker, had a vasectomy in 1976 had not been raised during the trial. Innocence Project lawyers at this point filed a motion to release the evidence in this case for DNA testing. Faced with more than compelling evidence of Mr. Honaker's innocence at this point, the prosecution cooperated providing samples which were sent to FSA for testing. The results of the testing showed that neither the victims boyfriend nor Mr. Honaker could have been the source of the sperm contained in the semen samples. Despite, this, Honaker's release was delayed, as Virginia law prohibits the intoduction of new evidence 21 days after a trial's conclusion. Governor George Allen finally signed Honaker's pardon on October 21st 1994, *after he was unjustly imprisoned for ten years.*

Near Death Experience Rolando Cruz and Alejandro were arrested and jailed for kidnap, rape and murder of a ten year girl in 1994. A Dupage County, Illinois, court jointly tried, convicted and sentenced them to death in 1985.

In 1988, both men made successul post-conviction challenges in the Illinois Supreme Court, which ruled that they, and a third co-defendant who was not convicted, should have been tried separately when it became clear that the prosecution was going to use their statements against one another. Upon remand back to the original convicting court however, the circuit court again convicted both men. When their caes were again appealed to the Illinois Supreme Court, the Court was deluged by *amicus curiae* (friend of the Court, positions) briefs saying that a convicted rapist-murderer had already confessed to the crimes alleged to Hernandez and Cruz.

Later, in 1995, DNA tests verified that neither Cruz nor Hernandez were the source of the semen found at the crime scene. Further, a sherrif's department lieutenant recanted incriminating testimony he hd provided in previous trials. The combination of all these factors resulted in the dismissal of both men's cases and their subsequent release. Both men served eleven years on death row, *for a crime they had not committed.* The outcome of this case was not based on DNA evidence, but rather, on a meticulous review of the facts in the case. The outcome in the Cruz and Hernandez case was obtained by a Professor of Journalism at Northwestern Uiversity and a Professor of Law at the same school, along with their students.

Barry Scheck feels that this combination of journalism and law schools is what's needed to overturn a lot of these unjust convictions. Scheck is currently in the process of assisting, The National Association of Criminal Defense Lawyers, in setting up, *Innocence Project satellite law clinics at The University of Missouri, (in Kansas City), Indiana University, Maryland Law School, and the law schools at New York University, Depaul University, Georgetown University and The University of Washington.*

The National Association of Criminal Defense Lawyers was founded in 1958 and has 9,500 direct members and 80 state and local affiliate organizations with 28,000 aditional members. Their mission is to ensure justice and due process for those charged with crimes and other misconduct. Their headquarters is in Washington D.C.

Concluding here, the next time you hear someone screaming after they are arrested that they are totally innocent, think twice about dicounting what they claim, for they actually may be just that, innocent. A lot of people tend, these days especially, to rush to judgement in matters where people are charged with crimes. That type of atmosphere does not produce justice but, too many injustices. For criminal justice to have a high degree of credibility and thus the confidence of the general public, the quality of criminal process and convictions, cannot be suspect. It is totally unacceptable to have police officers making arrests so it looks like they are doing their job well with the quality of a lot of their arrests meaning little. In the long run this winds up costing taxpayers much more than it would if solid convictions are sought and obtained in all cases brought by prosecutors. Clearence of high profile cases, where political pressure is on the police to find the person who committed the crime, should not result, in picking anyone up, to lessen the pressure in matters like that. Further, prosecutors, should back out of cases, without hesitation, where it is apparent that the individual being charged with a crime, is totally innocent, instead of

Bernard Paul

playing a numbers game with peoples lives, so they can advance their careers. Public policy should never include, convict at any cost, regardless of the facts of the case. Regretably, too much of this has gone in the the recent past fueled by politics and a lot of over-zealous prosecutors and the current aggressive law and order policy in our country.

I fear Barry Scheck, and Rev. James McCloskey will be overturning many more unjustly obtained convictions in the future, In otherwords, there will be no lack of legitimate cases for them to work on. The services Mr. Scheck and Rev. McCloskey offer free of charge are of great importance in our society. What they have instituted should have the respect of all Americans who actually believe in criminal justice and the proper application of the law in cases that warrent such. "Politics As You Like It" will return with more commentary on Sunday, January 10th 1999. See Ya All Then! Your comments are welcome in the guestbook for this page.

****<u>Credit and Attribution</u> Is Given To The National Association Of Crminal Defense Lawyers For The Case Studies Used In This Commentary-Ms. <u>Cheryl Amitay-Special Counsel for Legislative and Public Affairs</u>-Washington D.C.

VOL. 2 NO. 9

POLITICS AS YOU LIKE IT

WHERE HAS ALL THE MONEY GONE? MILLIONS RAISED TO HELP THE HOMELESS:HOMELESS PROBLEM CONTINUES IN AMERICA UNABATED:THE CRIMINALIZTION OF HOMELESSNESS IS THE RESPONSE FROM AUTHORITIES IN THE UNITED STATES

I know, most everyone has heard just about enough regarding homelessness in the most affluent and technologicaly advanced nation on earth, where as a country one of the things we take pride in is solving problems. Results are the bottom line in solving probelms and those results should be capable of satisfying at least to some degree all parties to a problem.

The probelm of homelessness in America is far from solved! Long after it was fashionable, to attend fundraiser's, write books, and watch people like Carol Burnett, play homeless people, on television specials, the way the problem is currently being dealt with, is a shame on our country and the Christian ethic most everyone would support, "Do unto others as you would have others do unto you".

I can't help but recall how Kenny Rogers (the famous country-western singer) raised millions of dollars for the homeless with his "Hands Across America" organization many years ago. Close to a billion dollars has been allocated through private and government funding in the past fifteen years to alleviate the problem of homelessness in America. Where has all this money gone? Rarely do I read of a program private or public that moves the homeless into a supported housing situation and then works with the homeless, to produce an indepedent living situation, where a person can obtain training, employment and their own housing and thus join the mainstream as contributing members of our society. Just what is the public policy objective with the homeless problem, to crush all the unfortunate people in that situation. Kick them while they are down and make sure they stay down?

Results, should not include the sweeping of the homeless problem under the rug and trying to act like the problem does not even exist. When the so-called solutions to homelessness as they are being implemented currently actually make the probelm worse and cost more than mainstreaming the homeless population, than a hard, long look must be taken at current public policy, to determine the direction that is being taken, and the long-term consequences of a public policy which essentially has no direction.

In a report released last Monday in Washington D.C., by The National Law Center On Homelessness and Poverty, it was noted, "that many cities are focusing on criminalizing homelessness and are failing to take advantage of exisiting constructive methods to treat homeless people for physical and mental problems and get them into housing and jobs". In plain and simple language, what would be in the best inetrests of the homeless, in the long term is not being done despite evidence that these methods would produce positive results. It's one thing not to have the wherewithall to solve a problem and entirely a different matter, when the solution to achieve positive results is staring you in the face, but government refuses to act. That's not sound public policy but deliberate neglect and irresponible government.

The advocacy group for the homeless in Washington D.C.; additionally noted in it's report, "that our nations homeless people are increasingly being harrassed by police and being driven from the streets in which they beg and sleep by cities putting meaness ahead of compassion". The report goes on to note, that the lack of affordable housing remains a prime problem in solving the homeless probelm. "While cities continue to crack down on homeless people, resources to shelter homeless people and to help them become self-sufficient are sorely lacking" the report further stated. The current report by The National Law Center On Homelessness and Poverty is the fifth since 1991.

Maria Foscarinis, The Law Center's Executive Director, said, " instead of sending the police in to arrest these people, you can provide resources". Ms. Foscarinis, went on to say, at a press conference held last Monday in Washington D.C., (parapharsed) "Criminalizing the homeless problem is a quick fix, but it's not a solution. People have to go somewhere".

Entwined with this sad state of affairs is the fact that currently, over two-hunderd and fifty thousand people in our country that are homeless comprise veterans of the military service in America. This is just unacceptable as it relates to this group of people who fought to preserve our way of life, in The Persian Gulf War, Vietnam, Korea, World War II and many other foriegn campaigns. Not that any group of humans beings should be homeless and that veterans should not. It is particularly annoying to know that this group is also homeless with little being done for them. Imagine, having fought for your country, and you you are now, back in the country in which you were born and defended to the hilt, and your homeless, in the cold bitter winter temperatures, with little to eat, and now the government you fought for sends police to harrass you because some citizen you fought for may have complained to the police that your prescence has offended his or her idea of what their neighboorhood should look like. Arrested for the way you look! Very interesting theory, right? Or perhaps some over-zealous "quality of life politician" decides your Honorable Discharge from the military, does'nt mean you are human? Sounds surreal, eh! Well it's not surreal and it's going on every day in our country today.

Many cities are currently resorting to new or old laws which restrict the use of public space and begging. "They are targeting the homeless for selective enforcement of the law and conducting sweeps to physicaly remove them". says The National Law Center On Homelessness and Poverty. What has America become for many of it's citizens, Calcutta, India?

Highlighted below are the way five municipalities are currently dealing with the homeless problem:

Atlanta, Georgia-Sweeps and crackdowns continue to occur with homeless people being removed from under bridges and moved along in the downtown area.

Chicago, Illinois-The city has made a concerted effort to arrest and prosecute homeless people for panhandling and is trying to remove them altogether from certain areas.

New York City, New York-There continues to be a crackdown on homeless people as the mayor focuses on quality of life violations, sweeps continue on an almost nightly basis

San Francisco, California-From January to November 1998 the police issued over 16,000 quality of life tickets, the majority of which were issued to homeless people. Police are taking pictures of people they claim are habitual drinkers and distributing them to liquor stores

Tucson, Arizona- City officials fully accept the criminalization policy and council members proposed looking into a plan to privatize the sidewalks which would allow business owners to keep homeless people off the sidewalks. Some homeles people were released from jail with travel restrictions

In concluding it's report last Monday, The National Law Center On Homelessness and Poverty, noted,(parapharsed) "that there are concerns about the use of public space which are legitimate". "Ultimately, no city resident homeless or housed wants people living or begging in the streets". However, The Law Center undescores, that rather than turning to the police, cities must concentrate on efforts to alleviate the problem of homelesness rather than concentrating on the symptons of the problem.

It is this commentators opinion, that the continued publicity regarding this national probelm, is necessary so the public does not forget about the problem or begin to see homelessness and the eradication of such as less than a national priority, above that of all national concerns, including the fight against crime. The definition of "eradication" as I use it here, does not mean letting innocent people die in the cold and starve to death, becuase politicians do not wish to tackle the probelm head-on by improving the lot of the people affected by this clamitity, who wish to help themselves out of homelessness. Affordable housing, and the lack of it, nationwide is a situation that did not come about without the aquiescence of our political leaders to begin with. In otherwords politics helped create the homeless problem and it can help bring it to an end, also. Real estate interests in our country did not run rampart in The United States, during the past twenty years without a green light from our politicians who have gained much from homelesness. In the war on crime, encouraging results have been obtained in recent years due to a concerted effort, on the Federal, National and Local levels. However, in the area of homelessness, results which would advance the interests of the homeless have not materialized. A shift in priorities regarding public policy toward the homeless is required at this time, so their plight can be resolved to the benefit of our entire society. The way the problem of homelessness is currently being dealt with is piece-meal and just a band-aid on a huge wound which will hemorrage into a major social disaster in the future, if not honestly addressed, at this time..

I would sincerely hope that we have the courage as a nation to finally stop playing games with this national disgrace of "homelessness" and to stop giving money and time to people and organizations who only seek to enrich themselves and not solve the homeless problem. The only conclusion I can come up with is that after billions of dollars raised both publicly and privately to end the problem of homelessness, is that the probelm persists at the same level that it did fifteen years ago. The money is just not getting to the people,(the homeless) it was meant to help. I stop short here of writing that the money meant for the homeless has essentially been stolen by those who received the funds and had a mandate both publicly and privately to help the homeless. I have not found the proof of that in my research for this commentray. However on the other hand I do know that in a traditional sense fund raisers no matter what, or whom they are raising funds for have excellent accountants, usually from the firm of Cooper & Lybrand, which is the class act in the accounting business. Accountants like that make a joke out of keeping two or three sets of books and might represent a client with fifty or sixty sets of books. They can move money off-shore quicker than the average person can say, "hey, just where do you think you get off telling me the stock you suggested I buy yesterday, which I bought, just went down 23 points" Just thought you'd like to know why charirties always need more money and the people they claim to help always for some reason need more help or never get any help at

179

all! Now off-shore investments in secret numbered accounts is not what this commentary is all about, but let me tell you, theres no better way to go. We're not writing about Switzerland here.Off-shore investing is much more sophisticated than sending a couple million off to a numbered account in Zurich, Switzerland by personal messenger which no longer has secrey laws that apply to The United States. By the time the IRS catches up with these poverty pimps, the paper trail, (if one can be found) goes all the way to Marakesh and back with the principals of the charity filing for bankruptcy in in the good old USA! The advantages of incorporating in The State of Deleware don't come close to this. With this off-shore stuff The CEO of the charitable non-profit corporation is found to be Mr. Bugs Bunny and Mrs. Mickey Mouse when the millions of pages of the non-profit organizations records are examined. Of course at this point the charitable organization needs charity. Bernard, how could you be so cynical and cruel? To heck with that! Let's start with The former CEO of The United Way, who was caught stealing millions a few years back. Need I write more?

I conclude here by noting that it's awful strange that after the huge sums of money, and other resources committed to ending the homeless problem in America, that we are still after 15 years of dealing with the problem, in the same boat we were, with little improvement in homelessness for all the so-called effort put into ending the problem. I called this the 2 + 2=5 syndrome and as long as the general public continues to beleive that 2 + 2=5. problems like homelessness will not go away. This may sit well with some, however I was brought up to at least add 2 + 2 which to me always equaled 4. "Politics As You Like It" will return in 4 weeks on Sunday February 14th 1999. There will be no scheduled commentary on January 24th or February 7th 1999 due to prior conflicting committments. See Ya All Then

VOL. 2 NO. 10

POLITICS AS YOU LIKE IT

A BRONX, NEW YORK TALE AND TRAGEDY:POLICE FIRE 41 SHOTS AT UNARMED MAN WITH NO PRIOR CRIMINAL RECORD:SHOTS FIRED FROM TEN FEET AWAY OF TOTALLY INNOCENT MAN:COMMUNITY AND CITY OF NEW YORK EXPRESS THEIR OUTRAGE AND SHOCK

REVISED EDITION WITH POSTSCRIPT

As a group of police officer's they are considered an elite group. The Street Crime Unit, (SCU) and it's four hundred members are officers down in the trenches of the fight to take guns and drugs off the street. They represent an aggressive style of law enforcement pioneered in New York City, which has led the way in the dramatic drop in the number of guns on the street and drugs sold, nationwide. Street Crime Unit Officers patrol in teams of two to four or five, in plainclothes and receive special training for their mission above that of the ordinary police officer. Last week in the Soundview area of the Bronx, (an area heavily populated by minorities, Black and Hispanic) four officers from The Street Crime Unit, just blew it, totally.

The race and ethnic background of the residents of the area where the incident happened, is noted here, because in the recent past, and in a historical sense a good majority of the types of incidents which occured last week in New York City and around our nation have involved black and other minority victims. Just by itself, with this recent incident is a clear example of police brutality, unlike anything that has been seen for a while in New York City.

The New York City Police Department prides itself, on the restraint it displays in the application of deadly force. However last weeks incident, and several other incidents in the past five years have brought into question the methods and justification for such methods regarding aggressive police tactics involving the use of deadly force.

The NYPD got a real black eye in the most recent case which involed a twenty-two year old black man who had come to our country from the West African nation of Guinea. Amediou Diallo's dream for opportunity and a piece of The American dream ended when four Street Crime Unit Officer's of The New York City Police Department shot at Mr. Diallo forty-one times with their nine millimeter automatic weapons and in doing so have created an international incident.

Four cowboys! With more training and a higher educational standard for the hiring of police officers in New York City. we now have this! Roy Rogers and Gene Autry, shoot em up, bang, bang. New York City has become Dodge City. Two years of college is now required for everyone who applys for the job. A nine millimeter handgun is seen as the elephant gun of handguns and can put a hole in a piece of steel to give you an idea of how powerful a weapon it is. It replaced the standard police 38 caliber gun, in New York City, because the police needed more firepower to match the better weapons that criminals were using in street crime.

Of the 41 shots fired, 19 hit Mr. Diallo, with 18 of the shots hitting him below the waist and one shot hitting him just above the heart. The shots were fired 10 feet away from where Mr. Diallo had been standing in the vestibule of the building he lived in.

This shooting of an unarmed man who was not threatening in any way has outraged all who live and work in New York City. What justification could the police have for shooting at an unarmed man 41 times? What occurred here is the equivalent to a mini-police riot!

A grand jury is set to convene next Tuesday or Wednesday to consider charges against the four police officers involved and The Federal Government in the person of The United States Attorny's Office and The Department of Justice and The FBI are also following the case very closely at this time.

A funeral service will be held this afternoon, (Friday, February 12th 1999) at an Islamic Mosque on the east side of Manhattan. Thousands of people are expected to attend the service including Mayor Rudolph Guilani and Police Commissioner Howard Safir. The family of the slain man has declined an offer by the Mayor to meet with him. Mr. Diallo, had been a devout Muslim and prayed five times a day.

What has been very disconcerting in this matter is the reaction of those involved and their bosses, New York City Police Commissioner Howard Safir and Mayor Rudolph Guilani. Mayor Guilani's initial response as far as I saw it, tended to diminish the seriousness of the incident with the exception of the amount of shots fired, the Mayor commented "this is no crisis, we will investigate and lets not rush to judgement" An innocent man gets shot at 41 times by people who are supposed to protect the public and that's no big deal, right? With the exception of a brief comment saying that there were no witnesses in the case, (it was later determined there were eight witnesses in the matter) Police Comissioner Safir left New York City 48 hours after the incident to attend a convention of The International Chiefs of Police in Los Angeles, California. He returned yesterday, one day early, to attend the funeral service being held this afternoon. A situation that could escalate into a major disturbance and the police commissioner leaves town 48 hours after it happens. Wonderful! Was this such a routine occurrence that Commsssioner Safir could leave town? I think not! The real possibility of an escalation of the tensions in this matter were there. Mayor Giuliani had canceled a fund-raising trip to the Midwest as a result of what had occurred and wanted to be available to help in any way he could to his credit. On the other hand, last year when he was running for re-election and was confronted with the torture of Abner Louima, by cops in a Brooklyn station-house, his reaction was much stronger than it was in the current incident. While torturing this poor soul, the cops indicted in the case were screaming, "It's Giuliani Time" as though The Mayor of The City of New York would condone the torture of a suspect in custody by the police.

Last week, also, across The Hudson River from New York City, in The State of New Jersey, two police officers had to bring under control a wild tiger. They shot the tiger, (an animal) once with a tranquilizing dart and one bullet from a gun, and the matter was contained. 41 bullets were fired at Mr. Diallo, a *human being,* who was unarmed and innocent! The explanation of the four officer's involved in this shooting; (parapharsed) "We thought he was reaching for a gun." They had been on patrol looking for a rapist.

A possible explanation was also offered as to why 41 shots were required to neutralize the threat this man represented to the officers as they deemed it. I call it The Rodney King Defense. With Rodney King in 1991, Los Angeles Police officer's, (most involved in that incident are now convicted felon's as they should be) contended that the threat Mr. King represented and their justification for hitting him repeatedly with their batons, was that Mr. King was still dangerous because he was not down and bounced up every time they hit him, meaning he had to be hit more, until he did'nt bounce up anymore. Makes perfect sense, right? A local all-white jury acquitted the officers involved in the King matter of all charges, mass riots occured after that and then a Federal Court jury convicted, and sent the police officers to prison where they belong. During the 1991 riots in Los Angeles the police whose behavior had created the riot could not be found in the area the rioting was taking place. The New York City version, could be that because of the many shots fired at Mr. Diallo, he was still standing, from all the bullets that were hitting him, making more shots neccessary. To both the aforementioned explanations, I say right, and my name is Donald Duck too. Quack, Quack. See, I go quack, quack, so I must be a duck right?

I am a strong supporter of law enforcement and have written such in a variety of commentaries that have appeared on this website, in the past. However, I don't feel the compulsion to support a bunch of irresponsible cowboys, who with their special training cannot determine whether or not a weapon is being pointed at them or not. This recent incident is ridiculous, as it is sad and tragic. If I were the New York City Police Commissioner all four officers would be fired on the spot. The act they committed speaks for itself, no explanation required, thank you. There is no explanation for shooting at an unarmed man 41 times, only the contrived, convoluted explanations that will be offered by the four attorney"s representing the police officer's involved in the matter. They of course, as it is their job to do, will attempt to defend an indefenseable act. Lawyers can be very good at this, but most see right through their fabrications on behalf of truly guilty clients.

Mr. Diallo's father, has called for the arrest and imprisonment of those responible for his son's needless death. When he was reached over the telephone in Vietnam, (where he was on a business trip) and informed of his son's death, he asked what his son had done wrong? He was told, nothing! The father then said, "he could not understand then why his son, had been killed by the police". The Diallo family is also having an independent autopsy performed on their son's body to determine what happened. That is in addition to an extensive autopsy performed last week by The New York City Medical Examiners office. Mr. Diallo's mother will fly back to Guinea with her son's bullet riddled body Sunday morning. The family has refused any offers of assistance from The City of New York and I believe rightly so. I would'nt want any help from a city, whose police officers had killed my son for no reason, either.

"My son was a good boy, well educated, and well mannered"; said the mother of Mr. Diallo. "He was a devout very religious Muslim who prayed five times a say," she went on to say. "He worked many hours on the street as a vendor selling books and videos and was a quiet, shy man, with an unassuming smile, the kind of a man you'd like to have as a friend' his mother also said.

Community leader Al Sharpton has demanded justice along with the family. One of the four officers involved in the shooting has apologized and pledged to co-operate fully in the on-going investigation. Police Commissioner Safir has recalled all four hundred officers of The Street Crime Unit for re-training. Below, are some incidents similiar in nature to the aforementioned that have happened in the recent past in New York City and these are the ones the public was told about.

Last year a drug dealer fleeing police was shot 51 times in the back. The justification for this was that he was a drug dealer

Several yaers ago in the Bronx, New York, Anthony Baez was playing touch football in the street when a fotball he threw, hit the police car of Officer Francis Livoti, a veteran police officer. This was according to Livoti sufficient reason to put Baez in a deadly choke hold from which he died. After waiving a jury trial Livoti was found not guilty on a variety of charges by a Judge who called most all of the police witnesses, liars. The Federal Government then prosecuted Livoti on civil rights violations and he was convicted there and sentenced to ten years in prison, where he belongs. He did not as a veteran police office have the discipline or restraint to ignore a harmless act, of some kid's football hitting his car.

The torture case involving Haitian immigrant Abner Louima, still brings chills to decent New Yorkers almost a year and a half after it happened.

The shooting by police of a disturbed grandmother with shotguns and many, many shots, Eleanor Bumpers many years back, still annoys many people. Deadly force used in this case was not required but was used anyway.

The murder of Michael Stewart by more than 7 transit police officers.

In all of these cases a black man or woman or Latino person involved.

Finally, I write here as a law-abiding citizen, who respects the very difficult job the police must perform, that any who would feel this type of behavior is acceptable, these days, will

most definitely join their (former police officer) hoodlum friends, where people go who commit these type of reckless, irresponible acts, to prison. This is 1999, not the mid-50's in The Southern area of The United Sstates and anyone who thinks we will go back to that type of treatment of human beings is sadly mistaken.

I further feel the actual restraint in New York City is being demonstrated by the memebers of the communities where these tragic events have happened and not the police. The fact that New York City has not had a major riot as a result of brutal and indifferent policing in minority communities, as other jurisdictions have had, is nothing short of a miracle. Now that is restraint! Restraint is not a police officer having the brains to ignore a kid's football that hits his car. That's common sense which Officer Francis Livoti did not have at the time of that matter. The New York City minority community should be commended for it's restraint, which in part comes as a result of Rev. Al Sharpton's ability to talk with leaders in the minority community and command their respect. In my opinion Rev. Sharpton deserves a Nobel Peace Prize. A lot of people may not like him, be he tells it like it is, helps keep a fragile peace here in New York City and fights for his people at all times. I can't help but respect and admire a man like that.

All in all this was a very sad and tragic incident. That the perpetrators of this matter were police officers sworn to protect us all should not undermine the severity or gravity of their act or the degree of justice obtained in the long run by those who demand justice in this matter. I feel badly for Mr. Diallo's mother and father, and for my home New York City, where an extreme and harsh political atmosphere has been instituted against those of minority extraction and those who live in poverty in New York City. New York City used to be a great place to live and have fun. I write from a reference point in that I've lived here the majority of my life. It is currently a very tense place to live, with a person never knowing what's going to happen next. Will the criminals get me or the police, a lot of whom are acting like criminals. This type of insanity, not publicly endorsed but created by the current Mayor of The City of New York, must cease It is just unacceptable. Should this Mayor become President of our country by some miracle, we will have the miltary patrolling the streets of our country for the slightest reason. He's a mean, un-compassionate man, autocratic and dictatorial in his poltical style and a reactionary extremeist who has no tolerance of people who do not accept and agree with his views. A one way Charlie who says, either you agreee with me or get lost.He is not open to new ideas or new ways of doing things. It will be his way or no way. He would fit perfectly into perhaps a South American dictatorship, but here in America, these type of people don't go very far. They were all over The South in the 1930's 1940's and 1950's. The baby boomer generation, (my generation) fought very hard to make sure people like this are exposed for what they really are, and don't hold political office or attain power. A few are still around like Trent Lott and Strom Turmmond, but their affiliations and real agenda today are sutle. People are hurting very badly as a result of many policies that were put into effect by this administration. If New York is to be a beacon to the rest of the United States then the police state type tactics endorsed by the current administration must end.

Once again, for any right-wing extremists out there who may read this commentary, There is no explanation for the shooting of an unarmed man by police 41 times. I don't even think avowed racist's could come up with an excuse for this very unacceptable behavior demonstrated by the police in this matter. Sad, very sad indeed!

"Politics As You Like IT" will return in two weeks on Sunday, February 28th 1999 with more commentary. See Ya All Then! Your Comments Are Welcme In The Guestbook For This Website.

POSTSCRIPT

The family of the victim of the police shooting in New York City last week announced late yesterday, (Friday) that they have hired O.J. Simpson dream team attorney Johnny Cochran to pursue a civil action for damages and to find out why the police shot their son. Mr. Cochran, commenting on his retention from Los Angeles,, California, said that he will reunite fellow dream team attorney's Barry Scheck and Peter Neufeld to assist him in the investigation he will be conducting on behalf of the Diallo family. Barry Scheck is currently, Professor of Law and Head of Clinical Trial Advocacy Programs at Benjamin N. Cardozo Law School in New York City. He also heads up The Innocence Project organization that has helped free many wrongly convicted priosners in the past years. Mr. Scheck is also a wrold class expert and pioneer of the use of DNA evidence to convict and exonerate criminal defendants. Johnny Cochran and Barry Scheck are also currently reprsenting New York City Police torture victim Abner Louima in his lawsuit against The City of New York. The four Street Crime Unit police officers involved in the Diallo shooting were indicted by a grand jury in The Bronx, New York, on Wednesday, March 30th 1999. The charges against all four included Second Degree Murder, Reckless Endangerment in The First Degree and Depraved Indiference To Human Life. All four were released on $100,000 bail, posted by their union, The Patrolmens Benevolent Association. They were immeadiatly after the indictments were announced, placed on suspension without pay.In a press conference held on the day of the indictments, all four officers claimed that they committed no crime by shooting at Mr. Diallo, 41 times. An element of Sccond Degree Murder includes the intent to murder another person. The prosecutor, Robert Johnson, will claim, that the amount of shots fired, in of itself, will establish the intent to murder Mr. Diallo. If convicted of the murder charges the oficers face life in prison. The lesser chargres in the indictment carry a maximum sentence of seven years in prison. The Grand Jury impaneled to hear the evidence in this case took eight weeks to return the indictments. During that period several thousand people protesting the shooting were arrested, while blocking the enterance to Police Headquarters here in New York City.

VOL. 2 NO. 11

POLITICS AS YOU LIKE IT

WHAT DO YA MEAN IT'S CLEARLY UNCONSTITUTIONAL? SO WHAT? JUST BECAUSE I MAKE THE LAWS DOESN'T MEAN I HAVE TO FOLLOW THEM:MAYOR OF THE CITY OF NEW YORK UPS THE ANTE ONCE AGAIN:SUSPENDS DUE PROCESS IN NEW DRUNKEN DRIVING LAW?

Q: What is the one thing that no one knows about New York City but that everybody should know?

A: "If 90 percent of police officers in New York City are decent, honest, hard working, public servants, that still leaves 4000 racist thugs with guns and badges running around with a license to kill."

Ron Kuby, Criminal Defense Lawyer and Former Associate of Late Civil Rights Attorney, William Kunstler

This week I invite my readers and visitors to this website to play a version of an old game that was called, "Twenty Questions". For those who are too young to remember the game, it was a simple game. You just picked a topic, any topic, and asked your friends questions about the topic. Whoever got the most questions right, won.

The answers here may be all too obvious to those who have been following the news across the nation in the past year. From Riverside, California to Bronx, New York, and in-between, instances of police brutality, have occurred with alarming frequency of late. Last week Attorney General Janet Reno said her office within The United States Department of Justice will launch an investigation into police abuses of the public.

It seems to this commentator, based on incidents he has read about in the past year, that in numbers more than usual, police officers in a variety of jurisdictions across our country have used deadly force in a lot of situations that did not call for it and in some situatons have used B-52 Air Force carpet bombing tactics, to contain a fly. The annoying distinction that surfaces in the majority of these "overkill" cases is the victim has been a memebr of a minority group. (Black or Hispanic)

In what can be deemed as an extension of my most recent commentary, before this one,

Commentary Of February 14th 1999 On Diallo Shooting

regarding the actions of four members of The New York City Police Department's, elite Street Crime Unit, in the Amedou Diallo shooting, I attempt to raise some points here in the form of some questions. Three and a half weks ago in New York City, the term, "police brutality" was taken to an entirely new level, (with the firing of 41 shots at anunarmd innocent man) and what happened must addressed. So here we go, not, "Twenty Questions" just a few, oaky. I encourage the readers of this commentary to sighn the guestbook of this page and offer some answers and solutions.

Question 1: A little over a week after police shot at Mr. Diallo 41 times, the Mayor and elected leader of New York City announced that The New York City Police Department would be switching from 9 millimeter bullets to hollow point bullets which would protect innocent citizens frm being injured when police were required to shoot someone. Is this the type of statement to make by an elected official a little over a week after an innocent, unarmed man was shot at 41 times by policer officers? Officers of what, "the looney bin?". In my opinion not only was the shooting highly irresponsible but so was the Mayor's subsequent statement.Statements like The Mayor made shortly after the incident only inflame the situation, not make it better and cool things down. Were I to make such a statement in a public fourm, I would be arrested and charged with inciting a riot.

Question 2: The four police officers who killed Mr. Diallo are still on the payroll of The City of New York, reassigned to desk duty pending the outcome of a grand jury investigation. Is this the apppropiate sanction, considering the circumstances. Is the shooting of 41 bullets an an unarmed, innocent man with no prior criminal record, reason enough by itself to do more than reassign the officers involved? My answer as written in my most previous commentary, a definitive, yes! There is no explanation for this type of "gangster" behavior.

I don't even think that actual gangsters working for mobster Al Capone in Chicago, fired 41 shots during infamous St. Valentine' Day Massacre..

Question 3: Is there not at the very least a reasonable presumption that can be made, by shooting at an unarmed innocent man forty one times, that this type of behavior would represent a reckless indifference to human life, a felony crime in many jurisdictions? I'll offer no answer to this question and your all on your own here!

Question 4: Last week The Police Commissioner of The City of New York, Howard Safir announced that an aggressive recruiting campaign would be instituted to hire more minority police officers in New York, considering that minority residents of New York City at this time represent sixty-five percent of all people that reside in New York City. Does this announcement address the use of excessive force against Mr. Diallo? Is there an assumption that minority police officers would not do what the four white officers did in this matter? What if this type of situation has nothing to do with who's doing the policing, but more to do with *"police culture"* and the us against them, syndrome. In otherwords if Police Department's across our country feel that the public they are sworn to protect is in reality their adversaries, then it would not matter what color a police officer was, in reducing incidents, such as the Diallo shooting. If it's us against them, then a black police officer could well have shot at Mr. Diallo 41 times too.

Question 5: An effort is going to be made in the future to require all police officers working in New York City, to be residents of New York City. Does this mean if you live outside a jurisdiction, you are less likely to do an effective job of policing and protecting the community you are assigned to patrol.?

Question 6: Is police brutality and the use of deadly force in situations that don't call for its application, issues of legitimate concern in The United States?

Question 7: This week New York City became the first area in our country to institute and enforce a drunken driving law, which calls for confiscation of a drivers vechile with no prior driving while intoxicated convictions. Twenty-Three cars have been taken away in the first week of this new law. The owners of the cars taken away make not get them back unless found innocent of driving while under the influence of alcohol. Further even if found innocent of the charges, the person would still have to go to Civil Court to get thier car back. Is due process being given the person whose car is being taken away by the police? Is an alcohol level above the legal limit, (.10) probable cause for police to take away a drivers car? Okay, what's right is right. I feel this new law is a good one and will save many lives. Yes, if a roadside test by police, determines that a person is clearly drunk and above the legal lmit of alcohol consumption, then, take that driver off the road. Why give him or her a second chance to kill someone, while they are driving drunk. A few years back, in a busy shopping area in New York City, some guy killed five people plowing his car into them, while driving drunk. Many, children have been killed by drunk ddrivers all over our nation. If you take away the car, you reduce the opportunity for an offender to drive drunk again, and endanger other people's lives. If your drinking, behind the wheel of a motor vechile is the last place you should be. This new law put into effect by The Mayor of The City of New York, last week, is an excellent one. It is not too harsh, nor is it uconstitutional. Get them off the road and keep them off the road. An over the limit alcohol test result is enough for me. How do you feel about this new law?

So there you have it, my version of "Twenty Questions" or seven questions. You don't have to answer all of them, take your choice.

"Politics As You Like iT" will return in two weeks on Sunday, March 14th 1999, with more commentary. See Ya All Then!

VOL. 2 NO. 12

POLITICS AS YOU LIKE IT

THE YANKEE CLIPPER:AN AMERICAN ICON AND BASEBALL LEGEND:JOE DIMAGGIO PASSES AWAY AT AGE 84:1914-1999

We lost an important part of American folkore this past week. Joe Dimaggio died at the age of 84. Part legend and part icon, Dimaggio exemplified a time in our country when everything was pretty good and the game of baseball was seen as just that, a game, and a lot of fun for both the players and the fans. Baseball has since evolved into a very big business where the average fan and supporter of the game has literally been priced out of even being able to attend a few games a year. Insult is added to injury when it is realized that most fans who cannot afford a ticket to see a baseball game today, were part of a group of fans who with their support in the 1940' 1950's and 1960's helped bring the game to where it is today.

This commentator has been a New York Yankee fan for the past forty-three years. When I first started following the team, they were in the midst of enjoying a streak of ten pennants in twelve years. In those days to win The American Leauge Championship, you had to finish first among eight teams. I spent many enjoyable afternoons at Yankee Stadium watching Mickey Mantle, Yogi Berra, Hank Bauer, Billy Martin and a host of Yankeee stars work their magic, under the leadership of another baseball legend, manager of that team Casey Stengel. At that time a box seat in the first ten rows, of Yankee Stadium, (field level box seat) between first base and home plate, or third base and home pate, (considered to be the best seat in the house) cost $3.50. Today the same seat costs $50.00. With parking, a few hot dogs and beers and maybe a scorecard and a Yankee yearbook, a day at the ballpark can cost over a $100.00. For a family of four, a day at the park, (with the aforementioned good seats) would cost approximately, $350.00. Just imagine that! You work hard all week, and you'd like to take your wife and kids to the ballpark, like your father did, and you get mugged for $350.00!

I never saw Joe Dimaggio play in person, or on television. However, I was always impressed, (when he was introduced at Yankeee Old Timer games) with his grace and humility. At Old Timer games, he insisted on being intoduced last and being announced as "The Greatest Living Ballplayer". He was also an intensely private man who guarded his privacy very zealously.

At a time when most important major leauge baseball records have been borken, Joe Dimaggio's record of hitting in 56 consecutive games in 1941 still stands. At his defensive position, center field, he was very graceful and seemed to glide when going to catch a ball. His lifetime career batting average in 1,736 games, was .325. Dimaggio played with The Yankees from 1936 to 1951 and played in 11 All-Star games and 10 World Series. In his entire career he struck out only 369 times while hitting 361 home runs. In contrast as far as striking out, Reggie Jackson, hit 563 home runs and struck out, 2,597 times.

Few in the history of baseball have played the game with such grace and elegance as Dimaggio did. He was considered an example of American, power, grace and skill by many, in all fields of life in our country at the time he played. In 1955, he was elected to The Baseball Hall of Fame, the highest honor a baseball player can receive. In the years after he retired from baseball, Dimaggio worked hard to protect his image and was very sensitive to anything written about him, or sung about him.

He has been written about by another legend, Ernest Hemingway, in Hemingway's classic book, "The Old Man and The Sea"and has been included in dozens of Broadway plays and films. Singer, Paul Simon's lyrics in the 1960's hit, "Mrs. Robinson", included Joe Dimaggio. "Where have you gone Joe Dimaggio, our nation turns it's lonely eyes to you"; Simon sang in a song from The Academy Award winning film "The Graduate". Years later Dimaggio met Simon in a restaurant and asked him what the lyrics meant. Dimaggio had thought the lyrics may have been derogatory. They were not, and Simon explained to Dimaggio what they meant. President of The United States Bill Clinton had this to say earlier this week in a tribute to Joe Dimaggio:

"America lost one of the century's beloved heros, Joe Dimaggio. This son of Italian immigrants gave every American something to believe in. He beceme the very symbol of American grace, power and skill."

Joe Dimaggio was born on November 25th 1914 in Martinez, Caiifornia, a small fishing village twenty-five miles Northeast of San Francisco. He was the fourth son and eighth of nine children born to Giuseppe and Rosalie Dimaggio, who had immigrated from Sicily to America in 1898. His father was a fisherman, and the family lived in a heavily Italian section, near the San Francisico, waterfront, the year Joe was born. Two of the other Dimagio son's became Major Leauge baseball players, by way of the San Francisco sandlots. Brother Vince (four years older than Joe) played 11 seasons in baseball and led the major leauges in strikeouts six times. Brother Dominic, (three years younger than Joe) played 10 seasons with The Boston Red Sox. Of the three baseball playing Dimaggio brothers, Joe was considered to be the best and a natural at the game.

Joe Dimaggio first started playing baseball as a shortstop (an infield position) when he was 14 years old, with The Boys Leauge Club, after he had dropped out of Galileo High School. His brother Vince at the time played with The San Francisco Seals of The Pacific Coast Leauge, the highest level of minor leauge baseball. Joe was only 17 at this time and it was 1932. In 1933, Joe's first full season with The Seals, he batted .340, hit 28 home runs and batted in 169 runs in 187 games. During this, his first season, he also batted safely in 61 consecutive games, eight years before he set the major leauge record in 1941 with The Yankees which still stands. *For those readers who may not be familiar with batting safely in a game, it means that you get at least one hit in every game. Doing this in baseball, is considered to be extremely difficult as evidenced by how few people have even come close to Joe Dimaggio's 56 game hitting streak record.*

When two baselll scouts (Joe Devine and Bill Essick) persistently recommended Joe Dimaggio, to then General Manager of The New York Yankees, Ed Barrow, Dimaggio was bought for twenty-five thousand dollars and five players from The Seals. Dimaggio was left with The Seals for the 1935 season, to heal one of his knees and polish his skills, He joined The Yankees in 1936 to play with other talented Yankees at that time, Lou Gehrig, Bill Dickey, Tony Lazzeri, Red Rolfe, Red Ruffing and Lefty Gomez. Dimaggio's contract with The Yankees for his first season called for him to be paid, eight thousand five-hunderd dollars. During his entire career with The Yankees the most Dimaggio earned was one-hundred thousand dollars a season. Today a lot of baseball players enjoy multi-millon dollar yearly contracts and some earn as much as ten or twenty million dollars a season.

On May 3rd 1936, Dimaggio made his delayed debut, for The Yankees against The St.Louis Browns. His start had been delayed by a foot injury. That season he went on to play in 138 games, hit 29 home runs, with 206 hits and 125 runs batted in while also batting .325. Dimaggio played that year in his first World Series, one of four consecutive World Series, he would play in since first

194

joining the team. <u>The New York Yankees as an overall team would go on to play in 23 out of 29 World Series through 1964, an incredible feat by itself.</u>

When Dimaggio, first started to play major leauge baseball he had to put up with prejudice and bigotry directed against him by his own teamates. Many of his teamates called him "Big Dago"; (an insulting term used to degarde those of Italian extraction) and Life Magazine' (a mainsteam publication and mirror of American life) in 1939, in publishing an article intended to be complimentary, noted that Dimaggio, "did'nt use olive oil or bear grease on his hair, but only water." The article went on to note that Dimaggio never smelled of garlic! Of course these comments written in Life magazine were highly insulting and not even remotely complimentary. True to Joe Dimaggio's demeanor. being a man of class and grace, he overgame, that state of affairs also. In 1939 he married an actress, Dorothy Arnold, with whom he had his only son, in October 1941, Joe Jr. He had two granddaughters and four great grandchildren. Dimaggio also served during World War II, for three years in The Army Air Force. He was a married briefly to Hollywood legend Marilyn Monroe and every year after Ms. Monroe's tragic death, Dimaggio, sent flowers to her gravesite. Dimaggio was known to have his "black sides" and could be very moody and sullen.

Dimaggio died last Sunady, (March 7th 1999) shortly after midnight at his home in Florida, He had come home after spending 99 days in a hospital, on January 19th 1999. While in the hospital, he fought massive lung infections and pneumonia and his death was mistakenly reported several times while he was hospitalized. A national vigil was held and hundreds of thousands of people all over the world prayed for his recovery, but it was not to be had. When he left the hospital on January 19th, Diamggio was weak with little hope for survival.

He was buried last Thursday, (March 11th 1999) in San Francisco, California, his hometown. The funeral service held was private and restricted by Joe Dimaggio's wishes, to members of his family, one longtime friend and his attorney, Morris Engleberg. along with The President of The American Leauge and National Leauge of baseball.

My oh my, how bright stars shine, when they shine. Then they fade. However, while they shine, the world obtains love and a true example of grace. Such was Joe Dimaggio's life. What he sgared with us was priceless. True hope and inspiration has no price tag. He was an inspiration to millions of people all over the world, who saw through him, that a better life was possible. Above his extremely talented, and fruitful career in the world of baseball, I feel his true legacy will turn out to be the hope he gave to millions. He was the embodiment of The American Dream, realized, at a time when that dream was attainable for many. As I noted earlier in this commentary, I never saw him play, in person or on television. He was not of or from my generation, but from the generation preceding mine. A generation that had lived through The Great Depression. Of course I knew of him as millions of other people did, also. The distinction for me, is that what I knew of Joe Dimaggio and what I did see of him, at Old Timers games, when he made brief appearances made me proud to be an American, and what my country stood for in the eyes of the rest of the world. We have a lot of work to do, to return our country to that standard. Another gem has left us, as far too many have in the past year and a half. Most certainly, the world became a better place with Joe Dimaggio here and his spot among the angels in heaven was something he earned a long time ago. This is a man who will not be forgotton, too soon. Rest In Peace, "Jolting Joe". "The Yankee Clipper" they called him. A man who gave light to the world and one of the last American heros. I'll miss him a lot!

"Politics As You Like It" will return in two weeks on Sunday, March 28th 1999 with more commentary. See Ya All Then! Your comments are welcome in the guestbook for this page. Your interest is appreciated.

Bernard Paul

VOL. 2. NO. 13

POLITICS AS YOU LIKE IT

GRASSROOTS ORGANIZATION VOWS ACCOUNTABILITY IN EXPEDITIOUS HANDLING OF VETERANS CLAIMS BY THE U.S. DEPARTMENT OF VETERANS AFFAIRS:THE NATIONAL VETERANS ORGANIZATION (NVO) OF LAS CRUCES, NEW MEXICO PROMISES RESULTS THROUGH POLITICAL PRESSURE

In two weeks, (April 11th 1999) the bi-weekly commentary that appears here will be written by guest commentator Linda Pierucki who hails from Jackson, Michigan. Mrs. Pierucki works as an over-the-road truck driver. We ran into each other when she signed my guest book with her comments about a commentary I had recently written. She then wrote me many E-Mails; which focused on her view of the importance of the constitutional rights we are all fortunate to have under The United States Constitution and the danger inherent in allowing those rights to be eroded.

I was struck with the clarity and honesty of her appraisal and invited Mrs. Pierucki to appear here as a guest commentator the week of March 14th 1999. She accepted my offer and we're all in for a big treat in two weeks. I think you'll find her views excellent and refreshing. Mrs. Pierucki's commentary appeared in the March 5th 1999 edition of The Jackson Citizen Patriot newspaper, The Voice of The People section, in her home town, Jackson, Michigan.

Her focus in the commentary addresses current seizure/forfeiture laws and the application of those laws at this time in various jurisdictions throughout The United States.

Thank you Mrs. Pierucki for accepting my invitation to appear as a "Politics As You Like It" guest commentator.

This Following Commentary Is "Politics As You Like It's" 50th Commentary Since Coming On-Line On July 28th 1997. I Sincerely Hope You've Enjoyed Reading Them As Much As I Have Enjoyed Wrting Them. Much More Thanks and Appreciation To The Technical Advisors For This Website From The Very Beginning And My Good Friends Eric & Denise Andresen of Davenport, Iowa and publishers of the very popular website, Web Tv Sig.<u>*WEB TV SIG WEBSITE LINK*</u> *When Denise first mentioned HTML to me, I thought HTML was an exotic pizza pie. Web Tv Sig is also featured in The Favorite Links section of this website. A real good visit. Love Ya both Eric & Densie-The Editor*

Exactly one year ago on this website I wrote a commentary on problems Veterans were having with The Department of Veterans Affairs hospital system in the Hudson Valley region of New York State. Veterans were perishing at the hospitals due to under staffing and cutbacks of almost all essential services. A subsequent investigation of the matter by The Department of Veterans Affairs, cleared administrators and policymakers within the VA of any responsibility or wrongdoing. A link to my prior commentary is below:

Politics As You Like It Commentary-Vol.1 No. 35-March 30th 1998

The suggestion for the topic of my commentary on Veterans hospitals had come from my good friend Jeff Gersten, who lives in Monticello, New York, Mr. Gersten also writes bi-weekly commentary for an excellent Internet Zine called Net4TV Voice. Jeff is coming up shortly on his first anniversary with Net4TV Voice. For an example of his great work a link to his columns is below:

Jeff Gersten's Columns For Internet Zine NetTv4 Voice

In the year since I wrote my prior commentary on one aspect of The Department of Veterans Affairs system,(here to after referred to as The VA) I investigated how the VA system in general treats those that file claims for monetary benefits who have fought in wars and a variety of campaigns to defend freedom and our way of life. What I found out was disturbing and it should disturb the readers of this commentary also.

The VA is the second largest Federal agency behind The Department of Defense (The Pentagon) Currently, it's annual operating budget is over 43 billion dollars a year. 17 billion dollars of the annual VA budget goes to run Veterans programs and for direct payments to Veterans injured while serving in the military and those Veterans whose disabilities are not directly related to their military service. In addition an extensive VA hospital system with facilities in all 50 states, treats qualified Veterans with honorable discharges from the military free of charge. The current Secretary of The Department of Veterans Affairs is former Secretary of The United States Army, Togo West. Secretary West was as Secretary of The Army recently involved with President Clinton's attempt to cover-up the burial of a friend who was a heavy campaign contributor in Arlington National Cemetery. The only problem with this was the person being accorded the honor of being buried in Arlington National Cemetery, *was not a Veteran.*

Bernard Paul

The VA also provides low interest loans to qualifying Veterans to purchase a home, and obtain education loans and rehabilitative vocational training. A national cemetery system is also operated by The VA that offers free burial to Veterans who have served their country honorably. Sounds real good right. Well lets see what happens, per se, when a Veteran these days attempts to secure some of these benefits from the VA. Below is an excerpt from a petition currently being circulated throughout The United States by a new organization based in Las Cruces, New Mexico, called *The National Veterans Organization (NVO)* The petition focuses on claims processing in general by The VA. This is the reality of what is happening currently to a good majority of Veterans who attempt to secure their benefits from The VA throughout our country.

When our country needed ordinary citizens to fight it's wars, we didn't hesitate o go. We fought to preserve our way of life and defend our nation''s values, often at the expense of our own bodies and minds. Our nation graciously promised to take care of those who suffered injuries and disabilities so that we could live a life of dignity, the same as those we defended.

Many Veterans have run into a stone wall when trying to obtain the benefits that were promised. We naively file a claim with The Department of Veterans Affairs Regional Office, thinking that if we have sufficient evidence to establish that our disability was incurred in service, the VA will grant our claims. This simply does not happen in the vast majority of claims filed.

The VA Regional Offices fail to follow up the laws as they are written, often ignoring overwhelming evidence in the Veteran's favor. This causes enormous grief to the Veteran and requires him or her to spend years supplying the same evidence over and over, appealing the merits of their claims to The Board of Veterans Appeals, (BVA) and finally to the Court of Veterans Appeals. (COVA) Over 46 percent of all decisions of the Regional Offices are remanded back from The Board of Veterans Appeals because of improper adjudication.(decisions)

The enormous number of faulty, negative decisions that have been overturned by The Court of Veterans Appeals bears out what most Veterans know: The Regional Offices of The Department of Veterans Affairs are doing what they want to do, instead of doing what the law says they should do. The claims adjudicators are poorly trained and regional office supervisors are unresponsive to the pleas from Veterans asking, if not begging, for justice. Telephone calls produce no results and letters go unanswered.

The laws currently on the books spell out what The VA must do when a claim is received. First, they must assist the veteran in developing his or her claim. They must put forth effort to obtain his or her military records. Then they must fairly, and according to law, adjudicate his claim and promptly notify him or her of the decision. In addition, they must grant the veteran a hearing, and listen to his plea face to face.

This seldom happens. Claims languish for months and even years with no or very little, development. Evidence is lost or misplaced. Claims are adjudicated incorrectly, or not at all. Hearing take months or years to be conducted. When claims are remanded back to the Regional Office either from The Board of Veterans Appeals in Washington D.C., or The Court of Veterans Appeals in Washington D.C., they sometimes languish for months or even years before being reajudicated in accordance with the Board's or Court's orders, even though those claims are supposed to take precedence over other, newly filed claims.

We are asking you to take a firm stand in support of ending this injustice. Please convene an investigation into the <u>lawless</u> practices of The VA Regional Offices, and, if it is necessary, take measures to remove those current VA officials and replace them with employees who are sensitive to the needs of the Veterans they are here to serve, and who will act in accordance with the law.

Respectfully;

The Under Signed Veterans of The US Armed Forces and Interested Citizens

Must Veterans who have served honorably in The United States Military, beg and plead for their benefits to which they are entitled to under law? It certainly looks that way, doesn't it? Is The VA really helping Veterans obtain their benefits in a timely and expeditious manner? Or are they like The Social Security Administration who set up shop in the 1930's hoping beneficiaries wouldn't live long enough to collect their benefits?

This situation is very similar to what I described in another commentary I wrote last year regarding the lawless behavior of The Social Security Administration in the handling of Social Security Disability claims in the early and mid-1980's. To read that commentary please go to the link below:

<u>Politics As You Like IT Commentary-January 12th 1998-Vol 1 No 24</u>

The National Veterans Organization was founded last year by United States Navy Veteran Doug McArthur. Currently the organization has a grass roots membership of over two thousand members. throughout The United States. Mr. McArthur who is currently 56 years old fell off an airplane wing while serving in the Navy during 1967. He hurt his back and neck in the accident. In 1980, because his injuries from the military started giving him serious problems he filed a disability claim or service connected compensation benefits with the VA, which was denied. He ultimately gave up that claim.

When the problem became worse in 1992, McArthur filed a new claim. In 1996, The Board of Veterans Appeals,ruled that the Albuquerque, New Mexico, office of the VA, had issued an incorrect decision and sent the case back to that Regional Office for a new review. Currently, a new decision has not been forthcoming almost three years after the case was sent there with orders from The Board of Veterans Appeals in Washington, D.C.

that a new decision be issued in a timely and expeditious manner by the Regional Office of the VA.

The genesis of Doug McArthur's new organization was as a result of this experience. His current claim has now been pending almost seven years. This is a man who served our country honorably. There is really no excuse for this type of treatment by a Federal agency whose mission is stressed as (paraphrased) "helping the Veteran". According to VA official, Tom Breen, "the department has been making headway against a massive backlog of claims".

The National Veterans Organization also maintains a full-time website where Veterans can obtain valuable information such as where to contact attorneys to help expedite their claims. A link to that website is below for a visit:

<u>National Veterans Organization Website</u>

If you would like to join this fine non-profit organization, the dues are ten dollars a year. The annual dues are being waived during 1999 to attract new members. So membership is free during 1999. For more information or to join you can write to the address below or call the telephone number below:

The National Veterans Organization Inc.

2001 East Lohman Suite 110-248

Las Cruces, New Mexico, 88001

1-(915) 759-6233

NVO is currently also considering the filing of a class action lawsuit in Federal Court, on behalf of the thousands of Veterans profoundly affected by this situation, If filed, the lawsuit will proceed sometime in May of this year. A massive public education campaign is also being planned.

A final note here on the use of attorneys by Veterans, when dealing with the VA and the National Service Organizations that have represented Veterans for years in proceeding involving The Department of Veterans Affairs.

For many years the VA has kept attorneys from representing Veterans, by limiting the pay an attorney could receive from a Veterans for his or her services to <u>ten dollars.</u> You didn't read that wrong! That's right, ten dollars. This effectively ensured that very few attorney's if any, would undertake a Veterans case before the VA. Currently a Veteran may not have an attorney represent him or her before the VA, until they have lost an appeal at The Board of Veterans Appeals level. The National Veterans Organization is a strong supporter of Veterans having the right to counsel at all levels of the VA decision making process.

Their main opponent? The National Service Organizations, such as The Disabled American Veterans, The American Legion, Veterans of Foreign Wars, The Jewish War Veterans and The Catholic War Veterans to note a few here. These service organizations overall have a horrible record of wining cases for the Veterans they represent. With office space, telephones ect. ect, ect. paid for by the VA in some 50 Regional Offices throughout The United States, many Veterans feel that the Service Organizations, don't and are afraid to put out 100 percent for them in fighting claims. In other words many Veterans feel that The Service Organizations are selling them out and are in bed with the VA.

Judging by the win to loss ratio of National Service Organizations, I would have to agree with those to say, "sellout" <u>Between, 85 and 90 percent of all cases where the National Service Organization's represent a Veterans at all levels of the VA claims process, the Veteran loses the claim.</u>

This sad state of affairs is not only ridiculous but unacceptable. As a matter if fact those statistics quite possibly would have the VA claims system as being characterized a "Kangaroo Court"!<u>Approximately, one out of 10 claims are granted? Does that sound right?</u>

It is the opinion of this commentator, (a United States Air Force Veteran, honorably discharged in late August of 1964) that the Service Organizations are a bad alternative to having attorneys represent Veterans at all levels of the adjudicative process. The time has come and is long overdue to have lawyers involved at all levels of the VA claims process. It's the fair thing to do. The last thing The Department of Veterans Affairs wants is attorneys involved at all levels of the process. That will take a good majority of the control over what happens to a claim, away from the VA. Currently, a Veteran that files a claim, must wait between four and six years, before he or she can bring an attorney into the process. A claim can take between a year and a year and a half to adjudicate on The Regional Office level. Claims are not being decided in 151 days as many Regional Offices claim. The time frame does not even come close to that. An appeal of an adverse Regional Office decision can take between two and three more years. If the Veteran loses on appeal, he or she then may bring the matter before The Court of Veterans Appeals, where he or she may be represented by an attorney.

Many, many Veterans just give up or die while attempting to navigate this process and that's a damn shame. If anyone should receive respectful and expeditious treatment when seeking assistance from our government, I would have to put our Veterans at head of the line.

With 243,000 employees nationwide The Department of Veterans Affairs claims of under staffing is a joke. Just how many more employees are needed to provide expeditious handling of claims filed by Veterans. Perhaps it might be a good idea to take a close look at the allocation of those employees and just where they work within the VA system. Without spending any more money, a more efficient use of the VA's resources and better training and pay for those directly involved in the decision-making process would be the solution.

Bernard Paul

There is no reason for almost half of all claims decisions that are issued by the VA to be contrary to the law.

I urge my reader to look into helping The National Veterans Organization, in it's just cause. The only requirement to join is that you be an honorably discharged Veteran of The United States military. To sign the petition that is now being circulated throughout The United States, you do not have to be a Veteran. Should you see an (NVO) member in your home town asking that you support (NVO) on this claims processing issue, by signing his or her petition, please do so. I assure you this is a bona fide issue and it is not being raised by a bunch of screaming malcontents. Those Veterans affected by this bureaucratic indifference need our help! Let's show them we are behind them one hundred percent, as they were behind us one hundred percent when they fought for us while members of the military. Shame on The Department of Veterans Affairs. Shame on you!

"Politics As You Like It' will return in two weeks,on Sunday, April 11th 1999, with Linda Pierucki's commentary, as a guest commentator here, from Jackson, Michigan. I will return in four weeks with more commentary, on Sunday, April 25th 1999.See Ya All Then! Your comments are welcome in the guest book for this page. Your interest is appreciated

VOL. 2 NO. 14

POLITICS AS YOU LIKE IT

**PROPERTY SEIZURE-A SLIPPERY SLOPE AND SOME RELATED
THOUGHTS FROM A SO-CALLED JANE SIX-PACK**

GUEST COMMENTARY BY LINDA PIERUCKI

This guest commentary is a re-print with permission of a guest column by
Linda Pierucki, which first appeared in the March 5th 1999 edition of The
Jackson Citizen Patriot newspaper. in Jackson, Michigan.

I've been watching with much trepidation the development of the situation
under which the city of Jackson works it's way rapidly toward an ordinance
allowing property seizure (vechiles) in instances of prostitution. I am in no
way debating the legal issues of prostitution, nor condoning prostitution. I am
sure this issue is of the up-most concern to residents in the neighborhoods
involved and am sure they deserve some form of relief/redress in the matter.
What does concern me is the increasing use of seizure/forfeiture as a method
of financing police departments throughtout the country.

There is increasing documentation that abuse of seizure laws has become
rampant throughout the states within which they are used. There are many
instances of such property falling into hands of individual officers and city
officials, being "lost in the system, ect. ect. Not long ago, Dateline NBC did a
feature on the seizure laws in Lousianna and the resulting miscarriages of
justice which created such hardship and scandal.

I'm sure many of you saw it. I would think that city officials concerned
with their political integrity would run screaming in the opposite direction
when such an ordinance was proposed. It concerns me that they seem so ready
to take such a step without much consideration.

Most people do not realize that a guilty verdict in most cases is not
necessary for the seizure to take place.

The seizure may well stand even if you are found not guilty. Some large law
enforcement agencies have increased their operating budgets tremendously by
relying on seizure laws, with the result that there is much opportunity and

incentive to make, "less-than-supportable" seizures and to concentrate less on actual law enforcement <u>while milking their new cash cow.</u>I would think our local police departments would be leary of putting themselves and their excellent reputations in such a position.

Far too many taxpayers applaud such laws as evidence their police department is "tough on crime" and is not demanding new tax dollars. They do not look at the larger issue. <u>That issue, my friends is "Due Process";</u> the heart of our judicial system. This is one of the fundamental rules upon which our nation was founded. The Fourth and Fifth amendment to The U.S. Constitution read: <u>Amendment IV</u>

"The right of the people to be secure in their persons, houses, papers and effects against unreasonable search and seizures, shall not be violated, and no warrants shall issue, but upon probable cause, supported by oath or affirmation, and particularly describing the place to be searched, and the persons or things to be seized"

Amendment V

"No person shall be held to answer for a capital, or otherwise infamous crime. unless on a presentment or indictment of a grand jury, except in cases arising in the land or navel forces, or in the militia, when in actual service in time of war or public danger, nor shall any person be subject for the same offense to be twice put in jeopardy of life and limb, nor shall be compelled in any criminal case to be a witness against himself, nor be deprived of life, liberty, or property without due process of law; nor shall private property be taken for public use, without just compensation"

We need no further erosion of our constitutionally-guaranteed rights. We see those rights prostituted daily in the interest of political correctness and increased security. Crime must be controlled, yes. But must we allow our fundamental rights as citizens to be eroded even further for such a minor crime as prostitution?

Think seriously before supporting such a measure. There was a nation not long ago whose citizens allowed their rights to be eroded bit by bit, till they awoke one day to find they lived under the most repressive dictatorship in modern history. One of those German citizens, in retrospect, wrote the following:

They came for the Communists and I didn't object-For I wasn't a Communist. They came for the Socialists, and I didn't object-For I wasn't a Socialist. They came for the labor leaders and I didn't object-For I wasn't a labor leader. They came for the Jews, and I didn't object -For I wasn't a Jew; <u>Then they came for me.</u>

by Martin Niemoler, German Protestant Pastor-1892-1984

Linda, adds this further comment in her E-mail to me of Sunday, March 14th 1999:

A quote often repeated by Benjamin Franklin in the foundational writings of the Republic, <u>paraphrased says</u>"Those who are willing to give up freedom for safety deserve neither safety nor freedom". Thomas Jefferson states words to this effect; "Government is the greatest danger to our freedom, and must be guarded against!"

Apparently, our founding fathers were wise enough to see that government's natural inclination is to abuse individual freedoms and warned us reeatedly against allowing that to happen.

Bernard Paul

I bow to their superior wisdom.

"Politics As You Like IT" will return in two weeks, with more commentary on Sunday, April 25th 1999. See Ya All Then! Your comments are welcome in the guest-book for this page. Your interest is appreciated.

Editors Note:Some very perceptive thoughts and ideas worth in my opinion further contemplation. Thank you Linda for giving me the opportunity to feature your comemntary on this website.

VOL. 2 NO. 15

POLITICS AS YOU LIKE IT

CARNAGE AND TRAGEDY IN LITTLETON, COLORADO:FIFTEEN PEOPLE DEAD AT HIGH SCHOOL:TWENTY-FIVE MORE HOSPITALIZED:NATION MOURNS INCIDENT AND LOOKS FOR REASONS

How can it be written that in our midst might be potential murderers that are just children? On Tuesday of this week in the small upper-middle class, affluent community of Littleton, Colorado, at Columbine High School, two young boys, one 16 years old, the other 17, shot and killed thirteen of their fellow students, and one teacher. The two boys then killed themselves. Twenty-Five others remain hospitalized in various degrees of serious condition. Armed to the teeth, the boys attacked with 2 shotguns, 1 rifle, 30 homemade bombs, and a handgun.

Our nation remains in shock, as to what happened. Reasons! That's what people say they are looking for. For this commentator, (from the baby-boom generation) all I can come up with. is that it is way beyond my comprehension that two young boys would be spending their days at home making pipe bombs that they intended to use against their fellow classmates. This incident is something I just cannot make any sense of whatsoever. Perhaps, those readers of this commentary who sign my guest book, can help me out with that?

A little over a year ago, in Jonesboro, Arkansas, two boys, one 11 the other 13, also shot fellow classmates. "Politics As You like It" wrote of that incident, calling for a return to basics. That commentary can be viewed by clicking on the link below:

<u>Commentary for week of April 6th 1998-TRAGEDY IN JONESBORO ARKANSAS:TWO CHILDREN CHARGED WITH MURDER:BACK TO BASICS</u>

Many observers might lay blame for what happened in Littleton, Colorado, on a popular culture here in America which gloifys violence. The Internet, (the vechile through which this website appears) has also taken it on the chin as a result of the shootings earlier this week. The two boys responsible for the carnage, had a website, that was essentially Neo-Nazi in nature and many commentators feel information was accessed by the two boys, on how to assemble pipe bombs, through The Internet. <u>In defense of The Internet and The World Wide Web, I'm sure most with agree with me, that The Internet is not being used by many people, to achieve violent agendas. There are, after all over 50 million people connected to The Internet here in The United States, and those who would call for regulation of The Internet due to incidents such as the one that occured this week, would be out of bounds in my opinion.</u>

The two boys who committed this horrible act were part of a group of boys that were called "The Trench Coat Mafia" by other students at the high school. The group, who attended school while wearing long black trench coats and baseball caps, worn backwards, were see as outcasts at the school. The group of about 10 boys expressed an intense dislike of jocks, (athletes) and minorities. They had been made fun of by many other students at the school. I don't know, I would think that youngsters make fun of each other as a natural part of their youth. So, nowadays, if your going to high school and someone makes fun of you, thats justification to go get your AK-47 assault rifle, and get revenge. Beautiful! Just Great!

The two boys just started shooting anyone who they thought was a jock or minority. To add to the evilness of their act they placed bombs beneath the bodies of those they killed so whomever would try to help them would be blown up. Another bomb was found yesterday, that was powerful enough to blow up he entire school building.

I'm cutting what else can be written about this incident short, because, I, like the rest of our nation am very disturbed by what has occured. I know it's my job as a cyber journalist, to offer a commentary, and perhaps offer objective views with a little analysis of the topic. I find that much too difficult to do with this event for I cannot analyze insanity. <u>In closing here, all I can further note, is that perhaps there is something very wrong, in a country that produces this and solutions must be found.</u> I never thought I'd live to see the day, that I must feel a teenager would represent a deadly threat to either myself or other children and adults..

My sincere condolences go out to the families and friends of those who lost their lives in this tragedy. My prayers go out to them also and that their lives may return to normalcy soon.

"Politics As You Like IT" will return in two weeks. with more commentary on Sunday, May 9th 1999. See Ya All Then! Your comments are welcome in the guest book for this page. Your interest is appreciated.

VOL. 2 NO. 16

POLITICS AS YOU LIKE IT

BI-WEEKLY COMMENTARY WILL RETURN ON SEPTEMBER 27th 1999 AT THE INTERNET ZINE NET4 TV VOICE

The Publisher and Editor of this website has accepted an invitation from the Publisher of the popluar Internet Zine, Net4 Tv Voice to join their staff as a contributing writer and feature Op-Ed columnist.

Beginning Monday,September 27th 1999 bi-weekly commentary normally seen here will be accessible from a link on the mainpage of this website which will take you directly to my commentaries at Net4 Tv Voice. Net4TV Voice currently has over fifty thousand visitors to their website every month.

I'm going to miss having control over the entire process of writing, editing, and maintaining my own website every two weeks as I did with "Politics As You Like IT".

However I look forward to working with the editors of Net4TV Voice, Kate Young, Nancy McPoland and Dexter Davenport along with the publisher of Net4 Tv Voice, Laura Buddine, to give my readers the best I can and some interesting topics too.

In the meantime, please take advantage of commentaries written in Volumes 1 and 2 at the commentary archives for this website which can be accessed on the mainpage for this site or by clicking on below.

Special Thanks are in order to my good friends and technical advisors Eric and Densie Andresen of Davenport, Iowa, who publsih their excellent website, Web Tv SIG and Jeff Gersten of Monticello, New York, who have been wih me since the beginning of this website in late July of 1997.

At that time I could'nt even spell the word Internet let alone define it, and HTML to me meant, perhaps a flavor of ice cream."Politics As You Like It' evolved many times due to the constructive sugestions offered by many readers in the past.

So on to better things with Net4 Tv Voice. <u>Want to take a little look at who I'll be writing for beginning in September</u> Click On Below To Go There

Bernard Paul

Commentaries Written For

Net 4 Tv Voice From September 1999

Through December 1999

Iacta Inc. Laura Buddine Editor
Downey California

Net4TV Voice
Coast to Coast
Bernard Wax

Just How Did I Wind Up Here?

This, my first commentary for Net4TV Voice, id dedicated to my good friends Eric and Denise Andersen who host the popular website WEBTV SIG from their home in Davenport, Iowa. Eric and Denise have helped thousands of "newbies" by answering the many questions sent to them. Without Eric and Denise, there is no way I would be doing what I'm doing here - New Media Cyber-journalism.

Well! It looks like I've arrived! Another overnight American success story. Well, not exactly, folks. Could I be the next Matt Drudge? Who knows?

Matt Drudge gained almost instant fame when, as an obscure employee at the CBS gift shop in Southern California, he picked up on the Newsweek magazine story (which Newsweek had killed) about Monica Lewinsky and President Clinton, and published the story on his Internet website. **The Drudge Report**. The rest is history, as far as Mr. Drudge is concerned! He currently hosts a radio program for WABC-Radio and also is seen weekly on his own interview program on The Fox News Channel. My hero, Matt Drudge: Keep up the good work.

However this column is not about Matt Drudge, (though I would be the first to admit that Mr. Drudge would make excellent copy) but about how this writer came to this Web site to become a regular contributing writer.

I've been on-line with WebTV for two and a half years. The Phillips-Magnavox Classic box had been on the market just five months when I bought it. Like most WebTV owners, I was looking for a cost-effective way to access the Internet. There were a lot of expensive computers to be had, with equally expensive software required to run them. WebTV solved the problem of cost, for me and thousands of others. One of the benefits immediately recognizable was the clarity of the WebTV picture; it was far better than pictures people were getting with their more expensive computers. Additionally, I was connecting to WebTV at 33.6 baud, about the same as conventional computers were connecting to the Internet.

Now, I'll admit there's a ways to go to bring WebTV into state-of-the-art computer technology. However, for me, the initial purposes for purchasing WebTV had been well served.

So, there I was in March 1997, with my new WebTV box and keyboard, and some very long wire. True to the promotions for the product, I set up my box and account with ease. A few trips to Radio Shack (to buy more wire and a coupler) and I was in business. However, within one week, my brand new WebTV was powering down for no discernable reason. I called WebTV Customer Support and was told everything except how to solve my problem.

At that point, (and I don't remember exactly how) I found Eric and Denise Andresen's Web site. I had heard that Eric and Denise helped people who were having problems with their WebTV units. I wrote them, and received a quick answer to my question.

Bernard Paul

Apparently there was a manufacturer's defect in some of the interlocking mechanisms, and the box needed to be exchanged. The new unit solved the problem. Eric and Denise saved the day for me the first time I met them. I call them my Special Angels.

In April of 1997I wrote Denise Andresen, outlining a concept for a user-friendly multi-faceted news Web site I wanted to call "Politics As You Like It." The space for the Web site was provided free of charge by Geocities Inc., a California company that recently merged with Yahoo, the Internet search engine giant. Geocities hosts the homepages of over three million people and is one of the most visited Web sites on the Internet. Last time I checked, Yahoo-Geocities was ranked fifth out of millions of Web sites in visitor traffic. Wow!

"Politics as You Like It" went on-line July 28, 1997, with a commentary about Massachusetts institute of Technology Professor of Linguistics and Political Science writer, par excellence, Noam Chomsky.

From July, 1997 to April 1999, 51 commentaries were produced within an editor. In September 1998, I went to a biweekly format, which became Volume II of "Politics As You Like It."

Two months after going on-line, I lost the entire Web site during Labor Day Weekend. I had inadvertently deleted the index.html page in my Geocities Editor. I did not know how important the index.html page was at the time.

So, there I was, out of business, with nothing to show for hundreds of hours of work. I was very upset and wanted to quit the whole project right there. Denise encouraged me to continue, and helped get the Web site back up and running.

The prime purpose of "Politics As You Like It" was to empower readers who visited the site and offer them points of view which were not available in the conventional media, broadcast radio, television, or print. The page eventually had over 7,500 visitors. However, one of the big disappointments was nominal weekly traffic, which averaged about 100 people a week. No matter what I did to promote my Web site, I just could not get the numbers I thought were acceptable, considering the work I was putting in.

Listings in major search engines like Alta Vista and a Link Exchange Banner Exchange account didn't help much either. With Link Exchange, I had thousands of visitors, but not one clicked through the banner ad for my Web site on other people's sites. I tried multiple search engine listings and that didn't produce much additional traffic either. I considered targeted advertising, but decided the cost was just not worth it.

I produced a 185 page edition (Volume I) of my commentaries and offered it for sale on the Web site for twenty five dollars a copy. The ad cost me twenty-five dollars a month. After six months, I did not have one Internet order to show for my investment. No longer able to justify the monthly expense, I reluctantly took the ad down.

Each commentary took six to nine hours to produce. While many readers and friends encouraged me to stick with it, I threw in the towel in April, 1999, shortly after writing a commentary on the Columbine High School shootings in Littleton, Colorado. I was totally burnt out and very disappointed with the traffic statistics from my Web site.

This does not mean I wouldn't suggest anyone else try what I did! Perhaps others will come up with ways to be more successful than I was. However, let me stress that promotion and marketing of a Web site is a very difficult proposition and a factor that should be very carefully examined before deciding to start a Web page where you hope to attract large amounts of traffic.

After all, it must be acknowledged that personal homepage webmasters do not have the resources of **The GO Network, ABCNews.go.com,** or **CNN.com,** who dominate the conventional media and are now trying to take over news coverage on the Internet as well!

It remains to be seen if major news organizations will be successful in the long run in delivering the news on the Internet and in matching the audiences they draw on broadcast television and radio. As a cyber-journalist I tend to believe that the television and radio news, and the public affairs entities have an uphill fight on their hands in terms of dominating the Internet, despite the huge resources at their disposal.

I believe a good many people came to the Internet to get away from the conventional print and broadcast media. Most were looking to this new form of communication as a way to empower themselves after being ignored or taken for granted by a good deal of the conventional media for most of their lives.

The key to domination of the market these days is a medium that doesn't speak to them, but allows for people to communicate with one another. Whether the ABC Television Network and their assorted "good old boy networks" around the world wish to accept it or not, inclusion is the name of the game, not the game they have been playing since they went into business in the late 1940s--exclusion!

As a result, television and radio networks, newspapers and magazines are literally fighting for their lives and forming partnerships with Internet based companies, just to retain some market share. The American Broadcasting Company (ABC) reported that six months ago that they had lost close to 20 percent of their viewing audience to the Internet in the last two years. Considering their snug attitude toward the general viewing public, ABC is lucky it wasn't 50 percent.

Some of the news stories I was writing about in "Politics As You Like It" were affecting me personally because of the horrific nature of the events. Once a journalist finds it difficult to detach him or herself from the their subject matter, it's time for a vacation. I felt it was time for me to "chill" as some people say.

About four weeks after I quit, my cyber-buddy Jeff Gersten, wrote me suggesting an alternative to my work at "Politics As You Like It." Little did I know that Net4TV Voice publisher, Laura Buddine, a.k.a. Dudette (I kind of like that handle), had been reading my commentaries for well over a year and liked my work.

In the next installment I'll write of what happened later, and how I may win a Pulitzer Prize for Internet Journalism. It's a category not yet created by the Pulitzer Committee at Columbia University who administer the Pulitzer Prize, the most prestigious award in print journalism.

Thank you for your interest and for taking the time to read this column.

You may contact the author by email: **bernard007@webtv.net.**

Welcome to Net4TV Voice
Meet your fellow users who crate Net4TV Voice in the **Masthead.**

Your Two Cents!
We want to hear what you think! Write to us at **Voice@iacta.com.**

Bernard Paul

Guestbook Entries for Publication

From Website Edition
Of
"Politics As You Like It'

1997

Net4TV Voice
Coast to Coast
Bernard Wax

Thoughts On Old And New Media
Part II

In my last column I tried to give everyone an idea of how I came to be writing for Net4TV Voice. When the idea was first proposed to me I was a bit reluctant to accept the invitation because I saw Net4TV Voice as a Zine primarily focused on the technological aspects of the Internet and WebTV. Several long telephone conversations assured me that Net4V Voice had no problem with my writing about anything my heart desired. At that point my eyes lit u and I responded with an unqualified yes!

I must say, even though I've been on WebTV and the Internet for nearly 3 years, there's an awful lot I don't understand about new technology and media. However, I feel I'm at the frontier of something that has a tremendous potential for individual empowerment, unlike anything else I've seen in my entire lifetime.

While many people believe there is unfettered freedom of the press in our country, just how free can that press be if they're funded by millions of dollars of advertising from outside sources?

Special interests permeate our society and special interests get what they pay for - the advancement of their personal or corporate political agendas. I don't know of a single American newspaper, television or radio station that doesn't have a Board of Trustees, publisher or editors pushing a specific political philosophy or personal agenda, and usually at the expense of their readership. Someone once said, "Freedom of the press belongs to those who own the press".

The amazing thing about the World Wide Web is that for a nominal outlay of money, each of us has the wherewithal for mass distribution of our ideas to the world at large. In the pat this was confined to people of significant means, but is now wide open to the average person. What we read, hear and see will be profoundly influenced by average people like you and I, not by advertisers' money, or special interests with private agendas, or people seeking to further expand their already powerful positions.

For the most part, those who call the shots in the conventional media endorse the exclusion of the same people that buy their newspapers, listen to their radio stations and watch their news reports on television. This is perverse elitism at it's worst. Yes, you can write letters to the editor and then some; but the important stuff, like deciding what news is covered when, is left up to those in the offices of editorial boards and news directors.

So, what do we get from these wise men and women in broadcast and print journalism? A few months ago I picked up a local paper in New York City, and on the front page was some story about Michael Jackson (it must have been major, it was on the front page of the newspaper)! I smiled as I plunked down my two bits thinking that someone at the newspaper had decided that on this day it was important that I know about Michael Jackson. Maybe the editor who made that decision was Janet Jackson. Why not put Bugs Bunny on the front page? It would give the same message to readers that the Michael Jackson story did.

Bernard Paul

The process that is used to decide what news I receive is based on what? Considering everything of major importance that was going on in the world on that day, someone decided John Q. Public needed to read about Michael Jackson and put the story on page one with a big headline. The American Society of Newspaper Editors would probably disagree with me and say that some highly complex process is involved in making decisions about what news is given to the public.

On the other hand, the potential of this new technology to end the status quo in the world of communications and make news worth reading or viewing again is both refreshing and invigorating. At the same time I also find it disturbing.

Microsoft Chairman Bill Gates (currently worth an estimated 85 billion dollars), in the beginning said, (paraphrased) "we'll change the way the world communicates." I don't know if that was Bill Gates' true intention or he just wanted a piece of everything that used his Microsoft software. Could he really have had any idea how much impact his company would have on worldwide communication?

The disturbing part are the individuals, groups and organizations who use the Internet to distribute messages of hate; or use this technology in other irresponsible ways that don't serve the overall interests of a peace loving, God fearing society who respect one another. Examples of this have been seen over the past two years as the Internet community has grown to over sixty million users in the United States. While I won't even attempt to define the parameters of Internet use, I believe many would agree that those who would use the Internet to injure others should find no avenue for their harmful activities.

The mechanisms are in place for the Internet community to police itself. Chat rooms where visitors hurl profanities at each other do not uplift, but only diminish the Internet in the eyes of many who have a vested interest in seeing the internet NOT succeed. In my opinion, those entities are the conventional media who have lost huge numbers of readers, viewers and listeners to the Internet in the past five years, which translates into the loss of the corporate bottom line - money.

The point is, unless the Internet strongly polices aberrant behavior on the Internet, our government will step in, claiming to save us all, and wind up trying to control every aspect of the Internet via heavy regulation.

Should that government intervention occur on a mass scale, we can all kiss our Internet freedom goodbye. Once such controls or laws are in place, they will not go away. Therefore, responsible, enlightened, uplifting use of the Internet should be a number one priority and I hope that all who use the World Wide Web will strive for that goal.

For too long many in the conventional media have treated the general public like children. Many editors and news directors feel that the public at large can be force fed anything, irregardless of the consequences to our society as a whole, which results in the irresponsible dissemination of news on a wholesale basis.

The quality of news coverage in our country has been in steady decline during the past fifteen years. During that time a circus atmosphere and tabloid mentality has infected news coverage in our country where sensationalism has replaced quality news coverage. Substance has been thrown to the dogs and the public now gets a steady diet of diversionary and irrelevant information with no real value.

217

We are fed a constant variety of gloom and doom, blood and guts, Hollywood glitz and totally useless information by many newspapers, radio stations and television stations, whose prime concern is money, not the people to whom they have a public responsibility.

The images sent into many homes by the electronic media every evening could make one think that planet Earth will only survive a few more hours, at best. The way most news organizations currently cover the news is an outright insult to the intelligence of viewers who only ask for a little reality and substance once in a while.

It's no small wonder that many in the public are uninformed as to important issues of the day. They are uninformed, not because they cannot read, write, think or evaluate, but because they are not being given the necessary information to make intelligent, informed decisions. This policy of de-information by a good majority of our conventional media is by design and ties in with the aims of the power structure in our country! "Keep em, dumb! They wouldn't know any better and wouldn't understand" is what the elitists preach! Sure, divert my attention from the real issues facing American society, for I wouldn't understand anyway. Well, the problem these days, even with the aforementioned policy of de-informing the public, is that far too many of us do understand.

The days of Walter Cronkite and Edward R. Murrow, (pioneers in the coverage and reporting of the news for television) are long gone and today's reporters of the news in the conventional media have a Dodge City, O.K. Corral mentality. Shoot em up, Bang Bang!

Only very recently have major news entities like CNN begun to address what the general public cares about or is thinking. CNN's possible concern over the mass of defections to the Internet has spawned a daily live program called, "Talk Back Love". It's nice to know that billionaire Ted Turner, and his Atlanta Media Mafia, are to hear what I think. Thanks Ted! Too little too late as far as I'm concerned. I had to wait forty years for you to want to hear what I think and have to say? No thanks, I'll use the Internet to get my points across, not "Talk Back Live" where your screeners will censor the calls and the topics.

Major media concerns, like NBC, CBS and ABC are owned and operated by major corporations like General Electric, Westinghouse and The Walt Disney Company. Their news coverage is of little concern to those corporations unless their news operations and shops by some error manage to do a repot critical to the parent corporation.

General Electric, owner of NBC, also manufactures materials use din nuclear weapons. So, NBC, with its public trust to inform me and make my life a little better, is owned by a company that contributes to the total destruction of our planet should nuclear war ever, God Forbid, become a reality. That's just great!

In spite of this, there are a few excellent, no-holds barred, cyberjournalists with Matt Drudge leading the way, to the chagrin of The CBS's, NBC's, and ABC's of the world. Yes, they have all tried to hire him, of late. Now Matt Drudge may resemble a muckraker in terms of his style of journalism, but I feel he's far from what Drew Pearson and Walter Winchell represented in the old days of getting the "scoop" at all costs. (Walter Winchell and Drew Pearson were feature newspaper columnists in the 1930's and 1940's. Drew Pearson wrote for The Washington Post and Walter Winchell for the New York World Telegram and Sun and New York Daily Mirror, both now defunct. Both Winchell and Pearson were known for their sensationalistic writing styles and both won the Pulitzer Prize, print journalism's top award.)

Bernard Paul

My hat goes off to matt Drudge for being who he is and having the guts to break the Monica Lewinsky - President Clinton story, after Newsweek found a reason to kill the story. Once again, as I wrote two weeks ago in my first column here, "Matt Drudge, my hero!"

So, in what I write for Net4TV Voice, I'll stay away from gloom and doom, blood and guts. My columns are not conservative, liberal, middle of the road, Democrat, Republican, socialist, leftist, reactionary, libertarian, sexist, racist, or tied to any political ideology or whatever labels our system uses to divide and stereotype us.

Rather, my columns are based on logic, common sense, and my calling it as I see it. My columns are not influenced by whether or not I'll have a job at the end of this week or next, nor are they influenced by sums of money that advertisers have paid me or my employer to push their personal or political agendas. Therefore, I would hope to make my readers think a bit, and ultimately, reach the idealistic goal of what journalism is: the practice of finding and getting to the truth.

If what I seek to accomplish and how I define the methodology of what goes into what I write puts me on a moral high ground in the field of journalism, that is not my intention. However, I would be the first to admit that all journalists should spire to the higher moral and ethical ground or position. Sadly, too many could care less and holding on to their social status and jobs is no excuse for producing crap, when one knows better.

In the twenty-one months I wrote commentary at my website, "Politics As You Like It" I felt I got to the truth of the subject matter I was writing about. This doesn't mean that if you disagree with any position I might take that you would be on my enemies list. I have no lists nor have I ever maintained one. My name is not former President Richard Nixon!

I have a healthy respect and admiration for other peoples' viewpoints and their inherent rights to have those viewpoints and I do not hold it against anyone when their views differ from mine.

Nor do I refuse to associate with those who do not share my beliefs, ideas, or politics. This is not to say that I'm totally politically correct, for political correctness (in my opinion), represents censorship of free speech. So, perfect I'm not! If you're looking for politically correct affirmations in what I write, you've got the wrong guy.

Tunnel vision along with tunnel hearing leads to darkness. No one's position, no matter how forthright it may be, is perfect. There are too many areas of gray to adopt positions based on black and white. Usually, black and white statements reflect personal interests, and a lack of true examination of an issue, not the truth. There are just too many sides to any given issue to reflect one way of thinking. Objectivity must be found in any issue before reaching the beginning of the truth.

So, I invite the readers of Net4TV Voice to go on this journey with me, in attempting to restore some ethics, morality and spirituality into the art of writing and journalism. It could prove to be a rocky ride, so I caution you to fasten your seat belt, for I have no insurance and am working without a net. Some of what I write of you may not agree with or like, but I promise you provocative, stimulating and interesting reading and the opportunity to think a bit.

Your comments are welcome in the guest book for this page, which can be reached by clicking below. Thank you for reading this column and I appreciate your interest. See Ya All Next Time! Peace and Love To All.

For Your Comments Click Here

October 10th 1999

Vol. 3 No. 2

Welcome to Net4TV Voice
Meet your fellow users who create *Net4TV Voice* in the **Masthead.**

Your Two Cents!
We want to hear what you think! Write to us at **Voice@iacta.com.**

Bernard Paul

Net4TV Voice
Coast to Coast
Bernard Wax

Gerry Spence Esq.: An Attorney Who Tells The Truth

Oft times, in these less than compassionate times, we as a nation are lucky to be blessed with a person who tells it like it actually is. Super lawyer Gerry Spence is one such person.

Born in Wyoming in 1929, he was the oldest child of missionary parents. While he was very young his mother committed suicide. After graduating from law school he represented an insurance company, something he did not like doing. He tells of his early life in one of his books Entitled, "The making of A Country lawyer."

In over twenty years as a criminal defense attorney, Spence has never lost a case. In civil law he has run up more million dollar jury verdicts for suing plaintiffs than any other lawyer in the United States. He has also written many books, all of which have been best sellers. Most of those books are listed at the end of this column.

Gerry Spence's wardrobe doesn't include the standard Brooks Brothers suit worm by many famous high-powered lawyers. At first glance you might think this man is a cowboy who works on a ranch somewhere. Over six feet tall, Mr. Spence wears a cowboy hat, along with cowboy boots and a trademark tan buckskin jacket. His voice is similar to that of the late John Wayne.

Currently, Gerry Spence splits his time between his winter home in Santa Barbara, California, and Jackson Hole, Wyoming, where he has his law office, with about 60 employees. He also appears as a regular commentator on CNN and on Court TV as a legal analyst.

Spence burst onto the scene many years ago with his spirited lawsuit on behalf of Karen Silkwood. The case centered around information that her employer (Keer-McGee) was contaminating her co-workers with deadly plutonium. She also had evidence of defects in the fuel rods of Keer McGee's breeder reactor.

Ms. Silkwood, intending to expose her employer, had arranged to speak with New York Times reporter, David Burnham when her car, a small Honda, was found smashed up against a concrete culvert, several miles from the Keer McKee plant where she worked.

A report by an accident reconstruction engineer concluded that her car had been hit from behind and she had been run off the road. Keer McGee claimed the cause of the accident, (they called it an accident, many to this day believe otherwise) was that Ms. Silkwood was very high on Quaaludes (a potent barbiturate). No criminal charges were ever filed and the actual cause of the crash remains unresolved.

Keer McGee had noted 574 incidents of worker contamination at its plant and had been cited 70 times for violations of worker safety rules by a federal regulatory agency. Despite this evidence, our federal government never levied a substantial fine against Keer McGee.

Ms. Silkwood's father, Bill Silkwood, brought suite against Keer McGee on behalf of Ms. Silkwood's estate and children. A search for a lawyer commenced and Gerry Spence was asked to take the case. The trial was held in Oklahoma City, before a Federal Court jury.

In a brilliant presentation of how Kerr McKee had contributed to the deaths of many employees and cancers in other employees, Gerry Spence won a ten million dollar jury award for punitive damages for the Silkwood estate. Appeals of the verdict went on for years. A settlement close to the original award was eventually reached, and Spence's name became a household word.

He went on to represent Imelda Marcos, wife of the former Prime minister of the Philippines, on a slew of criminal charges and won her acquittal before a Federal jury in New York City. Spence also won a nationally prominent case involving Randy Weaver, whose wife, child and dog were shot and killed by government ATF (Alcohol, Tobacco and Firearms) agents wile they were attempting to enforce an arrest warrant against Mr. Weaver.

I believe the honor, morality and integrity of Gerry Spence really stand out in his statements on social and economic justice in the many books he has written. In my opinion it takes a lot of guts to tell the sometimes awful truth about the country we live in. Below is an except from one of his many books, "Give Me Liberty, Freeing, We, The New American Slaves"

"You don't believe you are a slave, but you are. Your master is the master of all of us, a kind of conglomerate corporate, governmental oligarchy that controls our country and controls the world. The theory of this book is that our country suffered from 200 years of slavery. Five of the first Presidents were slave owners. George Washington owned 300 slaves. Congress at that time was dominated by slave owners. The first slave ships came to this country in 1619. The very structure of this country was created as a slave state. And though it is a more subtle kind of slavery, in many important ways, the American people today, are still slaves They work for corporations, they are numbers, digits, We don't elect our representatives - that is a myth. We don't own the media. We don't have a voice. We don't dare speak out. And though we have freedom of speech, no one can really hear us"

Character assassination can be an art, as long as you're not on the receiving end. Here are a few of the labels applied to Gerry Spence by those who do not agree with his views on social and economic justice. Un-Patriotic, Un-American, Communist, Socialist, Reactionary, Troublemaker, Malcontent, Pinko, Anti-family, Anti-social, Anti-community, etc. I, for one, admire and respect a man who attempts to address some of the horrible truths of American life and history. It takes a lot of guts to do that. Remember, you are not taught true American history in school, only a very sanitized version of what occurred during the first one-hundred and twenty five years of this country.

As a point of information, note that the same twenty families that were running this country in 1825, (they were called robber barons) are still running the show. Their names are no secret. Rockefeller; Vanderbilt; Harriman; Mellon; Getty; Rothchild; old money with old ideas that never go away, because their money keeps them in control. This group of non-progressives, (now there's one of my own labels-) have over 95 percent of all the money in America. That leaves 5% for the rest of us.

Finally, here is another excerpt from a Gerry Spence book entitled, "From Freedom To Slavery - The Rebirth Of Tyranny In America" published in 1993 by St. Martin's Press.

"We are not free. Nor have we ever been. Perfect freedom demands a perfect vision of reality, one too painful for the healthy to endure. It requires that we be alive, alert and exquisitely aware of our raw being. Faced with the pain of freedom, mans begs for his shackles.

222

Bernard Paul

Afraid of death, he seeks the stultifying boundaries of religion. Afraid of loneliness, he imprisoned himself in relationships. Afraid of want, he accepts the bondage of employment. Afraid of rejection, he conforms to the commands of society. If our knowledge of freedom were perfect we would not choose it. Pure freedom is pure terror."

Most of what we all go through on a day to day basis here in America is gently explained by Mr. Spence in his excellent books. He does offer solutions and I will use that as the hook to get my readers to buy one of his books or go to the public library and pick one up.

In an interview that Gerry Spence did with The Santa Barbara News press in June of 1997, he was asked who had been his mentor. Spence replied, "Franklin Roosevelt" "He was a great orator." Spence often imitates Roosevelt. "I still admire Roosevelt. He is the only President during my lifetime that had a program that somehow forwarded the interest of the American people" said Spence.

Below is a list of most of the books Gerry Spence has written. I've read half of them and highly recommend his writings if you would truly like to cut to the chase.

The Making of A Country Lawyer

How to Argue and Win Every Time: At Home, at Work, in Court, Everywhere, Every Day

With Justice for None: Destroying an
American Myth

From Freedom to Slavery: The
Rebirth of Tyranny in America

Of Murder and Madness

Trial by Fire: The True Story of a
Woman's Ordeal at the Hands of
The Law

Bernard Paul

O.J. the Last Word: The Death of
Justice

Gunning For Justice (Out of Print
At Amazon.com)

Gerry Spence is a man's man. He pulls the mask off of things many American shave taken for granted for too long. Brainwashing is an awful state of affairs. When one falls victim to the never-ending onslaught of rhetoric that our media and government heap upon us, we are left without the ability to think logically and evaluate what is going on around us and what is happening to us. If you wish to be deprogrammed from the status quo which has left you blind to the truth, I ask that you do yourself a great service and examine what Gerry Spence has to offer.

Your comments are welcome in the guest book for this page, which can be reached by clicking below. Thank you for reading this column and I appreciate your interest. See Ya All Next Time! Peace and Love To All

For Your Comments Click Here

October 24th 1999

Vol. 3 No. 3

To Top of Page

Welcome to Net4TV Voice
Meet your fellow users who create *Net4TV Voice* in the **Masthead.**

Your Two Cents!
We want to hear what you think! Write to us at **Voice@iacta.com.**

Bernard Paul

Net4TV Voice
Coast to Coast
Bernard Wax

"The Insider", Mike Wallace and "60 Minutes" Bite the Bullet

What caught my attention about the film "The Insider" was the large number of four star reviews and Al Pacino in a leading role. In the past, I've enjoyed every film I've seen with Mr. Pacino; the last one was "Donnie Brasco", about an aging Mafia soldier. The fact that Mr. Pacino is a native New Yorker (born and raised in the Bronx, New York like myself) perhaps colored my choice a bit to see his movies. However, I don't think you would get too much of an argument if you said that Al Pacino is one of the finest movie actors in the past thirty years.

My second reason for going to see "The Insider" is that I've had a desire to work in the news business for a long time, (having studied broadcast and print journalism in college), and knowing the film focused on a situation involving the highly rated CBS program "60 Minutes", its legendary correspondent, Mike Wallace and one of his producers, Lowell Bergman.

The magnitude of "60 Minutes" cannot be understated. A weekly one-hour program, it has been consistently in the top ten for the past twenty years. Close to forty million people tune in every week and advertisers pay top dollar to run their commercials in it. To understand "The Insider" requires understanding what "60 Minutes" stands for.

CBS News is seen as being the news operation that set the standard for the way news is covered and reported on the air. This tradition of excellence goes back to the beginning when Edward R. Murrow, Mike Wallace, Fred Friendy (Producer) and Don Hewitt (Executive Producer) were part of the "Murrows Boys" group. CBS News and especially "60 Minutes" have a tradition of integrity, ethics, and accuracy that is second to none in the broadcast news business. An attempt to soil that reputation occurs in the film, "The Insider".

While the film questions Mike Wallace's reputation as a broadcast journalist, I don't feel it comes close to undermining the reputation. Mike Wallace has commented he's not very happy with the way his role was depicted and is very upset with the producers and directors of the film. "The Insider" is a fictional account of what happened but uses the real names of the parties involved.

The film's director, Michael Mann, has admitted that dramatic license was taken with portions of the film. This writer does not understand how one can take dramatic license with a story that is true and uses real names, and then call itself a fictional account of the events that took place. I guess we'll leave that for the lawyers, but perhaps one of my readers has an explanation that would like to post in my guest book (the link is at the end of this article).

"The Insider" is about tobacco company executive Dr. Jeffery Wigand, (played by Russell Crowe); the company he works for - Brown and Williamson Tobacco Company, (the 3rd largest tobacco company in The United States), "60 Minutes" Producer Lowell Bergman, (played by Al Pacino) and Correspondent Mike Wallace (played by Christopher Plummer). Dr. Wigand was a research scientist for Brown and Williamson who discovered his employer had prior knowledge that their cigarette products were harmful to the consumer but continued manipulating the nicotine level to make them even more addictive. If this information was released to the general

227

public it would have disastrous consequences to Brown and Williamson's bottom line: the ability to sell product and make money.

They certainly were not paying Dr. Wigand to uncover this disturbing information, and he was summarily fired. In order to receive a decent severance package of benefits from Brown and Williamson, Dr. Wigand was told by company brass to sign a confidentiality agreement that he would not divulge anything he had learned - or his benefits would be revoked. The official reason that Brown and Williamson gives for Wigand's termination is "his failure to communicate properly." A man with a Ph.D. can't communicate? Reluctantly, Dr. Wigand signed the confidentiality agreement and found another job as a teacher.

At some point, "60 Minutes" Producer Lowell Bergman received an anonymous envelope that spilled the beans on Brown and Williamson. Bergman, a left-winger at heart and former radical journalist with Ramparts Magazine, seemed out of place as a producer with "60 Minutes." He obtained permission from Don Hewitt to pursue the story and Mike Wallace was assigned to handle the interviews. Eventually Bergman tracked down Dr. Wigand, but Wigand flat out refused to talk, citing his confidentiality agreement. Brown and Williamson were so worried about Wigand, they called him in a second time and forced him to sign a supplemental confidentiality agreement, as a condition of his continuing to receive his benefit package.

Lowell Bergman finally convinced Dr. Wigand to do the interview and the segment was taped. Dr. Wigand told a convincing story of how Brown and Williamson knew the harm their product would and could do. Wigand, as the film's name notes, is the "ultimate insider."

In the net year or so the Wigand interview with Mike Wallace is put on the back burner and does not air. One of the reasons comes out at a meeting between the "60 Minutes" staff and their in-house lawyer. The problem was that if CBS aired the interview, as a third party they could be held legally liable if Wigand had told the truth and CBS could be held liable for violation of Dr. Wigand's confidentiality agreement. All Dr. Wigand did was tell the truth and nothing but the truth.

A CBS lawyer suggested that if a way were found to put Dr. Wigand's confidentiality agreement into the court record of a tobacco company lawsuit in the State of Mississippi, then that confidentiality agreement would no longer be considered confidential in the eyes of the law and CBS could air the interview without liability. This tactic was not considered sound and CBS top brass ordered the interview killed. Dr. Wigand's interview never was broadcast. However, the fact that he gave the interview nearly destroyed his life. He was followed, death threats appeared in his e-mail and all kinds of strange things started happening to him. Ultimately his wife even left him. Brown and Williamson tried to further discredit Dr. Wigand by exposing a shoplifting conviction he had when he was very young and the fact he had once tried drugs - also when he was young.

Picture this for a moment: a tobacco company whose product could be responsible for killing millions of people and they decide that a shoplifting conviction and a brief interval of drug use is something that should impeach Dr. Wigand's credibility. Don't you just love that?

The film suggests that Mr. Wallace, in not protesting the killing of the story, was not as great a newsman as everyone thought. At the time of these events Mr. Wallace was 78 years old. In the film he says that he did not want to lose his job and wind up working at National Public Radio for the balance of his career. However, in terms of Mike Wallace selling out, this is all poppycock! A watered down version of the story eventually was broadcast without Dr. Wigand's interview. Mike Wallace strongly condemned the decision by CBS to not air the interview with Dr. Wigand. I believe Mike Wallace's actions were not different than any other reasonable human being's actions would be in the same situation.

While all of this was going on, the Westinghouse Corporation offered to buy CBS from then owner Lawrence Tisch. The offer, which was going to be accepted, would allow Mr. Tisch to walk away from CBS with ten times more than he had paid for the company when he bought it. Additionally, Brown and Williamson was threatening a massive fifty billion lawsuit against CBS if they broadcast Dr. Wigand's interview. The mere filing of the lawsuit would have caused Westinghouse to withdraw their offer to buy CBS. Lawrence Tisch would have been out on the street, and you can bet Brown and Williamson would have fired anyone even remotely connected with Dr. Wigand's interview.

Under these conditions, where there would have been no CBS and the literal survival of the owner of CBS and "60 Minutes" were at stake, I doubt very seriously whether anyone could blame Mike Wallace for not threatening to quit if the story was not broadcast. I would find it quite unreasonable for anyone to suggest that Mike Wallace did something that made him less of a news correspondent and that is precisely what the film suggests very erroneously, in this writer's opinion.

Taking business considerations into account, Mike Wallace bit the bullet. I believe many other people in the news business would have done the same thing. I can understand why Mr. Wallace is upset with the film and its portrayal of him.

Finally, this film is worth seeing even with the distortions of the story that I saw. The acting is superb and the dynamics that go on inside CBS News and the Brown and Williamson Tobacco Company take the viewer into a world rarely seen on the screen.

The last film that came close to what "The Insider" is about was "All The President's Men", the story of Washington Post newspaper reporters - investigative journalists, Bob Woodward and Carl Bernstein and their work on the Watergate debacle during former President of The United States Richard Nixon's administration.

I would recommend this 2 hour and 38 minute film. The film is fast paced and held my attention. "The Insider" actually takes you inside and with the one exception as to the dramatic license taken with Mike Wallace's role, is an excellent film.

Lowell Bergman, the "60 Minutes" producer who was caught up in all this, currently works for the award winning Public Broadcasting System's (PBS) investigative journalism program "Frontline" and teaches broadcast journalism at a college on the West Coast. Mike Wallace continues to do excellent work as a Senior Correspondent with "60 Minutes" and despite "The Insider's" inferences regarding his journalistic integrity is held in very high regard by his peers. Dr. Wigand is still trying to put the pieces of his life together. Brown and Williamson Tobacco Company continue to sell cigarettes despite a recent court settlement against the tobacco industry for two hundred and thirty-six billion dollars. Lawrence Tisch? Well, I'm not sure just exactly what Mr. Tisch is doing these days, although I am sure that his position is better than it would have been if he had decided to broadcast Dr. Wigand's interview.

Very Riveting Movie. You will not be disappointed if you go see it.

Your comments are welcome in the guestbook for this page, which can be reached by clicking below. Thank you for reading this column and I appreciate your interest. See Ya All Next Time! Peace and Love To All.

For Your Comments Click Here

November 21st, 1999

Bernard Paul

To Top of Page

Welcome to Net4TV Voice
Meet your fellow users who crate *Net4TV Voice* in the **Masthead.**

Your Two Cents!
We want to hear what you think! Write to us at **Voice@iacta.com.**

Net4TV Voice
VoxPop:
A Reader's Opinion

Dragging One's Feet Refined To An Art
Coast to Coast
Bernard Wax
(November 7, 1999)

On November 11th we will celebrate the last Veterans Day of this millennium. The debt of gratitude we owe our country's veterans, who have fought to preserve our way of life and freedom, cannot be measured.

Many veterans leave the military with profound injuries, most of which are directly related to their honorable service to our nation. The U.S. Department of Veterans Affairs, (hereafter referred to as the DVA) is entrusted with the mission of assisting veterans in obtaining the variety of benefits they earned as a result of their military service.

The U.S. Department of Veterans Affairs is a massive cabinet level agency, which employs over twenty thousand people and has an annual operating budget of forty-one billion dollars. With eighty regional offices nationwide and one-hundred and seventy-two veteran's hospitals, the DVA is second only to the Department of Defense in yearly monetary allocations given by Congress to run a Federal agency.

With the apparently ultra-conservative, mean-spirited, trend toward those in need, (which translates to the implementation of many social programs in a very uncompassionate way) the question remains, do we really want to abuse those who have honorably served our country in various military campaigns? (This is not to say that abuse by bureaucracy at any level is an acceptable state of affairs).

This then rings up the question: Why do we currently have 270,000 homeless veterans in our nation? I know this homeless problem has been beaten into the ground for the past twenty or so years and the general public is very tired of hearing about it. For some reason, this writer feels that the homeless veteran problem should continue to have a very bright light shining on it and I hope my readers feel the same way. So I hope I don't burden you with this subject matter. If you do feel burdened, I offer my sincere apology and ask you to read on anyway, for the plight of our nations homeless veterans is worth of great public concern. Why does this situation exist?

Most of the facts quoted in this column come from the National Veterans Organization, (NVO) a non-profit grass-roots organization is headquartered in Las Cruces, New Mexico. NVO's Founder and Executive Director is Douglas McArthur, a U.S. Naval veteran. His organization has over three thousand members across the United States. NVO's mission, according to Mr. McArthur, is to exert pressure on the Department of Veterans Affairs to process veterans disability claims in a timely manner.

Mr. McArthur, who is currently 56 years old, fell off an airplane wing in Italy in 1967 and hurt his back and neck. When that injury began giving him serious problems, he filed a disability claim with his local veteran's regional office in Albuquerque, New Mexico in 1980. He gave up when his injury became worse and later filed a new claim in 1992. In 1996, the

Bernard Paul

Board of Veterans Appeals in Washington D.C. sent Mr. McArthur's claim back to the Albuquerque regional office for a new review. Currently, Mr. McArthur awaits a regional office decision on a claim returned on appeal over three years ago. The telephone number of the National Veterans Organization if (915)759-6233.

One of the DVA's darkest secretes is their ability to accurately process claims in a reasonable amount of time. This is one of the significant factors contributing to the huge amount of homeless veterans. Consider this: nationwide, the average time it takes a DVA regional office to process a valid claim of disability benefits which can include monthly payments of up to $1,989.00 a month) is 717 days (that's almost two years). Now I'm not claiming that all veterans' claims for disability benefits are valid; just that many have merit and are erroneously denied by regional offices. Forty-three percent of appeals are returned to the issuing regional office because of errors. Twenty-five percent of these claims are later granted by regional offices. The average resolution time is 714 days.

There is something wrong with a system that works like this, especially where a veteran is involved. Let me explain! The veteran claims system is supposed to be based on a non-adversarial basis with the agenda to make it as easy as possible for the veteran to prove his or her claim.

However, the current statistics pertaining to grant-denials of disability claims show otherwise. The VA system, as it is working these days, shows an 'us against them' mentality exhibited by Department of Veterans Affairs decision-makers.

The reason the VA system is supposed to be non-adversarial is to honor and thank the veteran for his/her military service to our country. In the veterans claims system, the lowest threshold of evidence is required to win. When I write 'lowest threshold', I begin with the level of evidence to convict in a criminal case, (beyond a reasonable doubt and end with the level of evidence required in a civil proceeding where one party is suing another. By a preponderance of the evidence, if the veteran is operating at the lowest threshold of evidence to establish his or her claim, then why re so many claims for disability benefits not granted?

"The DVA delays wreaks havoc in the lives of veterans", says Trey Daly, a senior attorney with the Legal Aid Society of Cincinnati, Ohio, whose office handles many administrative appeals for veteran's disability benefits. Mr. Daly, Esq. goes on to say, "When the DVA incorrectly denies disability benefits, vets who honorably served their country are often left without income, without medical care, sometimes without a place to live, without their dignity."

Tom Breen, an official with the Department of Veterans Affairs offered these comments when asked about this claims processing problem at the Department of Veterans Affairs: "Over the past several years the department has been making headway against a massive backlog of claims." Mr. Breen went on to say, "the backlog has been climbing again, not only locally here in New Mexico, but nationally. Staff losses in the past year have caused our office to lose ground in processing veterans claims" (paraphrased quote). Department of Veterans Affairs spokesman, Kenneth McKinnon noted, "The average veteran's claim has been pending 151 days, nationwide." This writer attempted to obtain further comment from various Department of Veterans Affairs officials by telephone regarding the situation in New York City and Washington D.C., on the morning of the day this column was written. I was told that no one was available to talk with me. So it seems the DVA is fully aware of the situation and is having difficulty resolving it.

While recent efforts have been made by DVA Under Secretary for Veteran Benefits and Services, Joseph Thompson, and DVA Secretary Togo West Jr. to make the claims process more expeditious, those efforts have not produced the bottom line in this matter, *results*. Meanwhile, far too many, (not that any level is acceptable) of our nation's veterans remain out in the street without a roof over their heads, as winter approaches. If this is not sad, and worthy of some focus and attention by the general public, I don't know what is.

Sid Hudson, a Vietnam veteran who suffers from Post-Traumatic Stress Disorder, (PTSD) said this: "the DVA seems to only grudgingly award benefits, nickel and dimeing veterans, hoping they will be satisfied with lower payments and ratings or delaying the awarding of benefits for long periods of time, hoping the veteran will go away" (paraphrased).

Another example of this disgrace is U.S. Army veteran Sidney O'Neal from Walnut Hills, Ohio. Mr. O'Neal served in the U.S. Army for three years, from 1967 to 1970. He filed an application for disability benefits in March of 1990. He suffers from Post Traumatic Stress Disorder (PTSD), was unable to hold a job due to his illness, and eventually became homeless while his claim for disability benefits was pending with the DVA. In April of 1998, 8.1 years after he filed for assistance, he finally received a small non-service connected disability pension. *8.1 years!*

Clarence Loper of Georgetown, Ohio, waited seven years and one month to receive 100 percent disability benefits from the DVA. Mr. Loper, says, "A veteran's claim dies when he does, which creates a significant financial incentive for the DVA to delay decisions". Sounds unbelievable right?

Now imagine that for a brief moment! A government employee, whose job it is to award you a Federal benefit that the law says you have earned by paying into that program for a good majority of your working life or serving your country in the military honorably, is sitting behind a desk somewhere, delaying your case. Is this what you get after risking life and limb to fight for your country and allowing yourself to be put in harms way? Put at the mercy of bean counters, who in most cases are your fellow Americans. Yes, sadly, it seems that way!

Bureaucratic terrorism is the term I have coined for this very unacceptable, sociopathic behavior, which is killing innocent people in our country every day. No one that does this goes to prison. No one is even reprimanded or spends even one day in jail. It's perfectly legal to kill someone through bureaucratic inefficiency and it happens in our country a lot more than most people think. It has to stop. All Federal, State and City agencies must be held totally and directly accountable to the people they have a public trust to. Our tax dollars pay their salaries and this they work for and with us; not against us.

The Department of Veterans Affairs, is not achieving its mandate, "To Care For the Veteran and His Family" (quote attributed to Abraham Lincoln, former President of the United States), has failed big time in it's responsibility tour nation's veterans.

Finally, in so doing it's job efficiently and responsibly, the U.S. Department of Veterans Affairs has created a huge homeless problem among our veterans all the social consequences that are collateral to the problem they created, such as crime, drug addiction, family problems and a host of other aberrant behaviors indicative of bureaucratic terrorism.

Now perhaps you, my reader, say this is just not so. Well, it is, when you take into account the logical extension of not granting valid veterans claims in an expeditious way. Most veterans seeking these benefits to begin with are without families or social support structures. This delay

Bernard Paul

can leave the veteran without the funds to purchase housing. Yes, at the risk to their lives they can stay in state or municipal homeless shelters. They choose not to and cannot be faulted for that decision considering the dangerous conditions at most of our nations homeless shelters.

For the most part they wind up homeless. Were a more timely way found to grant valid veterans disability claims, the veteran homeless problem would see dramatic reduction. Since no concrete effort is being made by the Department of Veterans Affairs to seriously address this problem, it would be safe to write that they have created the problem by allowing the foot dragging to continue.

Unless the general public expresses outrage at this situation, it will continue unabated. That's what I've tried to do here and I urge you, my reader, to take a few minutes of your time to do the same. This week a bill was introduced in Congress, which would reaffirm the mandate to assist all veterans in claims they file or have pending with the DVA. Due to recent Court decisions, a veteran has no help at all from the government he or she fought for in developing a claim for benefits. The entire burden falls on the veteran.

I ask you to write the Chairman for the House Veterans Affairs Committee in Washington D.C., Rep. Lane Evans (D) Ill.-17th Congressional District, and express your outrage over this disgraceful way of dealing with our nation's veterans. Your e-mail will make a difference and you will honor our nation's veterans and yourself by showing the support they have earned and deserve. They were there for us when we needed them. Now let's be there for them as we approach the last Veteran's Day of our century. Rep. Evan's e-mail address is below. It will only take a minute to send him a message in support of our veterans. Thanks much!

Rep. Lane Evans **e-mail** or address Chairman of the House Committee On Veteran Affairs; Washington D.C.

This column will be sent to Rep. Evans' office in Washington D.C. and I will be sending a separate e-mail to Rep. Evans' inviting his response. Any response I receive from Chairman Evans will be posted here in a future column. Should you not see that response from Rep. Evans, it can be safely assumed that he shoes not to respond.

In support of our nations homeless veterans, Miss America, Heather Renee French visited and held a press conference on October 29, 1999 at the Homeless Veteran's Standown, Drop-In Center Shelter House in Cincinnati, Ohio. You too can help by sending your E-mail to Rep. Lane Evans and expressing your concern regarding the matter written of here.

Your comments are welcome in the guestbook of this page, which can be reached by clicking below. Thank you for reading this column and I appreciate your interest. See Ya All Next Time! Peace and Love To All,.

For Your Comments Click Here

November 7, 1999

To Top of Page

Welcome to Net4TV Voice
Meet your fellow users who create *Net4TV Voice* in the **Masthead.**

Your Two Cents!
We want to year what you think! Write to us at **Voice@iacta.com.**

Bernard Paul

Net4TV Voice
VoxPop:
A Reader's Opinion

Senator John McCain: Campaign Finance Reform's White Knight
Bernard Wax; Coast to Coast
(December 5, 1999)

Well, here we are in another presidential election year. With a little over two and one half months to the first primary in New Hampshire, things are heating up on the campaign trail.

On the Democratic side are Vice President Al Gore and Bill Bradley, former United States Senator from New Jersey and New York Knicks 1970's basketball star. It is not clear at this time who the front runner is; however many political pundits think Bill Bradley could beat out Al Gore for the Democratic nomination.

In this writer's opinion, the most interesting race is no the Republican side. Texas Governor George Bush Jr. (son of former President George Bush) has lost his huge lead in the polls against Arizona Senator John McCain. The other Republican candidate is millionaire businessman and Fortune magazine owner, Steve Forbes.

The Reform Party's candidate is Pat Bucannan, former Nixon speechwriter and nationally syndicated columnist. Other possible candidates are real estate magnate Donald Trump of New York, Minnesota Governor Jesse Ventura of the World Wrestling Federation fame, and Texas millionaire businessman, Ross Perot.

However, even with Governor Bush's sixty million dollar campaign war chest and his strong support inside the Republican party, the big story is how Senator McCain has pulled dead even with Bush. If Mr. McCain wins the New Hampshire primary, he could give George Bush, Jr. a real run for his money. Currently Senator McCain is campaigning very heavily in New Hampshire, spending a lot of time and money there.

John McCain's popularity combines many complex social, political and economic factors. In recent times, we in America have been searching for a real hero. Sixty-two year old John McCain more than fits that bill. A graduate of the United States Naval Academy in Annapolis, Maryland, he served aboard the aircraft carrier USS Forrestal during the Vietnam war and was a prisoner of war at Hoa Lo prison in Hanoi from March of 1968 through Christmas of 1970 (33 months).

During his captivity, McCain was beaten, starved, denied decent medical care and not allowed communication with other POW's. This treatment bent him a little out of shape but never broke his spirit, a testimony to the man's inner strength, character and courage.

Recently, his POW experience has been made an issue as to his suitability for becoming President. Critics claim McCain's temperament is suspect. A cheap shot in my opinion. Leading that chorus was Trent Lott, who was reported to have been affiliated with a KKK type group during his political career.

John McCain has been serving his country since the age of seventeen. As an elected official from his home state, Arizona, his political agenda cuts across party lines, and many endorse his long term goals for the Untied States: the restoration of political integrity to political offices, the reform of government in general and renewal of the American dream.

Senator McCain has a reputation for telling the truth (unlike many politicians I've seen in the past thirty-six years). I know, most of my readers may feel there's no such ting as a politician who tells the truth. However, after you examine some of John McCain's statements and positions, you might say to yourself, "this guy's for real".

The centerpiece of Mr. McCain's candidacy for President is government reform; and in particular campaign finance reform. One of the realities of life is that money fuels politics. Without money it is very difficult to get elected to anything. McCain calls our campaign finance system corrupt! At this **website** he states:

I think that most Americans understand that soft money - the enormous sums of money given to both parties by just about every special interest in the country - corrupts our political ideals whether it comes from big business or from labor bosses or trial lawyers"

When was the last time you heard an elected official in our nation say that?

The **Federal Election Commission's** web site lists those who contributed the most money to political campaigns in any given state during the years 1997-98. This will give a clearer picture of what John McCain is talking about when it comes to campaign finance reform.

For instance: in my home state of New York, leading the list of contributors for 1997-998 is Phillip Morris Inc. with contributions to political candidates of $1,437,019.00. Second is an individual contributor, Bernard L. Schwartz with $8781,000.00 and third is the giant drug company, Pfizer Pharmaceuticals Inc. with $440,000.00. That's almost two and a half million dollars contributed by just three donors.

Stack that up against the average American. Most of us, because of lack of money, are completely shut out of the political system while those special interests with big money get their agendas implemented.

Senators and Congresspersons tie up much of their time catering to these special interests, leaving little time for the average taxpaying, working constituents for whom they are supposed to be working. The rationale for all this? Running and getting elected and re-elected to political office is a very expensive proposition.

Since most everyone who runs for political office is not a multi-millionaire, we will continue to have a system that is weighted towards those with huge sums of money to contribute to candidates for political offices. Is this government for the people, by the people as it was meant to be by the founding fathers of our country? Not by any stretch of the imagination. Absolutely not! What it actually represents is government by the few, for the few and the rest of us be dammed!

Senator McCain has been getting a lot of heat from his fellow politicians for raising the campaign finance reform issue. Some of those politicians stand to lose an awful lot if McCain is successful in reforming the campaign finance system. On the floor of the United States Senate a few weeks ago during a heated debate regarding campaign finance reform, Senator McCain was asked to name specific individuals who were responsible for abusing the campaign finance system in our nation. His reply was that "names were not necessary because essentially the entire system of financing elections was corrupt and unfair" (paraphrased quote).

238

Bernard Paul

My solution to this issue? Well for one, I would have all elections financed solely by the Federal Government.

Secondly, I would have all the major media outlets: broadcast, print and Internet, provide free time to any candidate that wanted it. In return for the free airtime, I would give substantial corporate tax break to those entities that provided the free airtime. This should reduce the cost of running for office by fifty percent considering the huge expenditures a candidate must make to get their message out through television, radio, newspapers and the Internet.

Next, I would ban all contributions to PAC's, (Political Action Committees) and limit the amount of any contribution to no more than five thousand dollars. This would put the campaign finance system within reach of a lot of working taxpaying citizens who, for the most part, pay the majority of taxes in our country. No, our corporations don't come close to paying the amount of taxes that working American spay every year. Not even close.

Further, I would means test contributions from the poor. If a person could prove that their annual income was under fifteen thousand dollars a year, I would require the Federal Government to double every dollar that person contributed (one dollar contributed would become three dollars). My proposals would allow the middle class and the poor in our country to actually have significant input in the political process and reap some real benefits from their participation in that process. My proposal would even the playing field by limiting the influence that special interests buy with their huge sums of money. They type of system I describe would bring over one hundred million people in our country into the process and go a long way toward ending voter apathy and hostility towards our political system. My idea would bring about true participatory democracy; government for the people by the people as our founding fathers meant it to be. "Literal Democracy" I would call it.

If I were successful in doing all I have proposed, I would have to hide under a rock on some island in the South Pacific to avoid being assassinated! How much money would the major broadcast networks and publishing outfits in the print business lose under my proposal? Too many zero's to figure that one out right now. How much would corporations in our country lose by not being able to treat their politicians like high-priced whores? Too many zero's on that one, too! Bring poor people into the process? They would hang me upside down - and then some.

Better left to Senator John McCain? Well, yes! Okay, John you do it. I like living and have absolutely no Secret Service protection nor can I afford private bodyguards who can shoot straight!

Senator McCain says he's deeply concerned about the direction our country is going and the current attitude of the general electorate. In my opinion, he has good reason to feel that way. Where I live in New York City, in a general election held five weeks ago, only eleven percent of those registered to vote chose to do so. What does that say? Senator John McCain's partial remarks to the graduating class at John Hopkins University in Maryland earlier this year sums it up:

"The Threat that concerns me is the pervasive public cynicism that is debilitating our democracy. I'm a conservative, and I believe it is a very healthy thing for Americans to be skeptical about the purposes and practices of public officials and refrain from expecting too much from their government. Self-reliance is the ethic that made this country great, not cosigning personal responsibilities to the state.

But healthy skepticism has become widespread cynicism bordering on alienation, and that worries me very greatly. Government is intended to support our constitutional purposes to establish justice, insure domestic tranquility, provide for the common defense, promote the general welfare and secure the blessings of liberty to ourselves and our posterity. When the people come to believe that government is so dysfunctional or corrupt that it no longer serves these ends, basic civil consensus will deteriorate to the point that our culture might fragment beyond recognition".

I think John McCain understands the way many Americans feel about the federal government. His acute awareness and willingness to try to do something about it is the hallmark of his candidacy for President. How successful he will be is up to the American voters.

Without social, economic and political justice in our country we are but an empty shell trying to portray our nation as something we re not and never could be. Something that looks good, sounds good, but never reaches true potential, due to the nature of the system itself.

As a columnist and loyal American I question whether the American Dream is something our government continues to support for all citizens. With jobs going overseas at a faster rate than ever before and new technology putting thousands out of work every month, what is our government going to do with the surplus labor force created by allowing corporations to take over our country? Does the American Dream for this and future generations mean six dollar an hour jobs, and 80 hour work weeks, just to survive?

I didn't' write live, I wrote survive. Even though many might disagree with me, I believe our government has an obligation to rein in the corporations and thus ensure a quality of live that is acceptable to this and future generations. That stance by our government would be consistent with preserving the American Dream for those who wish to pursue it.

John McCain wants to address that deplorable state of affairs and should be given an opportunity to do so, if there is any semblance of fairness left in our nation. A close look at Senator John McCain's candidacy for President is warranted because he is forcing us to face what is actually happening and that takes a lot of courage and sacrifice.

As we approach the new millennium, business as usual cannot be the order of the day if we are to survive as a nation and command the international respect this country deserves. Indifference to domestic problems does have its price. Fiscal responsibility should not equal cuts that pull the rug out from under Americans who wish to be included in the American Dream and are willing to work hard to achieve that goal.

If fiscal responsibility and accountability is the real order of the day, then why not cut our defense budget by fifty-percent since we no longer have a Cold War to fight? Domestic tranquility is essential to an effective foreign policy. An international crisis every four or five weeks combined with those trying to figure out where their next meal is coming from and/or how to pay their rent or mortgage is a prescription for trouble.

Take a look at what Senator John McCain has to say, You might be as pleasantly surprised as I was. Please note, this column is not an endorsement of Senator John McCain's candidacy for President. I have not yet decided whom I will vote for next November. However, I do like what McCain has to say. I feel we are very fortunate to have a man of John McCain's caliber running for the office of President.

Bernard Paul

Your comments are welcome, in the guestbook for this page, which can be reached by clicking below. Thank you or reading this column and I appreciate your interest. Se Ya All Next Time! Peace and Love To All.

For Your Comments Click Here

December 5th 1999

—

To Top of Page

Welcome to Net4TV Voice
Meet your fellow users who create *Net4TV Voice* in the **Masthead.**

Your Two Cents!
We want to hear what you think! Write to us at **Voice@iacta.com.**

**Guestbook Entries from Authors
Website on the World Wide Web
@ http:www.geocities.com/Capitol Hill Lobby/2492
1997-1998-1999**

Bernard Paul

Don - 08/22/97 15:56:33 GMT
My URL:http://www.g eocities.com~fifty57/
My Email:fifty57@geocities.com
Where Are You From?:Rochester NY
Political Party Affilation(Optional):Republican and proud of it!!!

Comments:

Here we have exactly what the mass news media is afraid of....Two way conversation. No longer do we need to sit and be "told what to think" Now of course their problem is to find a way to "filter" and "control" the internet for the sake of the "children" This will work for the general populace who cannot take any responsibility on their own and still need to be told what to do. but I suspect the times are a-changing, slowly but that's how we got here. The country has always swung from left to right and back again. I never expected to see the GOP in control of the house and it's apparent they are not use to it, still…it's a change. How Bill can hang on is a mystery to me, he is so transparent I don't see how he can fool anyone. Maybe the second revolution is started, this time in cyberspace. So let them all fret, beside's they are so much fun to watch as they slowly self-distruct. Sooner or later they will overdo it and people will wake up. Thanks for cruising by my site and I'll be back.

■■■

Christopher Alex - 08/22/97 01:18:04 GMT
My URL:h ttp://www.angelfire.com/ca/revup/index.html
My Email:primestar@webtv.net
Where Are You From?: Sheridan, Wy.
Political Party Affillation(Optional): Rep.

Comments:

First, i like what you have done on your new look. I think what Ted K. was talking about when he refered to "Cheap Techology" is the fact that we the people, news casters and politicians have both forgotten about, we are able to communicate for pennies on the net. They have a fear for the arena of idea's that the net generates. It almost feels like big brother government can hear or find us when we disagree with its policies. While Washington is making liberal dicisions on how they are going to take care of us and protect us from ourselfs, we are here on the net hollering like hell, but its th only place left to holler.

■■■

John - 08/19/97 17:35:52 GMT
My URL:http://www.ucl.ac.uk/~regojpb/
My Email:No thanks I gave at the office
Where Are You From?: London UK
Political Party Affillation(Optional): Socialist

Comments:

Here I am on a return visit and I've just read your column re. ABC news. As you state it's oh so easy to blame someone else rather than accept your own responsibility, if they're losing the oh so important market share well it's up to them to improve, not limit the competition. Call me a cynic but I also wonder if this rant ha more to do with market share and profit than journalistic integrity? Of course there's mis-information "out there" on the net but it's a mere reflection on real life and all we have to do is apply our judgement as we do in real life. The net has provided people with something to blame for their own lack of responsibility. For example if people are concerned about porn being readily available to their children, well rather than trying to coerce the government or companies into censoring what may be legitimate (though not tasteful) how about taking responsibility for a change and surf the net with your kids to keep an eye on what they access etc. Kids have far more intelligence than we credit and more than likely able to hack any filters hat parents stick onto the browsers. Anyway all I'm trying to say is that responsibility starts off with the individual and not the government or a multi-national. John........(climbing off of his soapbox)

▪▪

Joe Pence - 08/19/97 14:40:00 GMT
My Email:joe1952@webtv.net
Where Are You From?: Baltimore Md.
Political Party Affillation(Optional): Rep.

Comments:

As always very interesting.

▪▪

Walter - 08/16/97 05:37:06 GMT
My Email:waleth2@webtv.net
Where Are You From?: Long Island

Comments:

Good page Bernard. Keep up the good work.

▪▪

~Laverne - 08/08/97 05:35:19 GMT
My URL:http://www.dzn.com/!lhindi/
My Email:Lhindi@dzn.com
Where Are You From?: TX

Comments:

Pretty interesting web site. I be sure to drop in often. Thanks! ~Laverne
JOIN OPERATOIN JUST CAUSE ADOPT A POW/MIA!
http://www.dzn.com/~lhindi/myhero.html

Bernard Paul

~Laverne's Homepage Poetry

•••

Charlie cancellieri - 08/04/97 22:42:41 GMT
My URL:http://www.geocities.com/southbeach/lights/8790 My Email:cccorna@webtv.net
Where Are You From?: nyc

Comments:
    BRAVO! BERNARD...YOU HIT THE NAIL RIGHT ON THE HEAD...THEY ARE
BARBARIC...I AGREE W/YOU 100%..AS A FELLOW NY'ER, I CAN RELATE TO WHAT
HAPPENED & I AGREE THESE F--KING ANIMALS SHOULDN'T EVEN BE HERE IN
THE 1ST PLACE!!! FOR THIS REASON I BELIEVE THERE WILL EVER BE PEACH
BETWEEN JEWS & ARABS...THEY ARE NOT HAPPY UNLESS THEY ARE KILLING
EACH   OTHER...&   WE   ARE   GUILTY   BY   ASSOCIATION   (LIKE   YOU
SAID)...EXCELLENT JOB...MAYBE YOU COULD DWELL ON THE POINT (OPINION) I
JUST MADE, IN YOUR NEXT ARTICLE...YOU CAN CALL IT "ELIGION: A PRELUDE
TO WAR"...BEEN GOING ON THERE FOR 5000 YRS

•••

Chuckies - 08/04/97 05:36:55 GMT
My Email: don't give this out
Where Are You From?: Florida
Political Party Affillation(Optional): not available

Comments:
    I think this is an interesting concept. Sorry to see that some of the people that stopped by to
read it, are so immature they have to use the profanity to be noticed. Doesn't say much for their
contribution to society! I appreciate the site and will be back often, thanks for doing it!

•••

1010111010 - 07/30/97 11:48:21 GMT
My URL:http://www.ucl.ac.uk/~regojpb/
My Email:yes I know
Where Are You From?: London UK
Political Party Affillation(Optional): Labour/Socialist

Comments:
    Certianly an interesting article and Chomsky sounds like a good lad. It seems to me at least
that the Labour party are sort of falling into the old ways of the tories, for example they are going
to bring in some freedom of information but that has been p t on the backburner now. Hope they
dont become corrupt so damn quickly! Anyway nice site and I'll be back! John.....

•••

245

Steve vogel - 07/02/97 01:41:13 GMT
My URL:http://www.angelfire.com/sc/hardhitters
My Email:hardhitters@webtv.net
Where Are You From?: denver, colorado
Political Party Affillation (Optional): working man's party

Comments:
i like what you do, keep exposing the corrupt leadership people have no one to blame but themselves they vote them in and dont vote them out voters are just as self serving as the politicians

Guestbook Entries for Publication

From Website Edition
Of

"Politics As You Like It"

1998-99

Bernard Paul

Visitor: Linda Pierucki
Reference: subscriber
Location: Norvell,Mi (small-town, America)
Website:
Web Info:
Contact;   llsp@webtv.net
Date: Mon, Apr 26, 1999 at 09:50:51 (EDT)

Comments: Bernard: Thank you again for your thoughtful insights into yet another major symptom of sickness in our society. I've thought long and hard about the horrible situation in Colorado, and gone through the gamut of usual reactions to this tragedy: nowhere have I been able to find a solution to these ills. This is a little long, but I feel I just have to say this -Maybe it's MY way of coping with grief. This will, unfortunately, happen again! A few issues that have NOT been discussed…A few years ago, I heard a psychologist remark that we currently live in a schizophrenic society (unfortunately, I dont remember who this psychologist was, but I felt his/her coments were extremely insightful). We live in a country of 'double-speak' and propaganda - we are TOLD things are one way, we SEE they are another. Witness the various Media 'Spins' aready placed on this tragedy to serve various groups' agendas and the inability of most of us to discern the truth of the incident. This creates a situation where we have real problems discerning reality. These children have been exposed to an unreal world all their lives. Large high schools are unhealthy for adolescents - the best and the brightest get perks, attention and team honors - the rest, including those with serious social-adjustment problems, often fall through the cracks. We promote these large school systems as successful as they have successful team sports, highly-honored debate teams, etc. We dont stop to think about the huge numbers of kids who didnt make the team, or receive the honors simply because there are only so many honors to go around. I believe these parents were TERMINALLY-UPWARDLY-MOBILE! These kids had everything money could buy, except love and attention, supervision and cookies and milk after school from a parent who asked (and really cared) How was your day? ust my thoughts on this…

••

Visitor: Mark
Reference: been here before
Location:
WebSite:
Web Info:
Contact: eagle109@webtv.net
Date: Sat, Apr 24, 1999 at 17:56:23 (EDT)

Comments: Not much can be said about this. I was off from work that day watching this live sige on tv. I was just in total shock. Long pause. Its just sad. I don't think much could have prevented this. These two boys were trying there best to be different and cause trouble they were just plain evil. In some of the other school shootings it always seem to involve the supposed nerds and i don't like to use that word because I was in that social classifaction in school and got picked on a bit I had a sevear dislike for jocks myself. I do think a lot of this would not happen if the social classes in school wernt so bad. You don't have to like each other but you can respect each other.

....

Visitor: Jeff Gersten
Reference: been here before
Location: Monticello, NY
WebSite:
Web Info:
Contact: JeffGersten@webtv.net
Date: Sat, Apr 24, 1999 at 08:05:42 (EDT)

Comments: This is so horrific that it is hard to even comment on it. I think it is time to crack down on the availability of weapons. The only purpose of sawed off shotguns and semi-automatic weapons is to kill as many as possible. These weapons are not for hunting or legitimate self-defense. There is no way that these minors should be able to obtain these types of weapon. Instead, as you pointed out, the media will blame the internet and video games. They could not have committed such carnage without so much firepower no matter what they entertained themselves with.

....

Visitor: Mark
Reference: been here before
Location:
WebSite:
Web Info:
Contact: eagle109@webtv.net
Date: Fri, Apr 09, 1999 at 21:03:55 (EDT)

Comments: I agree with everything you wrote. I've been against the seizure laws all along for the most part. A compromise would be if found absolutely quilty of the crime selling drugs out of a house for example the house could be seized and sold and the money donated to charity not the police departments. This would cut down and some of the not so tight cases where police just want the money. As far as The Constitution goes its pretty much out the window now days. It doesnt exist anymore. Theres not any real answers to this its just more sad commentary on the state of this country.

....

Visitor: Mark
Reference: been here before
Location:

Bernard Paul

WebSite:
Web Info:
Contact: eagle109@webtv.net
Date: Mon, Mar 29, 1999 at 21:42:17 (EST)

Comments: This is pretty pitiful. The government has no problem taking but they don't want to give unless its some type of welfare for the lazy. Veterns are very deserving of the benefits and they shoul get them. One problem is the government has promoised more than it can deliver social security, medicad, medicare, welfare, veterns benefits. All that money has to come from somewhere. I don't know the answer the whole thing is just a mess. The veterns should get priority over the welfare slobs and others.

■■■

Name: Sergei
Sent: 09:17 - mon 8 nov 1999

It would be nice to have a column from someone representing the opposite point of view. I hope that this goofy left-winger is not the "official" political voice of Net4TV. I wonder why Mr. Wax did not mention Gerry Spence's $10 million dollar estate in the Bahamas? I wonder how many servants this "man of the people" has working for him there? Typical left-wing BS.

■■■

Name: Betty Green
Hometown: Los Angeles
Sent: 12:10 - mon 8 nov 1999

I am a 12 year Vet and I think your column is very onesided. With all the points you raise, you don't back them up! You make the VA sound like an 'evil empire' outside of the government. Do you know how many Vets work for the VA? Where did you get your info from? You should be ashamed. It should be a crime to write stuff like this. You have made me very angry and I hope you do your own research more thouroughly before you blast out at the next agency! This sounds like a parody from Saturday Night Live, get real!!!!!!

■■■

Name: Douglas McArthur
Homepage: http://www.nvo.org
Hometown: El Paso TX
Sent: 07:00 - wed 10 nov 1999

Apparently the last poster to this guestbook has not had many dealings with the VA Regional Office, or perhaps she works for the VA. I'm one of the vets that was mentioned in the VA article and I can assure you that Bernard just lightly brushed the VA problem. VA adjudicators are poorly trained and inadequately supervised. I represent veterans in their claims and I see these problems on a daily basis. The problem isn't getting better, it's getting worse.

■ ■

Name: frances
Hometown: Lincoln, IL
Sent: 22:40 - wed 10 nov 1999

Bernard,
I can attest to the fact that the government does not take care of their own. My husband gave 20+ years and his life trying to get retired with a good percentage of disability from his injuries. He fought and was granted 40% and given 10 days to get out but died the next night on active duty.
The military claimed he was not ill enough to get more % and acted as though he did not deserve the 40% granted. But that was their way to get rid of him because he would not give up the fight……..HE GAVE IT ALL.
Keep up your work and a great thanks from us widows also.
BEEN THERE AND DONE THAT!!!!!!!!!!!!!

■ ■

Name: Linda Pierucki
Hometown: Norvell, Michgan
Sent: 10:16 - mon 15 nov 1999

Bureaucratic Terrorism is the perfect term for the way the Federal Govt treats ALL of it's citizens! It's particularly distressing when veterans are treated with this total lack of respect, having given their good health in defense of our country. It seems the larger our population of veterans gets, the slower and less 'human' our treatment of them gets. I sure don't see the IRS dragging their feet when it comes time to collect the tax dollars that are supposed to go to support these services - but it seems to be becoming more and more common to delay services, usually for political reasons, til the "Problem" either dies or goes away. Then, that elected/appointed official can pompously brag that he/she 'cut expenditures', secure in the knowledge most Americans wont look past the numbers to the true human toll these delays cost. Our current 'commander-in-chief' doesn't hesitate to send our military to defend the elite's policies/financial interests around the world, yet refuses to even pay current enlisted personnel or arm and train them adequately. Is is any wonder we are so shorthanded that the draft is seriously being considered again? Concerned citizens must not only voice their opinions, but must actively seek to elect representatives who will act with honor and gratitude toward our military, both past and present. The political and financial elitism that currently infects our nation's leadership has nothing to do with Fudalistic Socialism! I certainly didn't vote for this change in our national outlook and intend to do everything within.

Bernard Paul

For Your Comments Click Here

—

To Top of Page

Welcome to Net4TV Voice
Meet your fellow users who create *Net4TV Voice* in the **Masthead.**

Your Two Cents!
We want to hear what you think! Write to us at **Voice@iacta.com.**

Politics As You Like It:
Commentary From The Internet
An Example of Writing from the World Wide Web

Guestbook Entries for Publication

From Website Edition
Of
"Politics As You Like It'

1997

Bernard Paul

Don - 08/22/97 15:56:33 GMT
My URL:http://www.g eocities.com~fifty57/
My Email:fifty57@geocities.com
Where Are You From?:Rochester NY
Political Party Affilation(Optional):Republican and proud of it!!!

Comments:
    Here we have exactly what the mass news media is afraid of....Two way conversation. No longer do we need to sit and be "told what to think" Now of course their problem is to find a way to "filter" and "control" the internet for the sake of the "children" This will work for the general populace who cannot take any responsibility on their own and still need to be told what to do. but I suspect the times are a-changing, slowly but that's how we got here. The country has always swung from left to right and back again. I never expected to see the GOP in control of the house and it's apparent they are not use to it, still…it's a change. How Bill can hang on is a mystery to me, he is so transparent I don't see how he can fool anyone. Maybe the second revolution is started, this time in cyberspace. So let them all fret, beside's they are so much fun to watch as they slowly self-distruct. Sooner or later they will overdo it and people will wake up. Thanks for cruising by my site and I'll be back.

••

Christopher Alex - 08/22/97 01:18:04 GMT
My URL:h ttp://www.angelfire.com/ca/revup/index.html
My Email:primestar@webtv.net
Where Are You From?: Sheridan, Wy.
Political Party Affillation(Optional): Rep.

Comments:
    First, i like what you have done on your new look. I think what Ted K. was talking about when he refered to "Cheap Techology" is the fact that we the people, news casters and politicians have both forgotten about, we are able to communicate for pennies on the net. They have a fear for the arena of idea's that the net generates. It almost feels like big brother government can hear or find us when we disagree with its policies. While Washington is making liberal dicisions on how they are going to take care of us and protect us from ourselfs, we are here on the net hollering like hell, but its th only place left to holler.

••

John - 08/19/97 17:35:52 GMT
My URL:http://www.ucl.ac.uk/~regojpb/
My Email:No thanks I gave at the office
Where Are You From?: London UK
Political Party Affillation(Optional): Socialist

Comments:

253

Here I am on a return visit and I've just read your column re. ABC news. As you state it's oh so easy to blame someone else rather than accept your own responsibility, if they're losing the oh so important market share well it's up to them to improve, not limit the competition. Call me a cynic but I also wonder if this rant ha more to do with market share and profit than journalistic integrity? Of course there's mis-information "out there" on the net but it's a mere reflection on real life and all we have to do is apply our judgement as we do in real life. The net has provided people with something to blame for their own lack of responsibility. For example if people are concerned about porn being readily available to their children, well rather than trying to coerce the government or companies into censoring what may be legitimate (though not tasteful) how about taking responsibility for a change and surf the net with your kids to keep an eye on what they access etc. Kids have far more intelligence than we credit and more than likely able to hack any filters hat parents stick onto the browsers. Anyway all I'm trying to say is that responsibility starts off with the individual and not the government or a multi-national. John........(climbing off of his soapbox)

• •

Joe Pence - 08/19/97 14:40:00 GMT
My Email:joe1952@webtv.net
Where Are You From?: Baltimore Md.
Political Party Affillation(Optional): Rep.

Comments:
    As always very interesting.

• •

Walter - 08/16/97 05:37:06 GMT
My Email:waleth2@webtv.net
Where Are You From?: Long Island

Comments:
    Good page Bernard. Keep up the good work.

• •

~Laverne - 08/08/97 05:35:19 GMT
My URL:http://www.dzn.com/!lhindi/
My Email:Lhindi@dzn.com
Where Are You From?: TX

Comments:
    Pretty interesting web site. I be sure to drop in often. Thanks! ~Laverne
    JOIN OPERATOIN JUST CAUSE ADOPT A POW/MIA!
    http://www.dzn.com/~lhindi/myhero.html

Bernard Paul

~Laverne's Homepage Poetry

●●

Charlie cancellieri - 08/04/97 22:42:41 GMT
My URL:http://www.geocities.com/southbeach/lights/8790 My Email:cccorna@webtv.net
Where Are You From?: nyc

Comments:
  BRAVO! BERNARD…YOU HIT THE NAIL RIGHT ON THE HEAD…THEY ARE
BARBARIC…I AGREE W/YOU 100%..AS A FELLOW NY'ER, I CAN RELATE TO WHAT
HAPPENED & I AGREE THESE F--KING ANIMALS SHOULDN'T EVEN BE HERE IN
THE 1ST PLACE!!! FOR THIS REASON I BELIEVE THERE WILL EVER BE PEACH
BETWEEN JEWS & ARABS…THEY ARE NOT HAPPY UNLESS THEY ARE KILLING
EACH OTHER…& WE ARE GUILTY BY ASSOCIATION (LIKE YOU
SAID)…EXCELLENT JOB…MAYBE YOU COULD DWELL ON THE POINT (OPINION) I
JUST MADE, IN YOUR NEXT ARTICLE…YOU CAN CALL IT "ELIGION: A PRELUDE
TO WAR"…BEEN GOING ON THERE FOR 5000 YRS

●●

Chuckies - 08/04/97 05:36:55 GMT
My Email: don't give this out
Where Are You From?: Florida
Political Party Affillation(Optional): not available

Comments:
  I think this is an interesting concept. Sorry to see that some of the people that stopped by to
read it, are so immature they have to use the profanity to be noticed. Doesn't say much for their
contribution to society! I appreciate the site and will be back often, thanks for doing it!

●●

1010111010 - 07/30/97 11:48:21 GMT
My URL:http://www.ucl.ac.uk/~regojpb/
My Email:yes I know
Where Are You From?: London UK
Political Party Affillation(Optional): Labour/Socialist

Comments:
  Certianly an interesting article and Chomsky sounds like a good lad. It seems to me at least
that the Labour party are sort of falling into the old ways of the tories, for example they are going
to bring in some freedom of information but that has been p t on the backburner now. Hope they
dont become corrupt so damn quickly! Anyway nice site and I'll be back! John…..

●●

Steve vogel - 07/02/97 01:41:13 GMT
My URL:http://www.angelfire.com/sc/hardhitters
My Email:hardhitters@webtv.net
Where Are You From?: denver, colorado
Political Party Affillation (Optional): working man's party

Comments:
    i like what you do, keep exposing the corrupt leadership people have no one to blame but themselves they vote them in and dont vote them out voters are just as self serving as the politicians.

Guestbook Entries for Publication

From Website Edition
Of

"Politics As You Like It"

1998-99

Bernard Paul

Visitor:	Linda Pierucki
Reference:	subscriber
Location:	Norvell,Mi (small-town, America)
Website:	
Web Info:	
Contact;	llsp@webtv.net
Date:	Mon, Apr 26, 1999 at 09:50:51 (EDT)

Comments: Bernard: Thank you again for your thoughtful insights into yet another major symptom of sickness in our society. I've thought long and hard about the horrible situation in Colorado, and gone through the gamut of usual reactions to this tragedy: nowhere have I been able to find a solution to these ills. This is a little long, but I feel I just have to say this -Maybe it's MY way of coping with grief. This will, unfortunately, happen again! A few issues that have NOT been discussed…A few years ago, I heard a psychologist remark that we currently live in a schizophrenic society (unfortunately, I dont remember who this psychologist was, but I felt his/her coments were extremely insightful). We live in a country of 'double-speak' and propaganda - we are TOLD things are one way, we SEE they are another. Witness the various Media 'Spins' aready placed on this tragedy to serve various groups' agendas and the inability of most of us to discern the truth of the incident. This creates a situation where we have real problems discerning reality. These children have been exposed to an unreal world all their lives. Large high schools are unhealthy for adolescents - the best and the brightest get perks, attention and team honors - the rest, including those with serious social-adjustment problems, often fall through the cracks. We promote these large school systems as successful as they have successful team sports, highly-honored debate teams, etc. We dont stop to think about the huge numbers of kids who didnt make the team, or receive the honors simply because there are only so many honors to go around. I believe these parents were TERMINALLY-UPWARDLY-MOBILE! These kids had everything money could buy, except love and attention, supervision and cookies and milk after school from a parent who asked (and really cared) How was your day? ust my thoughts on this…

▪▪▪

Visitor:	Mark
Reference:	been here before
Location:	
WebSite:	
Web Info:	
Contact:	eagle109@webtv.net
Date:	Sat, Apr 24, 1999 at 17:56:23 (EDT)

Comments: Not much can be said about this. I was off from work that day watching this live sige on tv. I was just in total shock. Long pause. Its just sad. I don't think much could have prevented this. These two boys were trying there best to be different and cause trouble they were just plain evil. In some of the other school shootings it always seem to involve the supposed nerds and i don't like to use that word because I was in that social classifaction in school and got picked on a bit I had a sevear dislike for jocks myself. I do think a lot of this would not happen if the social classes in school wernt so bad. You don't have to like each other but you can respect each other.

■ ■

Visitor: Jeff Gersten
Reference: been here before
Location: Monticello, NY
WebSite:
Web Info:
Contact: JeffGersten@webtv.net
Date: Sat, Apr 24, 1999 at 08:05:42 (EDT)

Comments: This is so horrific that it is hard to even comment on it. I think it is time to crack down on the availability of weapons. The only purpose of sawed off shotguns and semi-automatic weapons is to kill as many as possible. These weapons are not for hunting or legitimate self-defense. There is no way that these minors should be able to obtain these types of weapon. Instead, as you pointed out, the media will blame the internet and video games. They could not have committed such carnage without so much firepower no matter what they entertained themselves with.

■ ■

Visitor: Mark
Reference: been here before
Location:
WebSite:
Web Info:
Contact: eagle109@webtv.net
Date: Fri, Apr 09, 1999 at 21:03:55 (EDT)

Comments: I agree with everything you wrote. I've been against the seizure laws all along for the most part. A compromise would be if found absolutely quilty of the crime selling drugs out of a house for example the house could be seized and sold and the money donated to charity not the police departments. This would cut down and some of the not so tight cases where police just want the money. As far as The Constitution goes its pretty much out the window now days. It doesnt exist anymore. Theres not any real answers to this its just more sad commentary on the state of this country.

■ ■

Visitor: Mark
Reference: been here before
Location:

258

Bernard Paul

WebSite:
Web Info:
Contact: eagle109@webtv.net
Date: Mon, Mar 29, 1999 at 21:42:17 (EST)

Comments: This is pretty pitiful. The government has no problem taking but they don't want to give unless its some type of welfare for the lazy. Veterns are very deserving of the benefits and they shoul get them. One problem is the government has promoised more than it can deliver social security, medicad, medicare, welfare, veterns benefits. All that money has to come from somewhere. I don't know the answer the whole thing is just a mess. The veterns should get priority over the welfare slobs and others.

∎∎∎

Name: Sergei
Sent: 09:17 - mon 8 nov 1999

It would be nice to have a column from someone representing the opposite point of view. I hope that this goofy left-winger is not the "official" political voice of Net4TV. I wonder why Mr. Wax did not mention Gerry Spence's $10 million dollar estate in the Bahamas? I wonder how many servants this "man of the people" has working for him there? Typical left-wing BS.

∎∎∎

Name: Betty Green
Hometown: Los Angeles
Sent: 12:10 - mon 8 nov 1999

I am a 12 year Vet and I think your column is very onesided. With all the points you raise, you don't back them up! You make the VA sound like an 'evil empire' outside of the government. Do you know how many Vets work for the VA? Where did you get your info from? You should be ashamed. It should be a crime to write stuff like this. You have made me very angry and I hope you do your own research more thouroughly before you blast out at the next agency! This sounds like a parody from Saturday Night Live, get real!!!!!!

∎∎∎

Name: Douglas McArthur
Homepage: http://www.nvo.org
Hometown: El Paso TX
Sent: 07:00 - wed 10 nov 1999

Apparently the last poster to this guestbook has not had many dealings with the VA Regional Office, or perhaps she works for the VA. I'm one of the vets that was mentioned in the VA article and I can assure you that Bernard just lightly brushed the VA problem. VA adjudicators are poorly trained and inadequately supervised. I represent veterans in their claims and I see these problems on a daily basis. The problem isn't getting better, it's getting worse.

■■■

Name: frances
Hometown: Lincoln, IL
Sent: 22:40 - wed 10 nov 1999

Bernard,
I can attest to the fact that the government does not take care of their own. My husband gave 20+ years and his life trying to get retired with a good percentage of disability from his injuries. He fought and was granted 40% and given 10 days to get out but died the next night on active duty.
The military claimed he was not ill enough to get more % and acted as though he did not deserve the 40% granted. But that was their way to get rid of him because he would not give up the fight……..HE GAVE IT ALL.
Keep up your work and a great thanks from us widows also.
BEEN THERE AND DONE THAT!!!!!!!!!!!!!!

■■■

Name: Linda Pierucki
Hometown: Norvell, Michgan
Sent: 10:16 - mon 15 nov 1999

Bureaucratic Terrorism is the perfect term for the way the Federal Govt treats ALL of it's citizens! It's particularly distressing when veterans are treated with this total lack of respect, having given their good health in defense of our country. It seems the larger our population of veterans gets, the slower and less 'human' our treatment of them gets. I sure don't see the IRS dragging their feet when it comes time to collect the tax dollars that are supposed to go to support these services - but it seems to be becoming more and more common to delay services, usually for political reasons, til the "Problem" either dies or goes away. Then, that elected/appointed official can pompously brag that he/she 'cut expenditures', secure in the knowledge most Americans wont look past the numbers to the true human toll these delays cost. Our current 'commander-in-chief' doesn't hesitate to send our military to defend the elite's policies/financial interests around the world, yet refuses to even pay current enlisted personnel or arm and train them adequately. Is is any wonder we are so shorthanded that the draft is seriously being considered again? Concerned citizens must not only voice their opinions, but must actively seek to elect representatives who will act with honor and gratitude toward our military, both past and present. The political and financial elitism that currently infects our nation's leadership has nothing to do with Fudalistic Socialism! I certainly didn't vote for this change in our national outlook and intend to do everything within

About the Author

The author is a graduate of Mercy College where he earned his Associates Degree in Behavioral Science in 1990 and Fordham University where he earned his Bachelor of Arts Degree in Media Studies with a Print & Broadcast Journalism Emphasis in 1992. A recent comment written on FEMA (The Federak Emergency Management Agency) was published in "The American Dissident" Journal based in Concord, Massachusetts. The author is a native New Yorker, having lived in New York City his entire life. He has additionally worked with ABC Sports, and produced daily news reports for WFUV-FM in the Bronx, New York. The focus of his training is Broadcast and Print News. Currently he works as a Free Lance Cyberjournalist and Political Consultant. The author is single and his hobby is studying various cultures of the world.

INDEX

www.ingramcontent.com/pod-product-compliance
Lightning Source LLC
Chambersburg PA
CBHW060526060326
40690CB00017B/3395